The Autobiography
of a Language

SUNY series in Italian/American Culture
_____

Fred L. Gardaphe, editor

The Autobiography of a Language

Emanuel Carnevali's Italian/American Writing

Andrea Ciribuco

SUNY PRESS

Cover image: Arianna Pagliara, *Landscape with Man and Suitcase*. Reprinted by permission of the artist.

Published by State University of New York Press, Albany

For information, contact State University of New York Press, Albany, NY
www.sunypress.edu

Library of Congress Cataloging-in-Publication Data

Names: Ciribuco, Andrea, 1986– author.
Title: The autobiography of a language : Emanuel Carnevali's Italian/American writing / Andrea Ciribuco.
Other titles: Emanuel Carnevali's cultural translation
Description: Albany : State University of New York, [2019] | Series: SUNY series in Italian/American culture | Revision of author's thesis (doctoral)—National University of Ireland, Galway, 2016, titled Emanuel Carnevali's cultural translation : an Italian in Modernist America. | Includes bibliographical references and index.
Identifiers: LCCN 2018040417 | ISBN 9781438475257 (hardcover : alk. paper) | ISBN 9781438475240 (pbk. : alk. paper) | ISBN 9781438475264 (ebook)
Subjects: LCSH: Carnevali, Emanuel—Criticism and interpretation. | Italian American authors—20th century. | American literature—Italian influences.
Classification: LCC PS3505.A72752 Z56 2019 | DDC 818/.5203—dc23
LC record available at https://lccn.loc.gov/2018040417

10 9 8 7 6 5 4 3 2 1

Contents

Acknowledgments

This book would not exist without the support of the people and institutions who accompanied me in the journey through Carnevali's works, which started as part of my PhD research. I would like to thank the National University of Ireland in Galway, which believed in me enough to grant me the Hardiman scholarship in 2011; and all the friends and colleagues who made it feel like home. In particular, Anne O'Connor and Adrian Paterson proved to be the best thesis supervisors I could desire, providing endless support and useful advice, motivating me constantly to pursue my research goals and improve the quality of my work. Their support and friendship, during and after the PhD, is invaluable.

Special thanks go to all the scholars who offered advice and guidance during the path that led to this book—especially Paolo Bartoloni, Beryl Schlossman, Loredana Polezzi, and John Paul Russo.

I would like to thank the staff of the archives who, in America and Italy, have facilitated the search of material on Carnevali. In particular, I would like to acknowledge the great and continuous help I received from Aurelia Casagrande of the Archivio Comunale di Bazzano in Valsamoggia (BO), Italy—who did all she could to make my search of archival material easier.

I am deeply grateful to the estates of Emanuel Carnevali, Ezra Pound, and Kay Boyle for allowing me to quote and discuss material present in the archives.

Vorrei ringraziare la mia famiglia per avermi insegnato il valore dello studio e del lavoro; per avermi incoraggiato e aiutato negli studi, anche da lontano dopo che avevo lasciato l'Italia.

Then there is Anna, whom I will never be able to thank enough. Our marriage is, without any doubt, the greatest thing that came out of all this.

This book is dedicated to all those people who, in 2019 as it was in 1914, choose to leave their homes and embark on a journey in search of a better life.

Introduction

Emanuel Carnevali, in Search of a Language

Emanuel Carnevali was an Italian intellectual in America, and an American writer born in Italy. Neither definition describes him completely, and his career is the story of a long, troubled passage across linguistic and national borders. This troubled passage, on the other hand, was strikingly fertile: it gave us one of the first Italian-American bodies of work to be recognized in American literary circles, as well as a crucial document of the many possibilities and challenges that come with choosing one language over another.

Carnevali was born in Florence in 1897, his childhood a prelude to emigration: raised by his mother, Matilde Piano (who was separated from his father, Tullio), Carnevali lived in Pistoia and then in the Piedmont towns of Biella and Cossato. After his mother's premature death in 1908, Carnevali was left in the care of his aunt Melania, and then of his father. He was sent to a boarding school in Venice in 1911 and then attended school in Bologna. Because of a conflictual relationship with his father, Emanuel decided to emigrate. In March 1914, he left for New York with his brother Augusto.

Carnevali lived in poverty in New York, doing menial jobs such as waiter and dishwasher. In 1917, he married another Italian immigrant, Emilia Valenza. He started writing poetry in English, and his first poems were published in 1918; soon he was publishing poetry, short fiction (most notably the series "Tales of a Hurried Man") and criticism in literary reviews. His work appeared in many of the most important literary reviews in the modernist circles of New York and Chicago, including *Poetry, a Magazine of Verse*, *The Little Review* and *Others*. After moving

1

to Chicago he was, for a very brief time between 1919 and 1920, the assistant editor of *Poetry*. He also translated a small number of Italian poets and intellectuals of his time (although not all of his translations were published). Carnevali rapidly established a reputation as poet and critic among American intellectuals, although he remained an outsider, and quite critical of modernist literature.

In February 1920, he experienced episodes of paranoia and delusion. Hospitalized, he was diagnosed with syphilis. He spent the following months between hospitals and clinics, with a brief experience living on the Indiana Dunes of Lake Michigan. When he returned to Italy in September 1922, the diagnosis was encephalitis lethargica, a neurological disease which left him affected by strong tremors for the rest of his life. Carnevali's health seriously compromised his career. He was hospitalized in Bazzano, near Bologna, where his father worked. Carnevali's American friends took to helping him financially (paying, for example, for a room in the Bologna clinic Villa Baruzziana in the years 1924–26). In 1925, his friend Robert McAlmon's Paris-based Contact Editions published *A Hurried Man*, a collection of his poems, short stories, and criticism written until that moment. Carnevali spent most of the following years in Bazzano, bedridden and gradually losing touch with the literary milieu. On the other hand, he kept writing until his death in 1942, always in English, sporadically publishing new poetry and fiction as well as translations from Pound (into Italian) and Rimbaud. The first six chapters of his memoir appeared in the 1932 anthology *Americans Abroad*: he never finished the work, but his friend and editor Kay Boyle collected it in the 1960s. Boyle's compiled *Autobiography of Emanuel Carnevali* saw the light in 1967. In 1978, the poet's stepsister Maria Pia Carnevali (with the help of opera conductor and Carnevali enthusiast David Stivender) collected and translated her own version of the memoir, together with other works by Carnevali, in the volume *Il primo dio*.

In the years after his death, Carnevali has drawn intermittent interest from intellectuals and scholars, going through a series of "rediscoveries." Giuseppe Prezzolini, in one of the essays of his 1963 collection *I trapiantati*, expressed his interest in Carnevali as soon as he heard about this forgotten contemporary of his, but he also lamented the scarcity of sources on him at the time. In the following years, dedicated friends, admirers and scholars rescued Carnevali from oblivion: Boyle, Maria Pia Carnevali, Stivender and the journalist and critic Gabriel Cacho

Millet, who did a great amount of work publishing Carnevali's letters (*Voglio Disturbare l'America*, 1981) as well as translating material left out by Maria Pia's edition (*Saggi e Recensioni*, 1994; *Diario Bazzanese*, 1994). This book would not exist without the dedicated intellectuals who almost singlehandedly rescued Carnevali from oblivion.

This book does not so much "rediscover" Carnevali as place him in the wider transatlantic context, looking at the challenges and possibilities that came with his choice of the English language over his native Italian. Carnevali's relationship with English—as an object of desire, a tool for literary assimilation, and the repository of Italian echoes and memories—is the fulcrum of this book. While he was hardly the only Italian of his time to write in English after emigration (his contemporaries Pascal D'Angelo and Arturo Giovannitti come to mind), Carnevali's case is exemplary for the symbolic power that the language had in his career. The fact that even after leaving the United States (where, after all, he spent only eight years) he kept writing exclusively in English denotes how much he invested in the language.

By writing in English, Carnevali could make sense of his troubled background as well as the hardship of emigration; at the same time, he could make a case for entrance into American poetry and into modernist circles. This meant having to do with different constraints, ideas of Italy that were projected onto him in America and that he had to navigate in the course of his career. His whole work was involved with the issue of how to bring an Italian experience into an American text, and how to do so without renouncing his individuality. This tension between the individual and the national in Carnevali's works, together with his very vocal presence in American modernism, make him one of the most relevant figures of the Italian-American exchange.

Carnevali's choice of English as a language also involved a continuous challenge, a confrontation with a linguistic system that needed to be accessed and decoded before it could be used. This aspect brings Carnevali together not only with other Italian members of the diaspora, but with every other translingual writer. The expression "literary translingualism" stands for the "phenomenon of authors who write in more than one language or at least in a language other than their primary one" (Kellman 2000, ix). Translingual writing is as old as literature itself: one must only think of the countless medieval authors who wrote in Latin while speaking their local vernacular in their everyday life, as well as more modern examples like Nabokov or Beckett. However, this phenomenon was largely neglected in the formation of modern national canons, the authors "safely" inscribed into American or Russian, Irish, or French genealogies. Translingual writing has come to forefront again in an age of migrations, postcolonial challenges and global discourses. There is no single way of writing across languages, since the strategies and possibilities of translingual writing are as many as there are languages in the world. One question, however, inevitably arises for all works: how much of the "first" language is still showing in the "new" language?

The first thing to note is that translingual authors do not necessarily use idiosyncratic variation of the target language, as one may think. Carnevali wrote a consistent part of his poems and fiction in what could safely pass as standard American English; others showed a clear Italian influence. All of those texts were the result of an approach to an unfamiliar linguistic reality, a language that was an end point rather than a starting point. The social and cultural factors that made him write in that style, the style of Whitman and Sandburg, speak volumes about the need for acceptance that come with translingual writing. When Carnevali, on the other hand, deviated from the norm, his deviations did not claim to represent the Italian-American variety of English that he could hear in New York (a claim that Pietro Di Donato, for example, could make). Carnevali's English was the instrument of an individual Italian hoping to make a mark in American literature, and using the elements of his background that he considered either relevant, or close to his heart.

The analysis of Carnevali's translingual writing must take into account several factors of the context—the Italian diaspora, American modernism, transnational channels of translation and criticism, Fascist cultural policy—together with the way in which bilinguals make use of their linguistic resources to fit their aims and the context. Following the evolution of Carnevali's language, this volume explores the different strategies that he developed to navigate all the constraints that came with his Italian background and with his American presence, without renouncing to his personal aesthetic goals. Carnevali's story is one of uncompromising individuality in the face of the modern metropolis; at the same time, it sheds light on the exchanges between Italian and American literature (those that happened and, as we shall see, those that did not). Besides, a study of the evolution of Carnevali's English through the years offers a chance to look at both the potential and the pitfalls of writing in a second language.

Carnevali versus Modernity

Carnevali's choice to become an American author—which he explicitly wrote to his first editor as he sent her his first poems—is at the basis of his writing. Saying simply that he chose English is not enough, however; this choice implied a series of other choices. The slang of New York, with its modernity and multicultural influences, was the first variety that he encountered. Soon, he started to read contemporary English and American literature, and when he started to write poetry of his own, he had to contend with the literary English of his time.

Writing in the years immediately after World War I, Carnevali was caught in the aesthetic challenges and calls for renewal that characterized modernism—albeit as an outsider. Writing his way into the New York and Chicago milieus, he became nevertheless a recognizable presence in the space of a few years (1918–1922). What is relevant in this sense is not merely Carnevali's presence alongside modernist masters (Carnevali's "Tales of a Hurried Man," for example, were serialized in *The Little Review* along with Joyce's *Ulysses* in 1920), but his specificity in relation to the modernist aesthetics, as he entered the modernist milieu precisely by flaunting his cultural difference.

Carnevali stood in relation to modernism, but modernism was far from being an identifiable whole, and even nowadays a univocal definition of modernism proves somewhat problematic. Its key element is, in any definition, a response to the modernity of the early twentieth century: "Modernity is a social condition. Modernism was a response to that condition" (Scholes and Wulfman 2010, 26). Modernism is inseparable from an idea of modernity, but its boundaries are equally blurry. Emerging as different responses to the challenges and aspirations of the metropolis, the art of the modern

> is a perpetually contested practice. It marks out no single zone of value, no single pattern of experience. It is an ill-defined collection of acts and responses—representation and abstraction, engagement and abstention, fascination and detachment, contemplation and critique—that has offered not one value but a region of commitments. (Levenson 2011, 9)

When I define Carnevali as an outsider of such an "ill-defined" cultural atmosphere, I indicate his critical relationship with the authors that would later be defined as "canonical" modernists: Ezra Pound, James Joyce, T. S. Eliot, William Carlos Williams. These authors were all native English speakers, and all of them readily included in the literary and critical discourse of Anglo-American modernity. Carnevali both criticized and appealed to them.

Modernism was highly concerned with language, and the exploration of its hidden potential, in "an acute awareness of the inadequacy of established literary languages" accompanied by "an unprecedented sensitivity to linguistic and cultural plurality and difference—an awareness, in short, of the condition of Babel" (Taylor-Batty 2013, 3–4). Carnevali's approach to "Babel" from the point of view of the emigrant was necessarily different from that of his modernist contacts. There is a fundamental discrepancy between Eliot's, Pound's, and Joyce's frequentations of different literary traditions in their stylistic evolutions, and Carnevali's use of English as a second language. For him it was, if not a matter of life and death, a matter of being recognized as an author or being forgotten, as were many Italian workers in the unforgiving American metropolis.

Several studies have recently "enlarged" the scope of modernism in ethnic and geographical terms (Caparoso Konzett 2002; A. Patterson 2008; Sollors 2008; Ramazani 2009). These "New Modernist Studies," as they have been called, are preoccupied with "local strains in parts of the world not always associated with modernist production" as well as with "situating well-known modernist artifacts in a broader transnational past" (Mao and Walkowitz 2008, 739). Situated in the same complex urban environment, modernism and avant-garde also coexisted with the rise of ethnic literature, especially in America. Authors from ethnic communities responded to the same metropolitan world that mainstream modernist authors were responding to, often focusing on similar themes (Sollors 2008, 60). At the same time, actual collaborations between American modernists and minority artists were rare. Carnevali was one of the few members of the immigrant masses who managed to create space for himself in English-language modernism, generating curiosity and diffidence in equal measure among the writers of New York and Chicago.

Being Italian, Carnevali had also privileged access to one of the traditions that his fellow modernists appreciated the most. He was highly conscious of it and often attempted to incorporate discussions of Italian tradition into his epic of the displaced migrant:

And as for spaghetti and ravioli, let me tell you once for all that parsley chopped fine and one small onion and . . . Yes, people do think that I am interesting! Characteristically an Italian, don't you know. And it's just what they want . . . the local color, that attractive and light way of talking . . . and those very extraordinary neckties . . . oh, perfectly charming! And, anyway, Dante died quite long ago, and there was a dash of Teuton blood in him, I bet! (E. Carnevali 1920b, 32)

Carnevali was content to include Dante, Petrarca, or Carducci in his fiction and criticism, but he was mostly interested in problematizing the relationship with modernity and with the American metropolis. When he rediscovered the Italian writers of his time, such as Papini, Slataper, and the other authors who wrote for the Florentine review *La Voce*, he immediately felt the desire to engage with them. He did so in the way that the distance allowed him, that is, by becoming a translator. Carnevali's translations may not have had a big impact on the popularity of Italian modernist authors in America, but they are important precisely because they attempted to create contacts between Italian and American/English modernism. One modernity is not enough to describe Carnevali.

Whereas Italian experiences such as Futurism have always been regarded as part of the modernist cultural climate, the term itself has encountered difficulties imposing itself in Italy. This is largely due to the presence of a nineteenth-century movement within the Catholic Church called *Modernismo*. The term has only recently entered the critical debate on Italian literature, providing with its "foreignness" an open category "to access the constellation of cultural phenomena which reflect, in complex and contradictory ways, on the experience of modernity in Italy" (Somigli and Moroni 2004, 4). Under the critical shift, authors and movements that were still categorized under the umbrella term of "decadentismo" or confused with the avant-garde have been placed within their European context (Luperini 2012). A reconsideration of Carnevali's translations and discussion of Italian modernists offers a unique perspective on the similarities and differences between authors who faced the same aesthetic and moral challenges in two different languages.

The aesthetic and moral challenges of making literature from the point of view of an Italian in America always involve, to a greater or smaller extent, the millions of men and women who crossed the Atlantic in the same years. Carnevali was conscious of being part of a great wave of emigration while, as we shall see, he sought access to American culture and literature exclusively on individual terms. Italian-American literature, though recognizable since the arrival of the first Italians in the New World, was largely born out of isolated efforts, and a clear view of the canon is "emerging" only in recent times (Buonomo and Russo 2011, 77).

He worked before Italian-American literature developed the ability to "think" itself, and an "Italian American vision" grew out of the "innumerable, even involuntary, returns that characterize immigrant Italian narrative as it registers its own passage through time and as it discovers and develops its own characteristic themes" (Viscusi 2006, 142). Carnevali developed his Italian-American conscience on his own, never putting much emphasis on being called "an Italian-American author," but always aware of the problem of being an Italian in American modernity.

Italian-American intellectuals in later decades often mentioned him as precursor. Viscusi praises his "mastery of international culture, which has become a lodestar for Italian American intellectuals" (2006, 178). Boelhower dedicated a good part of his study on immigrant autobiographies in the United States to Carnevali's *Autobiography* (1982). Other scholars have considered his immigrant individuality in relation to the modernity of America (Domenichelli 1998; Buonomo 2003), analyzed his relationship with American modernism (Ricciardi 1986; Templeton 2013), or compared him with other migrant authors (Fracassa 2005). Scholarly work on Carnevali so far seems to be inspired by his peculiar life story, narrated in vivid detail in the *Autobiography*, as well as the author's polemical confrontation with American literature.

Valesio cast Carnevali in the role of a quasi-mythical antecedent of Italian poets in America, precisely in virtue of the fact that he could not identify either with Italy, America, or the Italian communities in America:

> Ma insomma, la ragione per cui Carnevali merita di essere ricordato come genealogia della poesia italiana contemporanea negli Stati Uniti è il suo aver vissuto e scritto nell'intervallo o interstizio tra diverse compagini sociali; il suo non essere stato né italiano né americano né italiano americano, ma veramente (cioè coerentemente, puramente—anche con la irresponsabilità che spesso si accompagna alla purezza) poeta tra i due mondi.[1] (Valesio 1993, 277)

Carnevali's individual response to the cultural shock of emigration, and his efforts to present himself as an Italian on his own terms, give rise to a crucial question of Italian-American literature: when an Italian emigrant writes, in what measure does he or she represent Italy?

In the volume, I often refer to the idea of *Italianità*. *Italianità* is an umbrella term expanding across and beyond the Italian peninsula to indicate a repository of cultural elements—always shifting, continuously redefined through the ages, but always assumed to be "inherently" Italian. It is a declination, in the Italian sense, of Benedict Anderson's famous definition of a nation as an "imagined community" (2006, 5)—a community that is postulated as eternal but that requires the active imaginative efforts of its members in order to exist. It is a problematic term whose definition is not easy or automatic. When Tamburri asked, "what exactly is this *italianità* that [Italian-American authors] are interested in re(dis) covering," he could only conclude that the term

> could be language, food, a way of determining life values, a familial structure, a sense of religion; it can be all of these, as it can certainly be much more. Undoubtedly, a polysemic term such as *italianità* evades a precise definition. (Tamburri 1991, 21)

Tamburri's intuition applies to Carnevali as writer of texts featuring several indisputably Italian elements (food, Dante, Italian clerical and anticlerical discourses, the Florentine modernism of *La Voce*, Fascism, and the Little Italies of New York and Chicago), but whose definition of *italianità* is elusive at best. The "polysemic" notion of *italianità* can be realized in the text only through a continuous act of translation in which Italian culture is not communicated as a whole, but elements are selected, transposed, and put in contact with elements of the target language. This contact always points to wider frameworks of nationhood and belonging, yet it can only communicate the precarious and momentary stance of the individual author speaking to a restricted public. Carnevali's reaction to the language and values encountered in America contributed to build and define his shape-shifting *italianità*, allowing us a glimpse into an individual conscience confronting the overwhelming largeness and contradictions of "national" culture.

Carnevali's *italianità* in translation is instrumental for a rediscussion of Italian-American literature going, as in the title of Tamburri's 2003 essay, "Beyond 'Pizza' and 'Nonna!'"—that is, beyond the simple reaf-firmation of easy-access signs of Italian presence in America. The risk, Tamburri states, is that of being stuck in old hierarchies of major/minor literatures and in the repetition of old dialectics instead of exploring

> the different nooks and crannies of our ethnicity as it has changed over the decades and across generations from a dualistic discourse to a multifaceted conglomeration of cul-tural processes transgressing Italian, American (read, here, also Canada and United States, as one indeed should), and Italian/American cultural borders. (Tamburri 2003, 163)

Carnevali's oeuvre was based precisely on the transgression of borders and the refusal of easy logics of identity, and his reelaboration of cultural staples aimed at writing itself into "major" literature without letting go of his Italian background. Carnevali was also aware of the dichotomy that Italian-American intellectuals experience between Italian literature representing a major influence over highbrow Western literature and an American milieu in which Italian-American writers have been often relegated within the constraints of "ethnic" literature. His work is an early response to the same risks and pitfalls for Italian-American litera-ture outlined by Tamburri almost seven decades later—and a testament to the challenges that a writer encounters when he or she attempts to inhabit the space between cultures while crafting a language, a style, and a statement.

The category itself of "ethnic writer" has been rethought in the past decades of scholarly debate, evolving from the original compartmentaliza-tion of "ethnic" literature as opposed to the "mainstream." In the 1980s, scholars started interrogating the notion in its limits and restrictiveness. Sollors in particular proposed to focus on the shifting notions of *consent* and *descent* competing in each text: "we may be better served . . . by the vocabulary of kinship and cultural codes than by the cultural bag-gage that the word 'ethnicity' contains" (1986, 39). The idea is that the transnational writer continually negotiates his or her existence out of multiple constraints, related to kinship (*descent*) or cultural positioning (*consent*). The writer's individuality is continuously measured against a diasporic community, which stands in relation to an absence (the home country) and the challenges of the host country. The "ethnic" literary agenda is never univocal, having to navigate a range of challenges and constraints that depend on two cultural environments that are usually taken separately.

The present volume is based on the idea that the negotiations between consent and descent happen not only *through*, but also *around* language—that language is more than a tool for the writer to state his or her position with respect to the forces of consent or descent, but a force of attraction of its own, symbolizing acceptance or resistance of different cultures. Languages carry with them intricate patterns of belonging and difference, individuality and nationhood, all of them evoked in the space of the text: choosing one over another, or combining one with another, is the operation at the heart of migrant writing. Carnevali grew up with no English and spent most of his adult life working to be recognized as an American writer; the present volume deals with what happened between one moment and the other, and the latter's consequences. Language became the place where his Italian background and the challenges of American modernity could be displayed or rewritten, exhibited or discussed, glorified or ridiculed. Carnevali's English became the place where all these opposing aspirations found a place, and all contradictions exploded.

A Language for the Outsider

The challenges of analyzing a translingual body of work is that of analyzing a text while considering the possibility of another mother-tongue text that never was (translingualism does not necessarily mean self-translation), and the implications of existing in relation to two or more cultural horizons. It is the challenge of considering as many as possible of the cultural, social, and linguistic constraints that the authors assimilated or resisted and that resulted in one single text. In this sense, Deleuze and Guattari's 1975 *Kafka. Pour une littérature mineure* is exemplary; it has often been quoted as a fundamental precedent for the study of translingualism, but also contested by comparative literature scholars because of philological or cultural approximations. The book used Kafka, and his position as a Prague Jewish writer composing in German, to analyze a "minor literature" in the sense of "that which a minority constructs within a major language" (Deleuze and Guattari 1986, 16). Deleuze and Guattari take the use of German by Jewish writers in Prague as a model for the "revolutionary conditions" encountered by "every literature within the heart of what is called great (or established) literature (1986, 18). This approach allows them to dedicate only a few hints as to the linguistic properties of "Prague German that was influenced by Czech" (Deleuze and Guattari 1986, 23). Scholars have criticized them precisely on these grounds: "what, after all, is this subversive 'Prague German' that Kafka wrote? Deleuze and Guattari offer no philological descriptors at all" (Corngold 2004, 274). Corngold warns the reader about the difficulties of claiming that the distinctive brand of German spoken in Prague was recognizable in Kafka's texts, as he always reportedly intended to write standard German (2004, 273).

Without the space to join in the specific debate, I would like to point out what the researcher of translingualism may learn from the case of Deleuze and Guattari. They have the undeniable merit of having underlined how an author's approach to a major literary language is influenced by the use of it as a second language. Yet they have been subject to criticism for asserting the theoretical abstraction while failing to engage directly with the author's language:

> although Deleuze and Guattari articulate their theoretical project through an apparently specific geography, history, and writer, they abstract the theory away from a genuine encounter with particular political contexts and historical situations. (Seyhan 2000, 27)

The specificity of the context, and the author's individual intention toward the use of language, is crucial in determining the linguistic strategy that the author employed, or at least its visible part in the text.

An important methodological point, when considering the strategies of translingual writing, is that an author moves between cultures that are fluid and permeable, not stable and distinct. *Italianità*, as underlined above, is not an unchangeable monolith; but the very fabric of the modern multicultural space is made of exchanges between cultures that are not easily defined. In the 1990s, postcolonial scholars advanced the idea that the movement of ideas and people across borders is better understood not as relation between separate and essentially "pure" cultures, but as a state of perpetual negotiation. Bhabha famously called this the "Third Space" of enunciation, where translation and other forms of textual transformation create an *inter*national culture, based not on the exoticism of multi-culturalism or the diversity of cultures, but on the inscription and articulation of culture's *hybridity*. To that end we should remember that it is the "inter"—the cutting edge of translation and negotiation, the *in-between* space—that carries the burden of the meaning of culture. (Bhabha 1994, 38, author's emphasis)

The idea applies to Carnevali and his struggles for intellectual freedom beyond the label of a "characteristic" Italian. When Carnevali used an Italian proverb in a short story set in Manhattan; when he wrote articles about Dante or futurism for American readers; when he translated the prose of Papini and the poetry of Govoni, he inhabited the space between cultures but did not bind himself to any of them.

More recently, scholars have criticized Bhabha's paradigm for its highly metaphoric nature and its lack of distinction between translation in the strict sense and transnational writing at large (Wagner 2012, 64). At the same time, the global nature of the modern world makes it necessary to understand the "various kinds of practices" traveling "from one cultural context to another and by doing so undergo[ing] processes of meaning-shifting, or rather, of an extension of meaning" (Wagner 2012, 57). Several linguistic practices can generate this type of meaning-shifting (translation, translingual writing, multilingual writing), and Carnevali practiced most of them. These practices are not the same, but they all involve a degree of linguistic transformation.

Metaphors of transformation are indeed powerful when it comes to describing an existence between cultures. Some use the metaphor of translation to describe migration as the experience of the "translated being" moving "both in the physical sense of movement or displacement and in the symbolic sense of the shift from one way of speaking, writing about and interpreting the world to another" (Cronin 2006, 45). The migrant engages in translation on an everyday basis; for him or her, translation is often a matter of life or death. This process "cannot be reduced to ethnic struggles floating free of history or economics, nor of the landscapes that from time to time come to embody them both," but it is always situated in a precise context of migration (Inghilleri 2017, 143).

The experience to be communicated is often one of displacement, trauma, and misunderstanding, so the task becomes one of translating "the source language of pain into the target language of the host country" (Hron 2009, 39). If most migrants feel the pain of leaving and the challenges of thriving or failing in the new home, the translingual migrant writer then becomes a special kind of migrant who "translates" this pain in a language that people in the new home will understand. This type of migrant writing reaches out to a linguistic Other—we may even say that the Other is the catalyst of translingual writing, because were it not for the new audience, there would be no need to make the effort of writing in the new language:

> If we consider the narrative that articulates the premigration self a source text, and the narrated self that emerges from the translating act carried out for their adoptive language the target text, language migrants are translating from the mother tongue to the foreign language. They are translating the self into the other. (Wilson 2012, 49)

The idea that translingual writing is in some way a translation of the self into a new language is a powerful metaphor, and it gives a good idea of the challenge involved. Like translation, it addresses a new culture and deals with the problem of carrying meaning from one code to another. And, like translation, it implies the risk that not all meaning can be safely rendered in a different code—that something may be, as the saying goes, "lost in translation."

Translingual writing may share features with translation, but it is not a translation. It lacks a tangible original: translingual writing is born, so to speak, in the target text, and all discussions of "faithfulness" usually associated with a translation are purely hypothetical. It is best described as a form of writing in his own right, with a conceptual nature that sometimes makes us think of it as translation. This does not mean that there is no link between translingualism and translation: the link is conceptual and also practical, as Carnevali (like many other translinguals before and after him) worked as a translator as well. However, what brings together all his efforts at the deepest level—the translingual writing, the literary translations, the intercultural criticism—is a close relationship with English and Italian. Therefore, the most pressing task is not the analysis of how Carnevali handled his "translation" from Italian into English, but how he handled his English and his Italian throughout his literary career.

When Carnevali was writing, bilingualism was still largely considered outside the norm as the imperfect sum of competencies, "two monolinguals in one person" (Grosjean 2008, 10). The status quo of nation-states in Europe equates originality and authenticity with one national language—and claims that authentic expression can only come in the mother tongue:

> The uniqueness and organic nature of language imagined as "mother tongue" lends its authority to an aesthetics of originality and authenticity. In this view, a writer can become the origin of creative works only with an origin in a mother tongue . . . (Yildiz 2012, 9)

This is still a very common belief in our time, but it is dispelled by the realization that, in times of global flows of people and words, new languages open up new possibilities rather than impairing one's use of a pristine, genuine mother tongue. Linguists have recently focused their attention on the possibility that different languages *add* to one's personality and one's set of expressive tools; their findings offer interesting suggestions and points of comparison for a scholar who embarks on an analysis of literary translingualism. The "wider implications of multilingualism in literature are still under-researched" (Gardner-Chloros 2013, 1101), and, while the present analysis is an eminently literary one, the study of a translingual author may not ignore the ideas that are being developed to explain the speech of individuals who have more than one language in their lives.

In her work on *The Bilingual Mind* (2014), Pavlenko starts her chapter on bilinguals' autobiographical narratives analyzing the claim that the Russian version of Nabokov's memoir somehow helped him add more detail than in the English version. At the end she wonders: "but even if the switch to Russian did trigger new memories, how generalizable is Nabokov's experience?" (2014, 190). This book does not intend to generalize Carnevali; rather, I intend to analyze him in his specific, idiosyncratic Italian and American context. The focus is on Carnevali eschewing his father's Emiliano-Romagnolo dialect, keeping Carducci's literary language at arm's length, and attempting to decode Manhattan slang and to conjure Whitman's rhythms. Chapters 4 and 5 in particular focus on a type of language that can only be Carnevali's because they appeal to the different localities and cultural spaces that he encountered in his journey. At the same time, finding similarities between Carnevali's memoirs and similar experiences in the research on bilingualism helps frame his operations within a similar set of challenges and opportunities faced by bilingual migrants before and after him.

This is a volume on how a man managed the two languages he spoke with a view to becoming a recognized writer. In this sense, a very recent understanding of bilingualism provides conceptual tools. This is based on the idea that "language users employ whatever linguistic features are at their disposal with the intention of achieving their communicative aims," regardless of those features being part of this or that language (Jørgensen 2008, 169). In this view, human beings "have *language*, and that is important. It is less important that some of us have *languages*" (Jørgensen 2008, 169–70, my emphasis). This idea applies to all areas of human life, but one can easily see a poet, and a bilingual poet such as Carnevali, agree on the grounds that poetry is concentrated in a particular effect on the reader, and its strength may in some cases take precedence over the national origin of the words themselves.

Linguists call this general understanding of human speech *languaging*, and the free movement of bilinguals across repertoires of words and phrases *translanguaging*. When a speaker experiences life in multiple contexts where multiple languages are spoken, he or she knows elements from more than one repertoire:

> Translanguaging is the enaction of language practices that use different features that had previously moved independently constrained by different features, but that now are experienced against each other in speakers' interactions as one new whole. (Garcia and Li Wei 2014, 21)

While the sociocultural tenets of the modern nation-state generally call for separate monolingual environments, translanguaging regards the operation that speakers do on an everyday basis across the world when they freely use the linguistic tools in their toolbox. In a literary analysis, this idea is particularly useful because of its focus on a linguistic performance rather than on some essential and ingrained national identity of the writer (Harissi, Otsuji, and Pennycook 2012, 527). As we shall see, while Carnevali only wrote in English, his English was influenced by the words and literary works he knew, and that came from America as well as from Italy and France. The audience was always American, but his Italian background showed more or less depending on the subject matter and the context. All his works, more or less idiosyncratic as they are, come from a choice (repeated in every word) between English and Italian. The idea of *italianità* does not disappear in this effort, but it often becomes problematic. American culture becomes a moveable and elusive target, a goal that was established by Carnevali—and several migrant authors before and after him—and that we may equate provisionally with recognition, the idea of being part of a canon. In both cases, the language is the tangible form of this movement between uncertain poles, and its catalyst.

This analysis works for Carnevali in its individuality—or rather, in the tension between his individuality and what was posited as "Italian" or "American." It does not directly involve the general history of the Italian language in America, of the many forms that countless dialects and the language of Dante took in the New World, and that as a general rule mark their speakers "as belonging in the contact zone between speakers of standard American English and speakers of Italian dialects" (Viscusi 2006, 28). This is the *Autobiography of a Language* (emphasis on the singular article) and, as such, is concerned with the language of Emanuel Carnevali, following it from the first memories of an Italian childhood to the odd and idiosyncratic English of a returning emigrant.

A Journey Across Two Languages

The five chapters of the present volume present the story of Carnevali's language in a chronological order.

Chapter 1 deals with Carnevali's childhood in Italy and with the problem of the "mother tongue." The analysis of Carnevali's texts starts with his posthumously published *Autobiography* (1967), searching for clues on the poet's linguistic upbringing, with a view to understanding the development of a translingual writer in relation to emotional and social circumstances.

The metaphor of the "mother tongue" is a common image that we use in everyday writing and conversation, but in fact it threads a fine line between the individual and the nation, between emotional and social constraints. Analyzing the factors that led Carnevali to abandon Italy and the Italian language means unveiling connections that invest the family history as well as nationalistic and identity tensions in turn-ofthe-century Italy—and the role that they all had in Carnevali's rejection of the mother tongue.

Then, by looking at Carnevali's recollection of his early years in New York, the chapter reflects on the migrant's linguistic and social ordeal. Carnevali's *Autobiography* sheds light on the struggle of Italians in New York from the point of view of one who attempted to make an entrance not only into the English-speaking American society, but into its literature as well.

Chapter 2 starts when Carnevali enters the stage as a published poet in 1918 and concentrates on the author as a linguistic outsider using a newly learned language to address a monolingual audience. Translingual writing is a process: the long and laborious acquisition of a set of linguistic tools, and the confrontation of a new (often monolingual) cultural context. To understand Carnevali's growing command of the English language, the analysis centers on selected linguistic strategies and key words in both his published and unpublished early writings. Carnevali's use of specific imagery and concepts (in particular the notion of "commonplace") in English illustrates how a translingual author can approach an unfamiliar language, communicate his experience, and express a stance with respect to the target culture.

The story of how Carnevali established a reputation in American literary circles and both adopted and rejected American models shows how translingual writing is never a straight process, but always a complex one involving personal factors as well as the context and editorial market. Carnevali addressed American literature with a strong will to make himself heard and carve out a niche for himself in a literature whose language he had learned in those very years. Judging by the critical opinion of colleagues such as William Carlos Williams, he managed to be recognized as a new presence in America.

After establishing a presence in the target culture, how does an author communicate his or her culture of origin? Does translingualism favor translation and make the author an intercultural broker? How does that interact with the author's individual agenda?

Chapter 3 considers how Carnevali communicated his Italian identity in the new culture and how he related to the Italian immigrant community in New York. Carnevali's criticism and translation strategies indicates a desire to represent *italianità*, but only in his own terms. He made a name for himself in American modernism as a critic and translator of Italian literature at a time where it was experiencing a revival among

English-speaking modernists. However, his treatment of Italian literary symbols also denotes an intention to engage critically with tradition as a means to affirm his individuality.

When it came to discussing fellow Italian migrants, Carnevali's ambivalent and provocative use of the racially derogatory term "wop" indicates an uneasy relationship with the Italian immigrant community. While he sometimes championed the rights of Italian immigrants against discrimination, his strategy of representation suggests that he considered his agenda as separate from the interests of the Italian community in New York as a whole.

The last section of the chapter considers Carnevali as a literary translator. During his career, he translated his favorite Italian authors into English for American literary reviews. Most notably, in 1919 he translated a small anthology of his choosing of poems by Papini, Prezzolini, Saba, Govoni, and Slataper from *La Voce*, an Italian modernist magazine that he greatly appreciated. The project showed Carnevali's transnational links and his agenda as a cultural mediator. The translations themselves are also an interesting document of the links between translation and translingualism, presenting strong Italian influences and showing the different challenges of translating into a second language.

The issue of the translingual writer as "transposing a culture" has been expressed from the beginning of the debate on translingualism. Carnevali's treatment of the Italian tradition, of Italian emigration and Italian modernism, respectively, reveal how that communication does not take place simply between two discrete cultures. Rather, it must consider personal interest, different group interests, and demands of the editorial market.

Chapter 4 follows Carnevali back in Italy: in 1922, severely ill with encephalitis lethargica, he returned, and in Bologna and its environs he would spend his last two decades. Despite his sickness, he continued to write. Carnevali's works from the late 1920s are ideal for analyzing the evolution of translingual writing in a changing context, as well as the strategies that made Italy communicable to the American audience. He created a unique language featuring several literally translated Italian phrases and idioms; that strategy enabled him to effectively represent the unique features of life in small-town Italy under the Fascist regime and even to challenge the mainstream discourse of Italian culture. This highly idiosyncratic language demonstrates the provocative potential of translingual writing: it defines Carnevali as an outsider in both Fascist

Italy and American literary modernism and shows translingual writing's strict dependence on the cultural context.

A returning migrant is a double exile. In a rigidly monolingual society, such as Fascist Italy, the return of a migrant can result in diffidence and exclusion. Chapter 5 focuses on the relationship between Carnevali and 1930s Italy, focusing especially on his last big enterprise as cultural mediator: a translation of Ezra Pound's XXX Cantos.

While Italian commentators either ignored Carnevali or (rarely) attempted to absorb him into Italian culture, his few remaining links with the literary milieu included Ezra Pound with his group of Italian contacts. Pound gave Carnevali the job of translating the Cantos: a job left unfinished for health reasons. The surviving drafts, as well as the only published "Canto," are extremely interesting for what they show in terms of the translingual's relationship with the task of the translator and with his mother language. At a time when the transnational dimension of modernism is increasingly recognized as a defining element of the era (Ramazani 2008; Mao and Walkowitz 2008; Sollors 2008), it is important to record this episode of transatlantic, translational vision, its goals and outcomes.

All of Carnevali's work in the 1930s, both translation and original writing, shows a progressive detachment from both his adopted culture and the culture of his birth. His journey across languages and cultures apparently ended in silence and oblivion in a boarding room in Bazzano (Bologna) in 1942. However, in the following years a small group of dedicated friends, editors, and scholars collected his published and unpublished work, making available to the contemporary public one of the richest and most diverse texts of Italian/American writing.

1

Translating Childhood,
Decoding America

On the first day of September 1917, Emanuel Carnevali sent a letter to Harriet Monroe, editor of the Chicago magazine *Poetry, A Magazine of Verse*. It accompanied his first poems and contained a statement that is crucial for our understanding of Carnevali's journey across languages, nations, and literary canons:

> I want to become an american [sic] poet because I have, in my mind, rejected forever Italy and its standards of good literature: I do not like Carducci and less D'Annunzio.[1]

Carnevali apparently intends to break off with Italian literature, here represented by the two most popular poets at the turn of the twentieth century. This first chapter is, in a sense, the story of this letter. An examination of Carnevali's memoir reveals details about his linguistic upbringing. The analysis of the early chapters of Carnevali's *Autobiography* allows the reader to connect emotions and language in his personal trajectory, tracing the reasons that led him to abandon Italy (and Italian) and seek a new existence in English. The final section of the chapter explores his adaptation to the New York environment until he announced his desire to become "an American poet."

It is important to note that these clues come from a posthumously pieced-together text, written several years after the events described. The first six chapters of Carnevali's memoir appeared in the 1932 anthology *Americans Abroad* under the title "The First God. A Novel." Most of the memoir never saw the light during the author's lifetime until Carnevali's editor, Kay Boyle, compiled it in the 1960s, together with reworked versions of the 1932 chapters and several sections from Carnevali's poems and essays.[2] This posthumous, stratified, and composite text is also our best chance to understand how English became Carnevali's language of choice.

While he wrote most of the memoir from his sickbed in the 1930s, Carnevali had always felt an urge to narrate his life and his emigration. In the 1917 "American poet" letter, Carnevali outlines his reasons for emigrating in the space of a few lines:

> Parents separated. I lived with mother till I was ten. Mother died. I was sent to father. Did not agree with any of his views: at sixteen, after much fighting and rebelling and crying, I decided I must go to America . . .[3]

At the very moment in which Carnevali is crossing the border into literariness, by discussing the publication of his first poems, he is also writing his own story in English for the first time. The story contained in the letter was the first version of Carnevali's translingual autobiographical narrative, featuring elements that would reappear in the 1967 text.

The letter mentions Tullio Carnevali's comment on his son's desire to emigrate: "Father said: 'A nemico che fugge ponte d'oro' that is 'Make a bridge of gold to a fleeing enemy.'"[4] This well-known Italian idiom remained for Carnevali a sign of the enmity between himself and his father. The 1967 text of the *Autobiography* reads:

> When I saw my father he told me he agreed to my going to America since, and these were his words: "For the enemy in flight we build a golden bridge." I understood. I was then the enemy of that big beast. (E. Carnevali 1967, 58)

Tullio's words were not the English that Emanuel used in the autobiographical novel, but the Italian that he quoted in the Monroe letter. The passage from the language of experience to the new language of writing is not only a more direct way of communicating this episode to the American audience. It also is a rewriting and reinvention of psychologically significant episodes: a process entailing a certain degree of risk, but also some potential. Recently, applied linguists have noted that writing in a different language in some cases may prove beneficial to autobiographical writing, having "emancipatory effect" (Pavlenko 2012, 2014), as we shall see.

Carnevali's *Autobiography* is, in its first part, the story of how emigration gave him new linguistic tools to affirm his individuality, but first he had to handle the extraneousness that came with them. The text contains much information on the author's relationship with both his first language and his language of choice, also relating to the time before he could write in English. After all, Carnevali's list of possible titles initially included *Religious Stammering* (Boyle 1967, 15), presumably as a reference to the author's belief in the power of the word as well as the difficult, "stammering" process of finding adequate words in the new language.

It is common for translingual authors to discuss their linguistic upbringing in their autobiographies, which are an epic of the author's journey across languages and cultures. As noted by De Courtivron in her anthology of translingual memoirs, these texts often surprisingly "echo one another, despite their radically different contexts and histories" (2003, 3). Carnevali's *Autobiography* confronts issues commonly encountered along the translingual journey, such as the way in which a different language may act as a tool for dealing with certain emotions or the importance invested in learning the new language by a migrant. At the same time, it is deeply immersed in the cultural conditions that generated it, containing much of the Italy and America of its time, interacting with each other on the unfamiliar terrain of Carnevali's English.

The first parts of the *Autobiography* follow Carnevali's troubled youth, his difficult relationship with his parents and with the Italian school system, his emigration, and the impact with the reality of New York in the 1910s. First encounters with American society and the English language proved traumatic to Carnevali, as it was for many immigrants in the city at the time. However, in a few years, he not only came to terms with the unfamiliar metropolis, but also found in its language an instrument to translate his troubled youth into a literary text and a lifelong goal: "to become an American writer."

1. Mother Tongues: Bilingualism and Emotion in Carnevali's Autobiographical Writing

The early chapters of Carnevali's *Autobiography* are a collection of brief, impressionistic glances into the perception and feelings of the child-poet (one thinks of Scipio Slataper's 1912 memoir *Il mio Carso*).[5] The 1932 text starts with what seems to be a first memory:

I remember a white room with white sunlight coming in from tall windows; in it my mother and an old lady, a very white old lady, are stooping attentively over me; I may have been from two to three years old. It was in the city of Florence. . . . (E. Carnevali 1932, 74)

While in a 1919 letter to Giovanni Papini, Carnevali proudly stated, "io sono nato A FIRENZE!" (1981, 91), the memoir downplays his connection to the birthplace of literary Italian. Rather, it concentrates on the early memories that defined his upbringing and set him on his course away from Italy. The different Italian towns (Pistoia, Biella, Cossato) where he followed his mother and aunt only serve as background: the core of this part of the narrative is the two women, Matilde and Melania Piano. With their strengths and weaknesses, these troubled mother figures are responsible for Carnevali's emotional upbringing; the 1967 version of the text underlines this at the very start: "This book contains all of my mother, or at least it should, for I am her son" (E. Carnevali 1967, 23). This claim seems to confirm Seyhan's impression that migrant autobiographies are in fact more than the expression of a single voice, but the product of "an explicit or implicit dialogue between the writer and the community, ancestors, or family" (Seyhan 2000, 66). Admittedly, Carnevali's attachment to mother (Matilde) and aunt (Melania) defines his decision to write poetry. However, this would happen in a language different from Italian—rather, the very core of the narrative is the abandonment of Italy and the Italian language. The book contains all of the mother, but does so without his *mother tongue*. Yet what does the metaphor itself mean for a translingual writer?

Few notions are as concrete and pervasive in human experience as the mother-child relationship. It is no wonder, then, that the language in which one is educated, and with which strong links are usually construed (in terms of emotive, political, cultural, and social belonging), is often understood and explained in terms of motherhood. Psychologists hold the metaphor to be "sans doute plus poétique que scientifique"[6] yet concur that there is a self-evident, powerful link between the language first heard during childhood and the development of speech (Amati Mehler, Argentieri, and Canestri 1994, 72). Some linguists explain this link through "language embodiment," a theory concentrating on the "integration of phonological forms of words and phrases with information from visual, auditory, . . . visceral modalities, autobiographical memories, and affect" in early childhood (Pavlenko 2012, 421).

In its cultural dimension, we do not notice that we are using a metaphor when we say 'mother tongue': as linguists would put it, this metaphor has such a high degree of "conventionality" (Kövecses 2002, 29) that speakers usually take it for granted as one of the conceptual tools with which they interpret the world. It is a metaphor nonetheless, threading the delicate line between the personal and the national spheres and continuously reinventing it. Through the "mother tongue" metaphor, we take the language of a community to be as crucial and defining of ourselves as our parents are. At this point, the translingual writer's abandonment "of the mother tongue—*Muttersprache, langue maternelle*, . . . *lingua materna*, [appears] tantamount to matricide" (Kellman 2000, ix).

The treatment of the mother-tongue metaphor obviously differs from author to author, yet the break of this maternal link is very often at the center of writing. Many translinguals associate the lost language of childhood with a "more real" voice that may "claim a greater 'reality'" than the acquired voice of writing, as is the case of Polish-American author Eva Hoffman (Besemeres 2002, 41). The universe as described by the language of upbringing is assumed in this case to be more "natural," thanks to the deep link of that language with earliest memories and perceptions. Recently, Yildiz made the overcoming of the "Mother Tongue" narrative the center of what she calls a post-monolingual understanding of literature: while the "notion of the unique 'mother' insists on one predetermined and socially sanctioned language as the single locus of affection and attachment," implicitly diverting focus from any other linguistic possibility, "different languages can and do elicit heterogeneous affective investment" and can be a legitimate source of artistic expression (Yildiz 2012, 13). An understanding of language ties that goes beyond the mother tongue exonerates linguistic exiles from the accusation of being both traitors of their linguistic essence and incomplete users of their new medium. It does so through countless strategies and reconfigurations across time and space—there is no unified way of going beyond the mother tongue, but it depends on the many interpretations of one's ties to the mother, to the language, and to the nation. The analysis of Carnevali's abandonment of the mother tongue must include the discussion of his own maternal figures and his own experience of Italy.

Carnevali's memoir displays the break from the mother tongue in terms of Matilde's silence and sickness. They represent both the emotional link between Carnevali's childhood and his poetry and the impossibility of writing in the language of childhood: "Listening to the silence that was the life of my mother, I hear the words of my poetry, the words with which I could make a wreath for her head" (1967, 23). The forgotten story of a fragile and emotionally unstable woman, addicted to morphine and a victim of domestic abuse, needs a son who will save it from oblivion and give it literary shape. This shape is in American English, which was not Matilde Piano's language, but which gave her son a literary voice. In this sense, the early chapters of the *Autobiography* are testament to how writing in a different language may not only represent the loss of a "first" language, but also open new possibilities and redeem previous obstacles to expression.

The text contains all the powerful emotions that Matilde inspired, combining attachment ("Mother, do you remember your little boy who never left you alone, who followed you everywhere . . .") with equally powerful distress ("My mother once caught influenza and she became crazy: she tried to give me a glass of water to drink in which she had put a dozen needles"). Carnevali often defines his art in terms of the expression of suffering and trauma, which is traced back to his mother in the *Autobiography* to the point that her drug addiction is linked to the painful "parturition of this poor champion, Mister Me" (E. Carnevali 1932, 76). The text seeks a dialogue between mother and son on the basis of a common history of sickness and trauma, yet acknowledges its impossibility: "Mother, I would give you now all the affection your misery claimed: but I too am sick and fully engrossed with my own sickness" (1932, 76). The mother's silence ("I think of your dead mouth") mirrors the poet's inability to find words to amend her silence: "What can I tell you of myself, mother, except that I have wasted in sickness a good half of my real life from fifteen up" (1932, 77).

There is no possibility of communicating with Matilde, but Carnevali can use English to commit his earliest memories, and the powerful emotions attached to them, to literary form:

> I do not know that I ever saw a finer mouth than my mother's. It was sinuous and full-lipped and sensuous, large but beautiful, and the great purity of the forehead I remember well. You must know that I was only nine when she died. (E. Carnevali 1932, 77)

This is the English description of an image that is deep-seated in the emotional world of Carnevali's childhood. English (and emigration) made it possible for him to go beyond the traumas experienced in his mother tongue and to write them for a new public: the "you" in "you must know" may be a rhetorical figure, but it ideally includes a new Anglophone interlocutor. Recent tests on bilingual individuals have found that they tend to "express more intense affect when speaking the same language at the time of retrieval that they spoke at the time when the event took place" (Dewaele 2008, 1761). Conversely, a new language can have a beneficial effect on writing,

> also in psychological terms, offering writers new, "clean" words, devoid of anxieties and taboos, freeing them from self-censorship, from prohibitions and loyalties of their native culture, and allowing them to gain full control over their words, stories, and plots. (Pavlenko 2014, 20)

Abandoning a language where childhood traumas were embedded enabled Carnevali to give literary form to the defining traumas of his childhood and to redeem the "silence" of the mother through the abandonment of Italian. Matilde does not speak a single line in the text, which expresses her emotional legacy through gestures, images, and a link to irrational and uncanny moments in the narration. On her deathbed, she hears bells ringing and interprets the sound rightly as the "atrocious habit in some little towns in Piedmont that when one is in agony the bells play a special music to fit the case," signaling with her hand that she is ready to die (E. Carnevali 1932, 77). A black cat is also seen near her deathbed (1967, 25). After her death, Matilde gains the qualities of an earthly goddess:

> Your head, in the little cemetery of that little town, rests against the wall. Beyond the wall an unkempt space of tall grass grumbling with all kinds of small and big insects. I saw you dead, you were beautiful with your face color of the earth. You inspired tranquility. (1932, 76–77)

Her grave becomes the only holy ground in a country with which the poet was looking to sever his ties. The language in which Carnevali describes this private cult is an English that draws on his Italian experience. From the Latin of the mass, he conjures the epithet of "Mater

Dolorosa" for Matilde, translating the cult of Our Lady of Sorrows into his family history. The link to a weeping Mary, devastated over the death of her son, is significant in relation to Carnevali's own illness and sense of approaching death. This epithet is not however in Italian, but in Latin and in an English translation that follows the sound and rhythm of the Latin original: "Mother, mother dolorous" (1932, 76). It is in this sense that English liberated the traumas of Carnevali's early life, giving him fresh words to represent and explain a very personal collection of feelings and images. Neither mother nor mother tongue could represent a stable center, a trusted system of reference; but the addition of English to Carnevali's life provided the opportunity to represent images in a fresh way and translate part of the soundscape of his childhood.

To understand the importance of Carnevali's abandonment of Italian and the possibilities that English offered, it is necessary to turn to another mother figure (his aunt) and to Carnevali's first published short story. No less troubled than her sister Matilde, Melania Piano took care of Carnevali for more than a year after her sister's death in 1908. Melania is a complementary mother figure, and Carnevali stated that she "might well claim that she had been responsible for . . . the education of [his] soul," concluding, "I feel she made of me a poet" (1932, 81). Even before the *Autobiography*, Melania already had a place in Carnevali's narrative universe—at the very beginning of it, in fact. The first of Carnevali's "Tales of a Hurried Man," a series of autobiographical short stories published in America between 1919 and 1921, centered precisely on Melania Piano, underlining her influence on the poet. Interestingly enough, she became "Melany Piano" in the story, with an imperfect Anglicization reflecting Carnevali's still incomplete and tentative adoption of English.

Melania lived in East Africa during Italian colonial expeditions and came back, Carnevali remembers, with "beautiful tales of hyenas, pestilence, devoted negro servants and Ras Alula and Ras somebody else" (E. Carnevali 1919i, 16). The fact that the atrocities of colonialism are construed as "beautiful tales" for children, and reprised in that form without question by the adult narrator, underlines the text's deep roots in childhood memories.[7] "Tales of a Hurried Man, I" describes Melania's life as another story of trauma and exclusion: after Africa, she found herself living in Italy as a single mother, struggling against exclusion: "Two children, not brothers, and the mother a lady, proud, now bitterly proud, but proud still . . ." (E. Carnevali 1919i, 17–18). Like Matilde, Melania is a mother figure who was both responsible for

the poetic upbringing of young Emanuel and struggling to adjust to the
Italy of their time. The end of the 1919 "Tale," after a description of
Melania's failure to affirm her individuality in a close-minded society,
presents Carnevali affirming his new poetic voice in English:

> There comes the big failure and some bend
> their heads
> over their chests
> like birds in the cold.
> . . . .
> But there are eyes in the world
> that see the dance of the absurd,
> and always someone
> who carefully listens to the great song of it.
> (E. Carnevali 1919i, 19)

Melania's demise foresees Emanuel's emigration and triumph,
expressed in the vigorous Whitmanian tones ("the great song of it")
of his new language. In the story, Carnevali's desire to write proceeds
directly from this surrogate mother figure: "This lady, Melany Piano, was
my mother's sister, my aunt. I'm in a hurry. I wrote this about her; I am a
writer and I write about persons and things" (E. Carnevali 1919i, 21). In
the redundant simplicity of this statement, there is the link between the
maternal figures of his youth, his genuine desire to turn life into literature,
and the desire to do so in a different language. Melania and Matilde
made him a "hurried man" with an urge to translate into literature the
events of his life and his impressions on "persons and things." This first
"Tale" expresses all the excitement of a fresh start in a new language:

> I'm on a journey beyond you and your things, you and your
> colors and words. On the mountains, over this city and that,
> I am the bird that has no nest, I am the happy stranger, I'm
> sailing under the sun. (E. Carnevali 1919i, 22)

The maternal figures that shaped his life around poetry and sorrow
made him into a bird with "no nest," without a homeland. Starting out as
an American writer, Carnevali describes himself as "the happy stranger,"
content to face the challenges of the new language and context.

Carnevali's *Autobiography* cannot point to the language of childhood as the lost language of stability and emotional refuge. However,

the two maternal figures are very present in the narrative, with a strong emotional influence on the production of a text written in a language they did not speak. They embody the "gift of writing" in the narrative, as it "comes from the dead, not only in the writer's personal experience of loss, but also in a more general sense of tradition or inheritance, simply what is passed on to us as writing" (Karpinski 2012, 96). The influence of the dead on the living is articulated through writing, preserving the memory of the dead and attesting to their past existences; writing is also cultural inheritance that the dead have passed on to us. In the case of translingual autobiography, this inheritance must be not only discerned (and in some cases rescued from "silence"), but also translated, to save it from oblivion. This "intergenerational . . . transmission of memory" via the "genealogical function of translation" (Karpinski 2012, 97) happens through English. Carnevali construes the "gift of writing" of his mother in terms of silence and frustration without investing the Italian language with redemptive powers. Mother and aunt represent, more than a lost mother tongue, a sort of "emotional kernel" (Ciribuco 2013, 45), which only English will turn into literature.

2. Leaving the Fatherland

Tullio Carnevali enters his son's book as "the most ignoble of men" (E. Carnevali 1932, 76). A state clerk, he was separated from Emanuel's mother; Emanuel got to know him only at the age of eleven. In the *Autobiography*, this character will be the catalyst of the author's hostility toward Italy and the object of the rebellion that will lead him to emigrate. In the chapters dedicated to the author's adolescence, various aspects of Italian society and culture of the time make their appearance, opposed to or ridiculed by the narrating voice. The chapters dedicated to the mother may have underlined, more than the mother tongue, its problematic loss; the chapters dedicated to the father describe the rebellion against Italy as the fatherland.

    Carnevali gives his father ogre-like features, such as a "most vicious laugh: he showed his teeth when he laughed, which gave him the aspect of a ferocious beast" (1967, 41). Interestingly, in the same paragraph his laugh is "the Romagnoli's kind of laugh"—a remark on Carnevali's distress in the region where his father brought him after Matilde's death. The mother—the poet's emotional kernel—has no specific linguistic or

geographical ties in the narrative, while the father is almost always associated with a fact of Italian language, culture, or society. The hostility
of Emanuel and his brother toward the father is expressed in links with
the Italian society of the early twentieth century:

> We called him Bissolati (a member of the Italian parliament),
> and made the iettatura gesture after him. But we could not
> love our father. That was our great tragedy. Something had
> willed forever that our father and we two should never come
> near to one another. (1967, 40)

The association of Tullio with Leonida Bissolati, Italian socialist
leader of the time, is not evidently motivated, nor is it intended to be.
Relegated in the specific context of Carnevali's childhood, its translingual
obscurity is only partially mitigated by the comment between parentheses.
The "*iettatura* gesture" is also culture specific and difficult to translate.
This ritual gesture, aimed at a person who is believed to bring bad luck,
is the sign of an opposition to the father figure still happening within the
limits of Italian culture. The passage underlines the opposition between
the English of Emanuel's writing and the Italian system of signifiers of
the fatherland.

Tullio Carnevali's speech is also heavily bound to place in the
Autobiography. When Emanuel breaks some bottles during a nervous
breakdown, he reacts with a harsh comment in Emiliano-Romagnolo:
"*I scienta tott!*" (1967, 57, author's italics). The sentence, which is Romagnolo for "they break everything," is not only lost to an Anglophone
readership (Boyle provides no footnote here), but also would be obscure
to most Italian readers. This insertion is not the signifier of an identity to
be claimed and displayed by the author. "There was," Carnevali remarks,
"great bitterness in that utterance and it gave me pain" (1967, 57). "I
scienta tott" in the English text may express only the author's distance
from the father as Tullio's very local speech enters, violently and for
a single sentence, a text that testifies Emanuel's translingual freedom.

Hostility toward the father in these chapters of the *Autobiography*
goes hand in hand with Carnevali's critique of the fatherland as he
engages with Italian cultural events in his youth and defines his stance
as an outsider. Italian culture is embodied, in the chapters relating to
Carnevali's adolescence, by the various schools he reluctantly attends and
the staples of *italianità* against which he measures his individuality. These

chapters are crucial for defining the translingual narrative as a narrative of emancipation from a discourse of national identity. They show how writing outside the borders of national language enables authors to criticize, disregard, or ridicule elements of the national discourse that are taken for granted within the nation. Carnevali's autobiographical narration reacts on personal terms to an idea of the nation as an *imagined community*, as would be theorized by Anderson in the 1980s—that is, a nation as a "cultural artefact" that overcomes the impossibility of actual communion between its members by imposing a narrative and symbolic apparatus (Anderson 2006, 5), an accumulation of signifiers of national identity. In this way, "the entitlement of the nation is its metaphor" (Bhabha 1994, 141). The translingual text needs to translate that metaphor in a different language, as the translingual author sees the imagined community that he or she left, from the outside. This reimagination of the author's links with the community is a rewriting of individual history outside the self-perpetuating discourse of a homogeneous national identity. It fits with Carnevali's own, very private rebellion against the fatherland, but in so doing, it stages difference with respect to the mainstream assumptions of *italianità* and creates a wider space for being Italian in a different way, in a different language.

Carnevali grew up in an Italy where political unification still left questions about the nature and homogeneity of national identity largely open. There, a national project emphatically based on the glories of the Roman Empire was being tested by economic crisis, mass emigration, and the mixed results of the colonial enterprise. Carnevali's take on issues of national identity is idiosyncratic at best. He was involved with the "Society for the Redemption of Trent and Trieste" as a schoolboy, yet this link with the *irredentismo* movement, which ideally would complete national unification by "redeeming" the Italian-speaking cities under Austrian control, is used to ridicule the self-affirming national narrative. Carnevali writes rather candidly of how he stole the subscription money ("I collected some money making new members and spent a happy Christmas with the appropriated funds"): that money, he comments, was "almost all [Italy] gave me" (1967, 61). Not only he could write, from the vantage point of his new language, of how he explicitly scorned the nationalistic ideal, but the very translation of the nationalist vocabulary into English serves to expose its artificiality, as "Redemption" taken out of its context loses the impact and relevance it had in Italian.

As for his engagement with Italian literature, Carnevali mentions "a girl schoolfellow whose sympathy I won by defending D'Annunzio against Manzoni," a critical discussion hardly impaired by the fact that "[n]one of us knew much about the two authors" (1967, 60). Futurism, the groundbreaking Italian avant-garde group, is received by Carnevali in Bologna in a second- or third-hand account, as he "wore a flowing necktie and was believed to be either an anarchist or a futurist, the two things being strangely linked together" (1967, 61). Carnevali's days as a provincial, teen-age "futurista" apparently consisted mostly of episodes of petty vandalism (1967, 61). Later on, in New York, he would write articles in which he explained Futurism as a movement "fostered by the hustling of many vacant souls, who made out of these exaggerations, etc. (which were all they could reach), a theory and a way of art" (1919a, 211). Carnevali the author would argue against what he deemed the bourgeois and superficial nature of Futurism under the influence of the *Vociani*. As a character in his own narrative, he treats the recent classics of Italian literature as empty shells for schoolroom debates, and the avant-garde as more fashion than substance. While "practically every young Italian writer . . . faced the challenge of overcoming the influence of Pascoli and D'Annunzio, and of Carducci before them" (Somigli and Moroni 2004, 18), Carnevali developed his own idiosyncratic views on what Italian literature was and should be and then cast himself as character in the translingual text to express them.

It is not casual that the literary texts he mentions in the early chapters of the *Autobiography* are non-Italian. In boarding school, an attendant gives him novels to read:

> He gave me *The Three Musketeers*, which I read in French, understanding more than one might imagine. It was the first book that I read in French and he lent me the book because its French is extremely easy. But right after that he gave me *Eugenie Grandet*, and *La Dernière Fée*, and he himself read to me the dreary, macabre, fierce poems from *Les Fleurs Du Mal*. (1967, 44)

French was, more than any other, the language of culture and social prestige in the postunification Italy in which Carnevali grew up. It is quite natural that it should be the first foreign language that he learned—and one with which he maintained a strong link for all his life, as demonstrated by his lifelong passion for Rimbaud. The image of the young Carnevali being guided into French literature, struggling with Dumas, Balzac, and Baudelaire, seems a prelude to his engaging with the English language. Carnevali, unsurprisingly, "loved to read" as a boy, displaying an omnivorous interest in poetry and fiction. His early contact with an American imagery comes through the adventures of *Nick Carter, Nat Pinkerton,* and *Buffalo Bill.* In the *Autobiography* he also recalls reading "some terrible appendix novels" (1967, 44): the phrase literally translates the Italian *romanzo d'appendice,* a form of nineteenth-century cheap, serialized fiction, similar to the dime novels he mentions. The calque identifies his understanding of the literary world as still related to Italian categorizations to some extent, even in a narration that has the abandonment of Italian at its core.

The chapters dedicated to Venice (where he studied at the Collegio Marco Foscarini between 1911 and 1913) perfectly illustrate Carnevali's desire to engage with *italianità* on his own terms, from the perspective of an emigrant and not conforming to rules and assumptions. Venice is the Italian city that he describes most extensively and with uncompromising admiration: "Nothing in Venice is unbeautiful. All is resplendent, all speaks of ancient artists . . ." (E. Carnevali 1967, 54). Only there Carnevali "finds a reality commensurate with his poetic vision and form for his concept of beauty and value in human love" (Boelhower 1982, 160). He sets Venice in comparison against the whole of America and its alienating modernity: "I would give away all modernity for one look at Venice. I would give away all the unlovely new things for a single look at you" (1967, 54). According to him, "the gondola belongs to no one but a poet" and is superior to the automobile (1967, 55). In the narrative arc of the *Autobiography,* the description of Venice prepares for the author's imminent move to New York, anticipating that emigration will fail expectations and cause further trauma. In terms of Carnevali's abandonment of Italian culture, it stands as a reminder that Italy can be beautiful, but that he would not experience such beauty on his terms:

> I mixed my love for the Grand Canal with my love for Giovanni Genovali. He and Venice were the two splendours of my life. When I had his hand in mine, I was happy. (1967, 55–56)

Carnevali's homosexual relationship with a classmate would ultimately define him as an outsider and mark his distance from the fatherland. His account repeatedly attempts to deny the stigma on homosexuality and frame it as a natural relationship ("In short, ours was the ordinary love affair"). This is the account of a moment of personal growth framed by a literary reference: "I know from *Jean Christophe* [sic] that such love-affairs between boys are frequent, and often are the most innocent and pure things ever." The reference to Romain Rollande's Nobel Prize–winning novel *Jean-Christophe* (1904–12) explains Emanuel and Giovanni's love within the borders of a literary success of the time. This is possibly used by Carnevali as a form of self-defense, "authorizing" homosexuality in the context of the narrative by the fact that it replicates a famous fictional narration. The English language enables him in the 1930s to write the story he had intended to conceal from the school directors in the 1910s.

Carnevali's sexual identity is in a constant process of definition and redefinition in the *Autobiography*, and the account often expresses confusion and contradictions at a linguistic level as well. In particular, he does not refrain from borrowing derogatory words from Italian to define homosexuality, as in this later episode of the *Autobiography*:

> I slept one night with him and he endowed me with the sweetest names, but there was nothing pederastic about it, for he was young and strong and loved women very much, and I did too. (1967, 259)

The term "pederastic" is a calque from the Italian *pederasta*, a rather common homophobic slur at the time. While contemporary Italian gender discourse still has a strong influence in Carnevali's choice of words, the English language offered him a chance to discuss his sexuality more openly—not because of English per se, but for the liminal position allowed to Carnevali as a translingual and an outsider.

The causal link between bisexuality and the desire to emigrate is evident in the narrative, as it was arranged by Boyle: Giovanni's refusal to continue his relationship with Emanuel triggers the latter's "first symptoms of hysteria" (1967, 57). This results in Carnevali being expelled, reluctantly moving to his father's house and finally writing him a letter: "I said that I was sick of his house, . . . that I had quit school forever and that I wanted to go to America as soon as possible" (1967, 58). In the 1967 *Autobiography*, Carnevali's bisexuality is the feature that sets his separazione from the fatherland in motion.[8] It causes Tullio Carnevali to utter the sentence that, since the embryonic account in the 1917 letter to Monroe, Emanuel associated with his refusal of the fatherland: *a nemico che fugge, ponti d'oro*. The sentence resurfaces in the narration of the 1930s and in its 1967 edition: "For the enemy in flight we build a golden bridge" (1967, 58). In 1917, when writing his story for the first time in a letter, Carnevali had translated the idiom as "make a golden bridge to a fleeing enemy." This was the translation of a young translingual striving for acceptance in the new language. The 1930s text comes after a long process of learning and adaptation and refines the 1917 version. Still, Carnevali's continuous retranslations and retellings of his own story keep that utterance as decisive for his separation from the fatherland. That idiom, inherently tied to the Italian language (it does not exist in English) and to the man who uttered it, set in motion the journey across languages.

Carnevali grew up in an Italy that was still caught in the process of defining its national uniqueness and in an age for which the existence of a national conscience itself entailed a certain nineteenth-century idea of the "foreign as one pole, exterior and other, and the domestic as its opposite, internally derived, infinitely supple, and uniquely authentic in subjective expression"—leaving no space for the translingual (Hokenson and Munson 2007, 142). As a translingual author, Carnevali could, looking back at those years, paint an ironic and idiosyncratic picture of his younger self at odds with this idea of national culture. The text subtly ridicules the staples of mainstream culture in turn-of-the-century Italy, complementing it with the young poet's aspiration toward the foreign. In the paragraphs that lead to emigration, the narrator lists staples of Italian food from cities where he did not grow up, emptied of their specificity in the accumulation: "Goodbye to ravioli of Milano, zampone from Modena, agnolotti of Turin, spaghetti *à la Napolitaine*, goodbye!" (E. Carnevali 1967, 62). At the same time, he remarks that "there is an intimacy with a country one has suffered in and it is this intimacy one misses most when away." This preludes a continuous effort to recuperate *italianità* in his own terms, which will be evident in his American years. But most importantly, the last passage of this part of the narrative confirms the deep emotional reasons for emigrating: "I must confess I felt no great sorrow or nostalgia, for Italy meant my father to me" (E. Carnevali 1967, 63).

3. The Immigrant and the Language of Modernity: Carnevali Arrives in New York

Emanuel Carnevali, aged sixteen, left for the United States hoping to find the expressive possibilities that he felt the fatherland denied him. Looking to affirm his individuality, he took the same route that hundreds of thousands of Italians took each year toward New York. To every Italian immigrant, "America first existed as a metaphor," a compelling yet distant image, reinforced by tales of returning migrants: "exaggerated accounts of their successes and failures were created so that through story the myth of America was created and through metaphor the myth was communicated" (Gardaphé 2004, 18). It took Carnevali a single glance to dispel the power of the metaphor:

> This was the long-dreamed of New York, this awful network of fire-escapes. This was not the New York we had dreamed of, so dear to the imagination, so cherished among all the hopes a man may hope: this dream of the dreamless, this shelter of all the homeless, this impossible city. This miserable panorama before us was one of the greatest cities in the world. (E. Carnevali 1967, 73)

His account subverts many staples of immigrant narratives, including the vision of the Statue of Liberty from the ship deck welcoming the "huddled masses yearning to breathe free." Carnevali does not find much hope in the vision: "one could admire the Statue of Liberty, if one had the stomach to" (1967, 73). Ellis Island, the port of entry, has figured in many immigrant narratives as the place where migrants' hopes were tested and their encounter with the foreign began. It is the founding myth of citizenship for foreign-born Americans: it marks their arrival just as Plymouth Rock marked the arrival of the Pilgrim fathers, Russian-American author Mary Antin once stated (Sollors 2008, 202). Carnevali strips this moment of mysticism when he records, with an annoyed tone, that Ellis Island officials "thought it very fine to ask every immigrant whether he had been to jail" (1967, 73). Thus begins the narration of Emanuel's encounter with the modernity of America and his attempts to face it in his own terms.

Viscusi remarked that Carnevali, although sensitive to the theme of linguistic displacement, "never speaks of his own difficulties while learning English" and rather "seems not to have experienced any" (2006, 178). A close look at the *Autobiography* reveals several passages that underline the linguistic and cultural displacement of Carnevali's early New York years. Carnevali admits to having very little knowledge of English when he arrived. He gained his fluency by surviving moments of miscommunication, misunderstandings, and a constant threat to his individuality. This struggle is part of the picaresque tale that would lead him to become, as an outsider, "an American poet."

To describe the linguistic reality of the modern metropolis, linguists recently have come up with the concept of *metrolingualism*, describing "the ways in which people of different and mixed backgrounds use, play with and negotiate identities through language" with a focus "not on language systems but on languages as emergent from contexts of interaction" (Otsuji and Pennycook 2010, 246). Concretely, the model describes real language interactions in the metropolitan setting, considering all the words and phrases from different linguistic origins used in the same conversation, not as deviation from a norm, but as an indication of how individuals use the linguistic resources at their disposal. It is very likely that the fabric of everyday speech in New York at Carnevali's time was a similar texture of misunderstandings, adjustments, combinations, and creativity. The *Autobiography* preserves the memory of that metrolingual fabric as part of the narrative; however, it does so from the point of view of its English-learning hero. In so doing, it stages another fact of migrant life: existence as a "translated being" (Malena 2003, 9). This fact is true at a metaphorical level (substituting the old culture for the new), but it also has a counterpart in the continuous operations of decoding the unknown, bridging communicative gaps and creating ease of understanding where there is none. Translation is a "question of real, immediate and urgent seriousness" for migrants, as "the ability to translate (autonomous practices) or be translated (heteronymous practices) can in some instances indeed be a matter of life and death" (Cronin 2006, 45). The metrolingual reality of New York enters the narrative at certain points, but the horizon of the text is that literary English.

Literary modernism, "friendly as it may have been to polyglot experimentation (with luminaries like Dos Passos, Pound, Joyce and George grousing multilingually around Europe's salons), . . . had little aesthetic patience for the arduous and unelite nitty-gritty of language learning" (Gramling 2016). This dichotomy will be a constant factor in Carnevali's career. As an intellectual, he would interact with some of the modernist experimenters, but the basic operation of his writing is that of learning a language not to expand literary possibilities, but to have the possibility to write literature. At the heart of his language learning are displacement and trauma, which in his American years took the forms of menial work and an indifferent metropolis. Of his first job, as a busboy in a restaurant, he writes: "I gave myself enthusiastically to it, working like a horse, and at night dreaming of the piles and stacks of dishes, dishes, dishes" (1967, 77). Carnevali's days as a waiter, dishwasher, and gardener all blur into one image in the narration:

> I dragged this weary body of mine, eternally tired, eternally ill, with a certain obstinacy from place to place. I had to live, but I had all of America against me, all this never-ending urge to work. (E. Carnevali 1967, 149)

The author's pain is described as both physical and psychic in the intercultural narration. America is associated, in both passages quoted above, with words conveying the image of weights and burdens. Of the English vocabulary, one word in particular is quickly learned and fetishized, recurring through the pages of the *Autobiography* written two decades later: "the JOB, that damnable affair, THE JOB. Nightmare of the hunted, THE JOB, this misery, this anxiety, this kind of neurasthenia . . ." (E. Carnevali 1967, 76). Carnevali capitalizes the word "job" in much the same way that Pietro Di Donato would in his 1939 *Christ in Concrete*: to cast "Job" as the personified antagonist of his Italian workers (Gardaphé 1996, 68). Carnevali and Di Donato use the typographic device not only to respond to the same socioeconomic predicament—which is a more pressing concern in Di Donato's highly class-conscious novel—but also to signal the close association between the predicament of the migrant worker and the language of the new world, where a common word like "job" may signify a whole world of distress and precariousness.

The pain felt by an immigrant, writes Hron, "is not transparent" (2009, 40), not easily seen or understood by the host community. In the new environment, they have no language to express their toils. The painful experiences often become conflated with the very image of the host country, as Carnevali does while recalling his sensations from his first months in the United States ("I had all of America against me"). The *Autobiography* is an interesting document of the migrant's interaction with the new reality and also a "translation" of those feelings into the language of the host country: "expressing pain is not a transparent act; yet, neither is it ineffable. Translation does not presume transparency; yet, at the same time, it does counter inexpressibility" (Hron 2009, 40). Translingual writing enables the migrant to counter the silence imposed by language differences and convey at least a version of his or her experience to the readership of the host country. It is not a "transparent" version of the migrant's experience. Yet it can be used as a tool to probe the early stages of linguistic and cultural displacement of a migrant. By the time Carnevali writes this "translation," he is an American author in possession of a literary language with which to frame and illustrate his suffering.

Carnevali's exposure to the linguistically unknown begins on the ship to America, awakening the poet not only to linguistic diversity, but also to its power and threat. On the ship, he meets Missio, an immigrant who poses as a nihilist philosopher and who had been a civil servant in the Belgian Congo. Missio—whose tales do not seem to show any regret for his involvement in one of the harshest colonial experiences—teaches the young Emanuel some words from an unspecified African language. The words ("*soka*," "*malam*," "*menemene*") are left untranslated and their meaning only indicated as "obscene." Carnevali, in retrospect, concludes that learning curses and "obscene" words is a crucial part of the learning of a new language:

> The first words one learns of any language are always the obscenities and the blasphemies. Because obscenities are half the vocabulary of the people and the thing which interests them the deepest. Organized beastiality [sic] is infinitely more comprehensible than organized beauty. (1967, 70)

The "beastiality" of language is threatening but more immediately appealing to newcomers, as taboo words are the key to a primal and powerful aspect of a language. To the young, culturally omnivorous exile, they must have exerted great fascination if he remembered them after two decades.

In New York, Carnevali encountered the "beastiality" of several languages and attempted to come up with some "organized beauty," but what emerges primarily from the narrative are the continuous attempts at understanding and making himself understood. He apparently created a small circle of friends, all of them linguistic outsiders: a French prostitute, a Dutchman, a German, and most importantly his brother Augusto, who briefly lived in New York before returning to Italy to fight in World War I.[9] Carnevali and the unnamed French girl start a friendship, where his previous experience learning French is put to good use, as is evident in the code-switching moments in the narrative: "we became good friends when her *souteneur* was not around. . . . She told me that her task was to '*soulager le genre humain*'" (E. Carnevali 1967, 88). Carnevali's German friend Mitterlechner, on the other hand, has his own way of bending English to his will to create his own slang and express his irredeemable difference:

> He called his landlady "a camel." He called me "a sucker." He called his doctor "a fraud." He called his sweetheart "a whore." He called his work "slaving." He called all Italians and Greeks rotten people. He called his *vaterland* the highest most civilized land on earth. (E. Carnevali 1967, 121)

While Carnevali and the French girl can establish a sense of community over their common predicament, Mitterlechner seems to make his brief appearance in the *Autobiography* mostly to remind the reader that speech created in a multicultural environment is not always informed by a desire to overcome difference and create communion; intolerance can also be brought into the picture and translated in turn. Carnevali rejects this view: "his love for his *vaterland* was most ugly" (1967, 121).

In spite of the amount of metrolingual exchange, incomprehension is a recurring element as Carnevali tried to decode the city of New York and its indifferent modernity. He recalls finding a room with an Italian landlady on the day of his arrival, but that did not prevent him from experiencing his first miscommunication:

> The landlady of this one was deaf as a bell, but she was Italian and she was the cook. There was a servant-girl who inevitably asked me if I wanted "Awful Pie." I tried to write down for her whatever I wanted, but to my surprise and indignation she never understood. (E. Carnevali 1967, 74)

In this case, the Italian landlady would be able to understand the author, but she is "deaf as a bell" (a literal translation of the Italian idiom *sordo come una campana*). The waitress, on the other hand, keeps offering what the author understands as "Awful Pie": the apple pie, a dessert which is often regarded as quintessentially American, is misunderstood by the disillusioned immigrant as "Awful." Once that migrant has become a migrant-author, he can reuse that misunderstanding for parody and comic effect. The misunderstandings staged in the narration may only be a fraction of the ones experienced by Carnevali upon his arrival in New York, but it is likely that they all provoked his "surprise and indignation" at the lack of a common code.

As Cronin underlines, "translating oneself into the language of the host community is not only a way of understanding how that community thinks and functions," but also a step toward the individual's inclusion in the community (2006, 53). Carnevali's early attempts at translating himself are often frustrated. He and his brother are kicked out by a landlord after he calls the landlord's wife his "mistress," which turns out to be a remarkable example of mistranslation: "I explained that in Italy women are always addressed as Signora which I believed meant 'mistress,' and no one would ever dream of calling a lady by her actual name" (E. Carnevali 1967, 91). Carnevali's mistake depends on an earnest will to maintain formality in shifting linguistic systems, yet in this episode he ends up being left out of the linguistic common space.

Carnevali's literary education progresses together with his acquisition of English as he complements his daily experience of dishwashers and sidewalks, street signs, and free-lunch counters with nightly reading sessions. He recalls "div[ing] fearlessly into George Bernard Shaw" and "[falling] in love with one word," although he did not get its "real significance: *disparagingly*" (1967, 92). As pointed out by Fracassa, the fascination for this word entails "l'autonomia del significante quale polo d'attrazione per il poeta straniero"[10] (2005, 144). The narration takes the sound of the foreign word as a symbol of the mystery that the foreign language represents before it is first translated and then familiarized. After the young, displaced migrant reader becomes a writer, the episode becomes part of an English narrative, testifying to the accomplished command of the language in which he could tell the story of how he conquered the foreignness, reducing it to an italicized English word within an English text.

The process leading to the start of Carnevali's literary career is now already in full motion. Carnevali begins writing, although his first experiments are destined to be forgotten. He initially writes film scripts—or, as he calls them, "scenarios"—with the help of his Dutch friend. These scripts, now lost, were apparently indebted to the *Grand Guignol* tradition, involving "a drastic muddle of love, death, crime, and malefactors" (E. Carnevali 1967, 94). They are soon replaced by poems. Carnevali recalls writing his first line ever while shoveling snow in Brooklyn: "As yet I wasn't a poet, I was only a reader, but there I wrote one line. I wrote: Love is a mine hidden in the mountain of our old age" (E. Carnevali 1967, 116). Carnevali's narrative construes his transformation from reader/learner to poet/producer as something that started with a single line: we may ascribe that to his later ideas on art and poetry, founded on a rejection of technique and an exaltation of the poet's sensitivity alone. We know, on the other hand, the long process of trauma and displacement that gave birth to this line.

The beginning of Carnevali's writing is also the beginning of fruitless visits to the editors of reviews and of rejection slips. A rejection slip from William Rose Benét testifies to his still unaccomplished acquisition of English: "He wrote me that my poems were 'turgid.' I was compelled to lose some precious time going to my dictionary to find out what turgid meant" (1967, 95–96). Finally an editor, A. R. Orage of *Seven Arts Magazine*, accepts two of his poems. What Carnevali fails to mention in the narration is that *Seven Arts* closed in 1917 before it had a chance to publish those poems. He then contacted other editors from the same circle, including *Poetry*'s Harriet Monroe: thus began Carnevali's relationship with the modernist literary circles of the United States. By this time, he is able to write in English, but the language still feels new and different, compelling him to use a dictionary. He will never eliminate the feeling that he is an outsider in America or the sense of economic and cultural precariousness that comes with being a migrant. At the same time, he will never stop interacting, from the outside and on his own terms, with Italy and Italian culture. What begins here, with the words "I want to become an American poet," is a career always in precarious balance between individual aspirations and the constraints of the nation, between echoes of Italy and the desire to be part of American literature.

2

The Newcomer
and the Splendid Commonplace

Using English as a Second Language

Carnevali published his poem "Colored Lies" in *The Forum* in January 1918, followed by a short collection of six poems, "The Splendid Commonplace," in *Poetry* in March of the same year. At this point he is hardly "an American poet," but he is on the way to becoming a recognized outsider, crafting his poetry and prose on the base of American models and polemicizing his way into modernist circles. From 1917 to 1919, he is both a language learner and a constant presence in literary magazines. Carnevali's first poetic and narrative experiments reveal the distance that he had to cover to master his language of choice: what the native speaker usually takes for granted may be a source of confusion or wonder to the newcomer, and even a "commonplace" may sound "splendid."

In a chapter of her recent *Translation and Migration* that deals with Ellis Island interpreters, Inghilleri remarks how, in the "liminal" moment of arrival, "when individuals are precariously positioned between their departure from one place and their arrival at another, *language becomes significant in a heightened way*" (2017, 57, my emphasis). In this situation, communication with people who speak the same language may become a "vital stabilizing resource" while "inter-lingual interactions provide migrants a voice" (Inghilleri 2017, 57). This "voice" does not come cheap, or naturally—especially when it ultimately has to fuel a literary effort.

Translingual writers, who share less linguistic common ground with their target audience, must engage in a direct, continuous process of negotiating grammar, vocabulary, and idioms to convey their meaning.

Kellman explains this aspect of translingual writing using Shklovsky's idea of *ostranenie*, the "defamiliarization" that is inherent to art:

> It is hard to take words for granted when writing in a foreign language. Translinguals represent an exaggerated instance of what the Russian formalists maintained is the distinctive quality of all imaginative literature: ostranenie, "making it strange." (Kellman 2000, 29)

According to Shklovsky, art implies the defamiliarization of the common, the "removal of [the] object from the sphere of automatized perception," causing "estrangement" and a "long and laborious" perception (1998, 6). In the case of the translingual writer, the textual object—his or her medium—is always out of the "sphere of automatized perception." The resulting text may or may not present a "strange" language to the monolingual audience: that depends on the degree of linguistic deviance the author employs. The translingual author, on the other hand, works in a permanent condition of estrangement with respect to the medium: the ground that he or she chooses to cover to get closer to the intended audience is up to the author. In this respect, Carnevali's relationship with everyday English is a particularly revealing example of the complex relationship between the translingual author and the linguistic medium.

This chapter explores Carnevali's nascent career through the lens of translingual analysis. It starts with his early works, which earned the young poet a place in New York and Chicago modernist circles, building a complex relationship that drew on both his display of cultural difference and the assumptions of the prevailing cultural milieu. Contemporary criticism, both by and about Carnevali, expressed this relationship in terms of linguistic, aesthetic, and ethnic boundaries.

For his part, the young dishwasher who read English books in the furnished rooms of Manhattan approached the established forces of American poetry both enthusiastically and critically—with Whitman as a model and Williams and Sandburg as mentors. The adoption of a style inspired by these poets provided him with tools fit to describe the American metropolis, which he often would bend and transform according to his own expressive needs.

The last section of the chapter deals with the opposite of literary assimilation. Carnevali's translingual repertoire is particularly apparent in the rhythms and the vocabulary of his New York poetry: what role could his native Italian play in poems and fiction that engaged with the American metropolis?

1. The Splendid Commonplace

For Carnevali, America was the land of the commonplace. According to his *Autobiography*, this impression took root from his first look at New York: "These famous skyscrapers were nothing more than great boxes standing upright or on one side, terrifically futile, frightfully irrelevant, so commonplace that one felt he had seen the same thing somewhere before." (1967, 73)

As noted in the previous chapter, this first impression is in stark contrast to the typical immigrant narrative, substituting disappointment for awe. Boelhower notes that Carnevali appears immune to the "metaphysical appeal so obvious in buildings like the Woolworth," reducing them to "their function, to a zero degree of semantic charge, the protagonist has no other choice but to dwell on their economic function" (1982, 165). His critique of skyscrapers fuels his wider assessment of the American urban environment as one devoid of philosophical power, unable to support the migrant's hopes of personal fulfillment.

There is a linguistic dimension to Carnevali's recollected first look at Manhattan. The passage recalls the poet's first attempt to organize and define the reality of America: in brief, to find a language to make sense of America. That language is the language of the commonplace. America appeared to Carnevali as a succession of basic functional shapes: in addition to the skyscrapers, the elevated railroad station is called an "unpretentious, unassuming little box" (1967, 74). The insistence on "boxes" may point to the freshly arrived Carnevali's lack of terms to describe and categorize the reality of New York. Writing the *Autobiography*, an older Carnevali who has mastered the English language still remembers that first basic impression of "boxes." Approaching a new language means also to "develop sensitivity to new features, shift prototypes, adjust category boundaries, and in some cases, acquire entirely new categories organized around distinct perceptual properties" (Pavlenko 2014, 71). Carnevali's early experience with the cityscape initiates the start of a "cognitive restructuring," to use Pavlenko's term, which leads him to resort to conceptual analogy. The result is a sort of defensive déjà vu, pinning down the cityscape to the already known: in recollection,

America felt "so commonplace that one felt he had seen the same thing somewhere before" (1967, 73).

Making sense of America involves, in the *Autobiography*, dealing with the impenetrable unknown and the trivial commonplace at the same time: America is a "land of easy mystery (easy because readily solved)" (E. Carnevali 1967, 74). The narrative of that first impact informs our understanding of Carnevali's literary career in New York. Raymond Williams describes the link between modernist abandonment of familiar environments and detachment from familiar modes of expression:

> The experience of visual and linguistic strangeness . . . raised to the level of universal myth this intense, singular narrative of unsettlement, homelessness, solitude and impoverished independence: the lonely writer gazing down on the unknowable city from his shabby apartment. The whole commotion is finally and crucially interpreted and ratified by the city of Émigrés and Exiles itself, New York. (R. Williams 1989, 34)

Carnevali's writing deals with the modernist tropes of "unknowable cities" and "shabby apartments." The linguistic and cognitive mismatches between himself and New York City were such that he could enter the world of modernist "Émigrés and Exiles" and criticize it from the inside. The commonplace was the fundamental notion he used to interpret his new environment, articulating the narrative of unsettlement and independence described by Williams through the eyes of a linguistic newcomer. The commonplace became part of Carnevali's language, appearing in his poetry and fiction and contributing to the discussion on the role of the poet with respect to everyday language.

The first poem of the "Splendid Commonplace" collection, "In This Hotel," powerfully presents the poetic potential of everyday language when used by someone who does not take it for granted. It is set, presumably, in one of Carnevali's New York workplaces and describes the headwaiter greeting every hotel guest with small talk: "Nice day to-day!" and "It will rain to-day!" In reiterating these set phrases, the poet expresses his desire to possess this habitual language and to extend its meaning:

> And I, who do not sleep, who wait and watch for the dawn,
> One day I would come down to the world.
> I would have a trumpet as powerful as the wind,

And I would trumpet out to the world
The splendid commonplace:
"Nice day to-day!"
And another day I would cry out in despair,
"It will rain to-day!"
("In This Hotel," ll. 13–20)

The poem is based on the reception and understanding of everyday English and its transformation into poetry. It is built on the reality of translingual existence, which involves not only a continuous sense of linguistic novelty, but also a sense of diffidence toward simple utterances in the new, alien language. In this case, the poet cannot simply replicate the headwaiter's small talk. From a translingual perspective, each successful utterance is a success, representing advancement into foreign and dangerous territory. This triggers Carnevali's desire for poetic transformation of everyday speech, turning his foreignness to his own advantage. Here the poet can invest everyday words with power ("a trumpet as powerful as the wind") to create the "splendid commonplace." Carnevali looks at the English language from the outside, and what he sees may be "splendid" or threatening. As an outsider, the translingual sees unexpressed potential in the most trivial expressions, and Carnevali often links this perspective with the creative power of poetry.

Another poem in the "Splendid Commonplace" collection identifies poets as "essences of the people's beautiful selves," violins "whose strings quiver . . . even when touched by the world's rough fingers" ("To the Poets" ll. 1–5). Carnevali's faith in poetry links his art form to a special kind of sensitivity to the everyday world and the possibility of redemption from that world's "rough fingers." Other poems from the same period concentrate on the unfamiliarity of everyday English. "Last Day," from 1919, describes a neurotic episode ("my hands / afraid / trembling / insanely" ll. 7–10) that is also a repudiation of the city environment: "I am listening to the great appeal of the things that have gone crazy" (1919b, l. 24). There is also an unnamed interlocutor, who utters "the incomprehensible commonplace: / 'All is well, / All is well.'" The soothing, everyday language should reconcile the poet with the city environment, but instead it becomes the impenetrable element with which Carnevali struggles to come to terms.

Two 1925 poems, inserted in his post-return collection *A Hurried Man* under the title "Commonplaces," show that Carnevali continued

to reflect on the hidden potentialities of everyday language, even after
he left America. The first, titled "How Are You?," considers the title
phrase from the painstakingly literal point of view of the language learner:

> I wish that you all be well,
> And that the sick ones of you get well;
> I want a big, fresh, clean world.
> Do you, too?
> Is that what you mean
> When you say:
> "How do you do?"
> "How do you feel?"
> ("How Are You?," ll. 1–8)

The poet plays here on the distance between a customary greeting
and the potential that the utterance has when taken literally by the
newcomer-poet. The second poem, "I Am Glad To See You," plays on
the same distance with bitter irony. The expression is taken to mean
"My life still missed / One aspect / And here you come / To fill the
longing for you . . ." (ll. 2–5). For the speaker, the phrase is made of
words "too plain to hide a lie: 'I am glad to see you'" (ll. 8–9). The
line implies that the phrase may lose force when uttered carelessly by
more accustomed speakers and therefore becomes a "lie." The role of
the newcomer-poet is to reaffirm the primary meaning of such phrases,
insisting on plain language.

Carnevali combined the linguistic migrant's "sense of inauthenticity in uttering what passes for idiomatic speech in the second language"
(Besemeres 2002, 29) with a poet's attitude toward language, seeking
poetic value in everyday phrases. The condition of the linguistic outsider
also enabled him to position himself as a poetic outsider in the modernist
milieu. In a 1918 letter to *Poetry* editor Harriet Monroe, written in the
form of a poem, Carnevali stated:

> And I'll go on making confessions
> Even tho I don't speak english [sic] well
> Even tho nobody gives a damn . . .

Half-jokingly, he acknowledges his status as linguistic outsider, although
his frequent use of spellings such as "tho" in drafts and correspondence

implies a degree of familiarity with the informal register of American English. Above all, he claimed his role as disruptive poetic force, intending to follow his path of choice even if he could be met with diffidence.

At the time, American modernists elaborated diverse responses to immigrants, ranging from reticence to cosmopolitan interest as they attempted "to establish new kinds of communities, foreign both to their (generally middle-class) upbringing and to contemporary consumerist culture" (Miller 2007, 455). New York intellectuals identified Carnevali as a poetic force coming from the outside, bringing his uniqueness to the literary community. They also had trouble adapting to this untamed force. On his part, Carnevali often used the aesthetic and ethnic boundaries between himself and the other writers to fuel his critique of modernism.

"As He Sees It" appeared in 1918 in *Poetry* as a letter in poetic form. A brief introduction by the author indicates that the poem was a parody of the stylistic clichés of literary modernism as he observed them in literary reviews. Interestingly, Carnevali (who then had only a handful of poems to his name) already characterized modernism as "his" area, writing, "Here is what I feel sometimes about our own stuff." Even more interestingly, the poem continuously refers to an alien "voice" in his throat:

> V
> A voice sings in my throat
> And rings like a fever
> Through my body
> That vibrates with pain.
> ("As He Sees It," ll. 15–18)

Even when not explicitly dealing with linguistic identity, translinguals may appear "painfully cognizant of the fact that in different languages their voices may sound differently even when telling the 'same' stories" (Pavlenko 2006, 3). In this case, it is tempting to identify the alien "voice" described by Carnevali with the English language. The poem's exploration of his divided linguistic self also expresses his struggle to bend the language of the commonplace to his artistic use:

> It's an old platitude, an old commonplace.
> You can't force an artist, what do you think?
> Modern

Modernity,
Modernism . . .
I am above my throat,
I have a right to forget . . .
("As He Sees It," ll. 53–59)

The poem reflects Carnevali's uncertainties in navigating the multitude of constraints and influences of the new modernist canon. He feels his new language as a foreign body within himself, bringing with it alien terminology and stylistic elements: in the end, Carnevali seeks refuge outside rationality ("Nobody home / The poet has left for the asylum").

Attempting to come to terms with the "splendid" (but also threatening) commonplace, Carnevali began a quest for purity of poetic expression, in which he identified strongly with Rimbaud. In quasimystical adoration, he wrote an essay about the French poet in 1919:

> This paper will not be criticism. Critics are dead leaves lying still while the hurricane sweeps by high above. To utter something while enraptured in the hurricane, that is the only way to compensate to me my not being the hurricane; and the only way to criticize a poet. (E. Carnevali 1919c, 20)

The essay considers the stylistic qualities of Rimbaud only briefly, focusing more on his status as an ideal poetic persona, the personification of youth—a vital force that names reality anew and defies social and moral conventions: "Rimbaud is the Advent of Youth. Almost everything else in the world is unbelief in Youth" (E. Carnevali 1919c, 20). As noted by Domenichelli, "through Rimbaud, Carnevali found that the achievement of poetry is the achievement of life that consists in knowing the ego and possessing it" (1998, 85). Still a young man himself, in exile, bisexual, estranged from his family, and dealing with a sense of linguistic extraneousness, Carnevali turned to his French role model: "Rimbaud is, in me, a prayer to things more beautiful than I, the perfectly soul-less things, the unconscious, beautiful things" (1919c, 24). Carnevali's youth, and his linguistic outsiderness, were tools in his assault on American letters. The language of the commonplace (a vernacular to which he must react, but around which he could also build an entire poetic world) catalyzed this opposition.

Fellow modernists were often baffled by Carnevali's novelty and by the strengths and weaknesses of his poetic of the splendid commonplace. In 1919, at a party hosted by poet Lola Ridge, he gave a speech that criticized the poets of New York. Carnevali then refashioned the speech as an article, which he sent to *Poetry*; it was rejected for being too harsh.[1] The article was printed for the first time in *A Hurried Man* in 1925 under the title "Maxwell Bodenheim, Alfred Kreymborg, Lola Ridge, William Carlos Williams" and later reappeared in a rearranged version in his 1967 *Autobiography* as "My Speech at Lola's." In a letter to Monroe, Carnevali called it "almost my declaration of war to anybody who does not write as I do."[2]

The speech is an example of his emotion-laden criticism; he claims that he wrote the essay "for [his] soul's sake," because "what [he] understood by literature was in danger of collapsing" (1925, 248). The issue is that of poetic technique as a threat to the poet's creativity: "I speak of your form, that half-and-half thing, that thing which cannot break loose from the cage of metrical rhythms and which clumsily strives toward the spontaneity of talk" (1925, 257). Disgusted with the present poetic debate ("If you are poets, as they say, I don't want to be a poet," 264), Carnevali questions the very artistic milieu he has just entered. The language of commonplace enables this critique, countering the sophistication of poetic technique with sheer creative power:

> I am the glorifier and the creator of the commonplace that made and make the world—I say, in the beginning there was the commonplace . . . I am a death and a resurrection, I am the same torment that is called everchanging life. I am a voice for the big sorrows of New York city. (1925, 266)

This incarnation of the "commonplace" testifies to the author's newfound confidence in using the unfamiliar language of America to create art and express his disruptive interpretation of poetry. Here, the commonplace assumes poetic power in the etymological sense of *poïesis* (creation)—it is the point of origin of the perceivable world in its everyday banality now remade and reimagined by the poet. Carnevali claims to be the "voice" of a city of outcasts and immigrants, and his role is to use the commonplace in a novel and disruptive way, proving irrelevant the stylistic and technical debates of his contemporaries.

Following his own artistic agenda, Carnevali was a linguistic outsider in an artistic milieu that existed alongside New York's immigrant
communities but often failed to engage with them. In this sense, the first
relevant critical appraisal of Carnevali's presence in modernist America
comes from the New York review *Others*. This short-lived magazine
(1915–1919), edited by Alfred Kreymborg, was particularly sensitive to
avant-garde modes and themes: "publishing the most unbridled free verse,
Others earned a reputation not only for technical innovation, but also for
social rebellion and sexual transgression" (Churchill 2006, 6). The review
was also attentive to minority cultures and engaged in a "performative
restaging of modernist identity and poetry with reference to New York's
immigrants," in particular the Jewish community (Miller 2007, 457).
Carnevali worked with the review in its final months and—if William
Carlos Williams's words are to be taken literally—accelerated its demise.

Others' final issue appeared in July 1919, bearing the words "For
Emanuel Carnevali" in bold letters on the front cover. Carnevali was
one of the issue's main contributors (the poem "Serenade," the short
story "Bogey Man," and "Leavetaking," a translation from Papini), and
the editorial by Williams explains *Others'* closure through his presence.
The essay describes Carnevali as an unrestrained poetic force, although
Williams appears dubious about his poetic accomplishments:

> What do I care if Carnevali has not written three poems
> I can thoroughly admire? Who can write a poem complete
> in every part surrounded by this mess we live in? The man
> is smashed to pieces by the stupidity of a city of s**tas**s.
> He will not allow me to take a line out of a poem . . . He
> is right. I am wrong when I yell technique at him. (W. C.
> Williams 1919, 3)

Williams identifies Carnevali's function in the New York milieu as demonstrating the superiority of life over poetry. Some imply that Williams
"must have seen in Carnevali a specter of his younger self" (Churchill
2006, 127). The essay was possibly influenced by Carnevali's recent speech
at Lola Ridge's or by a similar performance on his part.[3] It constructs
a lexical dichotomy between Williams, Kreymborg, and the *Others* on
one side and Carnevali on the other. The former are linked to poetic
technique and old age: "we older can compose, we seek the seclusion
of a style, of a technique" (W. C. Williams 1919, 3). Carnevali, on the

other hand, is "young," and that is precisely the reason why "his poems will not be constructed, they cannot be." Williams's dichotomy between style and poems that "cannot be constructed" seems to enact, from another point of view, Carnevali's ideal of the splendid commonplace.

Referring to Carnevali's passion, and to the avant-garde origins of *Others*, Williams concludes that the review must close down because it "has been blasted out of existence" (1919, 3). Of course Carnevali did not single-handedly cause the review's closure. Churchill reports that Kreymborg sought collaborations with other literary circles, causing a rift between him and the original group until "Williams seized the editorial controls and issued the July 1919 number, in which he pronounced *Others* dead once and for all" (2006, 58). Carnevali was nevertheless a catalyst: Williams perceived himself and his contemporaries as "too comfortable, complacent even, with the state of modern verse," intending to "not just . . . move outside of his comfort zone, but to raze it to the ground," and "Carnevali's critique . . . gave Williams the nudge he needed" (Templeton 2013, 149). Nevertheless, the editorial is an acknowledgment ("We salute you") of a pure, undiluted poetic force that dealt with basic facts of life, armed only with a sense of novelty and awe for those very same basic facts: "I believe he will go crazy or quit rather than write in a small way" (W. C. Williams 1919, 4).

Carnevali's first efforts were a poetic attempt to make sense of strangeness, overcome the immigrant's sense of linguistic displacement, and turn it into a strong artistic statement: one that could shock and disrupt the very literary milieu to which he sought access. Yet, for all his efforts to present himself as detached from schools, styles, and manifestos, Carnevali was very much a part of the modernist debates of his time. Although an outsider, he proved his relevance to the central discussions of the day. His attempts at the splendid commonplace, as we shall see, contain much of the America and Italy of his time.

2. "Because he was a foreigner": Literary Style and Linguistic Assimilation

As Carnevali's poetry and criticism started to appear in reviews like *Poetry*, *Others*, and *The Little Review*, he drew closer to his aspirations of becoming an American poet. Yet what kind of American poet would he be? One entry point to this question is to consider the American poets Carnevali admired. His 1917 "programmatic" letter to Monroe contains a rather composite canon of influences (Whitman, Poe, London, Waldo Frank, and James Oppenheim) and a statement: "I believe in free verse."

In his 1938 memoir *Being Geniuses Together*, Robert McAlmon (who published Carnevali's *A Hurried Man*) commented on Carnevali's literary allegiance:

> I concluded that it was because he was a foreigner that he so passionately loved Whitman, and later Sherwood Anderson and Carl Sandburg. Neither Anderson nor Sandburg ever rang true to me. (McAlmon 1938, 136)

Interestingly, he implied that "because he was a foreigner" Carnevali appreciated quintessentially American poetry, which the American modernists had already left behind. Modernism was in fact a period when American poets became preoccupied with the search for different poetic models from Europe and Asia, aiming to reconnect with ancient traditions and hoping to refine their own poetry through technical and sometimes philological research. Ezra Pound wrote in 1909: "mentally I am a Walt Whitman who has learned to wear a collar and a dress shirt (although at times inimical to both)" (2005, 188). Then, in a 1913 poem, he addressed Whitman as his "pig-headed father" while acknowledging that "[i]t was you that broke the new wood / Now is a time for carving" (Pound 1913, ll. 6–7). Yet at a time when "writers like Ezra Pound, H. D., and T. S. Eliot were fleeing American provincialism in favor of European culture and sophistication, Carnevali was running in the other direction" (Templeton 2013, 131). Much of his poetry and criticism is imbued with Whitman and his model of free verse, and many of his literary contacts also claimed to follow in Whitman's footsteps.

Poetry, a crucial element in Carnevali's literary education, declared its explicit allegiance to democratic aspects of Whitmanian poetics, sporting a quotation from Whitman on its back cover: "To have great poets / there must be great audiences too." These words expressed the inclusiveness and democratic spirit of American verse as the editors intended. Poets like Carl Sandburg, who also wrote for the magazine, were interested in renewing modern poetry's links to Whitman. Sandburg "enacted Whitman's idea of language" emanating from the people, as his "use of American idioms . . . suggests that he not only wants to speak *for* the people, he wants to speak *like* them, too" (Redding 2010, 684, author's emphasis). In a review of Sandburg's poetry, Carnevali praised this inclusion of street language into literary English as "a purely and originally American language . . . and a language of today" (1921a, 267).

Carnevali was not alone in his appreciation for the poet of *Leaves of Grass*: some of his Italian contemporaries entering the American literary scene were also susceptible to the influence of Whitman. Pascal D'Angelo's poetry acquired "the universal ambition that makes him first Italian, then American" from models "somewhere between Whitman and [Shelley's] Prometheus" (Viscusi 2003, 49); Arturo Giovannitti is believed to have taken Whitman as a model of social activism as well as "high-flown language" (Marazzi 2012, 26). Nor was the popularity of the American bard limited to Italian-Americans; Sollors called Whitman "the formal prototype, the adoptive ancestor, of ethnic modernists" (1986, 258), who in general appreciated Whitman more than their native counterparts. This may have something to do with the naturalness and inclusiveness of his style: "Whitman meant Poetry, Art, the Canon; but he also meant Brooklyn and the plebes" (Ferraro 1990, 12).

Whitman may have occupied a space within the American canon that made him appealing to migrant poets not only on a social level, but also because of the stylistic repertoire he had built to describe those social instances. Described as "long-line free verse" (Beyers 2001, 40), the most evident feature of Whitman's style is the length of the line; it also tends to sport long lists of elements together with strong assertions in a prophetic tone. Both characteristics seem to "encourage . . . enthusiastic and often syncretic religious philosophies" (Beyers 2001, 40). This feature is linked with the poet's democratic or universalist beliefs, elevating each element in the list to poetic dignity. In the light of recent developments in the study of bilingualism in a urban multicultural setting (translanguaging theory), it is easy to understand why this form may have appealed to migrant poets: as the modern urban space "allows multilingual individuals to integrate social spaces (and thus 'language codes') that have been formerly practiced separately in different places" (Garcia and Li Wei 2014, 24), the most open and inclusive expressive form may appear the most appropriate to discuss the migrant's predicament. While complying with the generally monolingual requirements of twentieth-century literature, migrant poets picked a form that was designed for inclusiveness, was not afraid to speak the language of the streets, and did not require complex stylistic shibboleths.

To Carnevali, this model of free verse was both a necessity, if he wanted to consider himself an American poet, and a new, open, inclusive form that could stage both the speech of the immigrant metropolis and the poet's reaction to it. His colleague Samuel Putnam commented that in the "constant bobbing up of . . . the every-day word, [Carnevali] is akin to the Sandburg whom he loves—and, beyond Sandburg, Whitman" (Putnam 1922, 11).

At the beginning, as Carnevali remembers in the *Autobiography*, he wrote "absurd, rhymed poetry which [he] sent to more than twenty magazines, getting nothing but rejection slips in return" (95). These poems were apparently influenced by Romantic clichés: "I even poetized that old drab mask, Pierrot . . . and then the springtime, and several other standard subjects" (1967, 95). He soon moved on to describe his environment and the struggles to balance artistic aspirations and immigrant life. Carnevali's first published poem, the January 1918 "Colored Lies," links the colors of Manhattan (the red of building facades and the blue, black, and gray of men's suits) to the notion of bourgeois respectability that the poet criticizes: the first of several poetic attacks on the urban environment. The poem has many rhyming lines and a structure that alternates three- and four-stress lines:

> The houses in a long row
> Have wind-burnt red faces.
> These coffins of motionless air
> With a fat, silly stare
> Beckon at the winds that blow
> A joyous insult in their faces—
> ("Colored Lies," ll. 1–6)

Carnevali was moving toward free verse, but his first published poems still denoted the need for a structure around which the words of his new language were cast, repeating insistently ("faces") as they built the poetic image.

Some of the rhymed poems would make it into the "Splendid Commonplace" collection. These poems resemble "Colored Lies" in their loose schemes, pairing long and short lines through insistent repetition of rhyming words, or even of whole phrases:

> Sweetheart, what's the use of you—
> When the night is blue,
> And I'm sad with the whisper of the skies,

And I'm heavy and I'm weary
With my many lies?
There is no music around me—
Not a sound
But the whisper of the skies . . .
("Sentimental Dirge," ll. 1–8)

These were the vestigial remains of his first experiments in poetry. In 1917, he said that "Sentimental Dirge" was "[his] first poem in rhyme and . . . second poem of all," written a month after he had begun writing in English.[4] He was conscious that his style was in continuous evolution:

> You see, this happens to be the case with young people—one year means a whole lot[:] in one year they can change radically. And I feel I did. So, people reading E. Carnevali of 1917 could not possibly claim to know E. C. of 1918: and I just want to enable people to make such same claim.[5]

Soon Carnevali developed a vivid, irregular, and assertive free verse, which is already visible in most of the 1918 "Splendid Commonplace" poems. In "His Majesty the Letter-Carrier," he portrays himself waking up early in the morning to wait for the postman:

Ah, there he is!
Who? . . . The letter-carrier, of course!
(What do you think I got up so early for?)
You never see him run—
He is so proud
Because he's got my happiness in that dirty bag . . .
("His Majesty," ll. 8–13)

The postman obviously fails to deliver to him the cherished letter of acceptance, that "letter from an editor that says / You're a great poet, young man!" (ll. 24–25). The poem ironically elevates the postman to a quasimythical figure, while the bits of dialogue with an imaginary audience break any rhythmic pattern, testifying that Carnevali was willing to experiment with his newly acquired stylistic freedom. His modernist parody "As He Sees It," on the other hand, testifies to a problematic adherence to the stylistic tenets of modernism. While he called modernist verse "our own stuff" in the poem, he also mocked some modernist techniques, such as Gertrude Stein's repetitions and those of his New York colleagues Kreymborg and Williams (Ricciardi 1986, 186):

> I
> A wondrous voice is urging me within
> And thrills me with a pain, alas! . . .
>
> II
> A wondrous voice urges me within
> And with a pain thrills me—alas! . . .
> ("As He Sees It," ll. 1–4)

The poem also reflects his anxiety with free verse:

> The throat and the pain,
> Which all rhymes with rain;
> But if it's a free verse
> It doesn't count.
> ("As He Sees It," ll. 32–35, author's emphasis)

The lines show Carnevali's fascination with the rhythms of English: the realization that "pain" and "rain" rhyme in English is expressed with a newcomer's surprise, followed by the puzzled comment that in free verse this "doesn't count." In 1918, he is an eager learner (of languages as well as poetic techniques) driven by the attempt to find his own voice, enthusiastic and cynical at the same time in relation to the different stylistic constraints that he witnessed and absorbed.

In his long 1919 poem "The Day of Summer," in which he engages deeply with the city of New York, Carnevali evokes Whitman as his predecessor: "O city, there lived in you once, O Manhattan, a man WALT WHITMAN" ("Summer," l. 251). Writing in the very same environment, Carnevali seeks a connection with Whitman as "a kosmos, of Manhattan the son" ("Song of Myself," l. 497). In the May 1919 issue of *Poetry* celebrating Whitman's centenary, Carnevali wrote his own homage—and his participation marked an important step in his literary assimilation into American letters. The poem in question, simply called "Walt Whitman," is quite a short homage at only four lines. However,

it does manage to contain both long lines and assertive statements in
this short space:

Noon on the mountain!—
And all the crags are husky faces powerful with love for
    the sun;
All the shadows
Whisper of the sun.
("Walt Whitman")

The poem displays sensitivity for the inherent force of nature that is found
in Whitman's poetry. Varzi remarks that the second line in particular is
true to the homage because "how Whitman himself put it: all truths wait
in all things" and while "we get only a few broken murmurs . . . every
murmur is significant" (2017, 369). In this way, Carnevali's splendid commonplace adheres to the path traced by Whitman. Carnevali's poems were
more often focused on the poet's inner world in a metropolitan context,
but this brief excursus into nature reveals the Whitmanian ascendancy
of his poetry. A few years later, in 1921 (when the American stage of
his career was nearly over), Carnevali wrote that every American poet
who does not follow in the path traced by Whitman is destined to a
brief life (1994, 45).

While it retains identifiable Whitmanian features from its earliest
stages, unlike Whitman's, Carnevali's poetry focuses almost exclusively
on the poet's inner world. The poems record the experience of the
surrounding environment, foregrounding displacement more often than
connection with the American landscape. Carnevali crafted a style that
drew lessons from the American poets he admired but was free and open
enough to let him express his dissent with respect to the culture and
society he was living in. In a way not dissimilar from what happens
when a style is disseminated and assimilated via translation, translingual adoption presents some formal and thematic features of the forms
that it reproduces, rearranged to fit a different sensibility and aesthetic
goals.

Carnevali's New York is one of multiple codes and narratives, all
perceived through the lens of his Old World background and expressed
in American free verse. Carnevali has an instinctive understanding of
urban modernity as "an awareness of the plurality of codes, a thinking

with and through translation, a continual testing of the limits of expression" in which translators and mediators walk like "flâneurs of a special sort" (Simon 2012, 6), but his poetry problematizes rather than celebrates the plurality of cultures:

> Not so . . .
> Not so disgusted after all.
> O altars of a little comfort, altars of a dyspeptic god gone
>   crazy in America for lack of
> personality (hamburger steak, Irish stew, goulash, spaghetti,
>   chop suey and curry!) O lunch-room counters!
> ("The Day of Summer," ll. 205–7)

Carnevali uses long-line free verse that lists and presents several elements (not unlike Whitman's lists), all of them making up the multilingual and multicultural reality of New York. Yet he underlines how the foods from all over the world lose their specificity in the melting pot of America. Boelhower observed that Carnevali in the *Autobiography* recalls "the complete indifference of the urban scene towards him, which he can only register and transcribe, not transmute or process" (Boelhower 1982, 167). Carnevali always sees New York through European eyes, as the place where hopes and expectations contend with the dangers of assimilation.[6] "The Day of Summer," analyzed in more detail below, represents Carnevali's most obvious effort to "process" his New York experiences, combining a record of the urban environment in long-line free verse with the impressions of the poetic *I*.

Published in 1919, shortly after he left the city, "The Day of Summer" takes up fourteen pages of the issue of *Poetry* in which it appeared. The long poem is divided into chronological sections ("Morning," "Noon," "Afternoon," "Evening," "Night") and follows Carnevali as he walks through Manhattan observing the people who rush through the streets. Mentions of poems titled "The Day of Winter" and "Preparations to a Day of Spring" in letters indicate that in 1919 Carnevali was considering writing a series of poems about the experience of different seasons in the city.[7] "The Day of Summer" was the only one of the series to be published. Alone, it constitutes a significant portion of Carnevali's poetic production while in New York and is his most convincing synthesis of the intimate, short lines of his first poems and Whitmanian free verse.

All the motifs of the early poems (the threatening cityscape, Carnevali's aspirations to become a great poet, the celebration of youth, and the critique of the bourgeoisie) are visible here.

Extended length, irregularity, and the inclusion of several voices from the streets of Manhattan are the apparent Whitmanian features in "The Day of Summer." Carnevali explored the possibility of breaking free of the limits imposed by metric, as lines expand into paragraphs. Preoccupation with the technique of free verse and the poetic speech of America goes hand in hand with Carnevali's description of urban displacement. Carnevali takes features from Whitman and Sandburg's free verse (the assertion of the poetic I, the inclusion of popular language) and bends them to his own aesthetic goals. The form of the poem, apparently free of any stylistic constraint, responds to the tradition of free verse in such a way as to symbolize Carnevali's difficult assimilation.

The beginning of the poem pits the city environment against the poetic ideal by bringing up a global poetic tradition before providing any context:

> How long ago was it
> The dawn pleased Homer?
> And Petrarca—was it among flowers
> Dew-full, tearful for the love of the dawn,
> That he sang his best song
> For Laura?
> (Carnevali, "The Day of Summer," ll. 1–6)

In these lines, we see Carnevali reflecting on issues that were central to modernism. In reacting to the unprecedented changes in urban life, many authors used literary tradition as a tool to explore the present. Modernism saw art as "the means by which to give structure and value to an otherwise formless modernity" and "restore a context to the chaotic reality of the moment" (Nicholls 1995, 173). This approach to artistic works resulted, in practice, in modernist works filled with references and quotations. In his own work, Carnevali expressed a modernist's characteristic sense of loss, a painful detachment from a time in which poetic words had a definite meaning and corresponded with living experience. As the poem goes on, this brief glimpse of an idealized past is replaced with traumatic modernity:

In New York,
These summer days,
It's a swollen-faced hour,
Sick with a monstrous cold,
Gasping with the death of an expectance.
(Carnevali, "The Day of Summer," ll. 11–15)

This kind of brutal juxtaposition is not dissimilar to Eliot and Pound's use of high culture references to expose a present void of meaning (see Pound's "the pianola replaced / Sappho's barbitos" in "Hugh Selwyn Mauberley" or Eliot likening clerks to Dante's dead souls in *The Waste Land*). Carnevali interprets New York from a cultural distance, which Ballerini linked to his Mediterranean, premodern background, in which "agisce ancora il mito, o quanto meno, la condizione psicologica del e per il mito" (1978, 420).[8] His references to a past tradition do not have the function of bringing tradition back to life, but instead represent an imperfectly erased Mediterranean background. The Italian "Petrarca," used instead of the English rendition Petrarch, is a remnant of an Italian education—and yet the reference is incomplete, as Carnevali does not mention any particular "song" (which he presumably uses to render the medieval form of the *canzone*). It is not Pound and Eliot's philological movement toward an ancient tradition, but the remnants of the same tradition that migration could not erase: it soon becomes clear that the soundscape of New York is the main focus of the poem.

Engaging with the reality of New York means confronting the language(s) of the street, establishing a relationship between the poetic *I* and such language. The sensorial experience of the city demands its own language: "Now has the deep hot belly of the night / Given birth to noises" (37–38), and the poet finds himself increasingly driven to find an adequate language to represent them. This introduces the problem of the urban language:

Stench
Of drenched clothes
And snore
Of married men.
Who shall ask the furnished-room poets to write
A song for the dawn?
("The Day of Summer," ll. 73–78)

The "furnished-room" is Carnevali's signifier for a whole lifestyle: that of the lower middle class who lived in small, rented rooms, economically precarious and alienated. Furnished rooms, representing emotional bareness and the negation of traditional homes, summarized Carnevali's New York. In a 1918 letter to Monroe, Carnevali called a group of drafts a part of his "furnished-room songs."[9] In the *Autobiography*, he would speak of life in New York as "my life in the rooming-house, the furnished-rooms of America" (1967, 74). The image stayed in his mind even after his departure from the United States. In 1928 he wrote a "Furnished Room Rhapsody" in which he claimed:

> Furnished room, you have held me in your arms;
> and what I paid for the embrace,
> what I lost,
> what I left behind going away,
> I alone know.
> ("Furnished Room Rhapsody," ll. 26–30)

The use of "I" and "you" underlines the close, emotional relationship between the poet and the environment in which he spent most of his American life, but the poem is mainly about the precariousness of furnished-room life ("it is a house without being a home").

Carnevali's language, absorbed in the streets of New York, revolves around a few key terms and phrases that he received and reused to create his own form of English. Biographers write with admiration of how he learned much of his English "affascinato dalla scrittura aperta dei giganteschi messaggi pubblicitari e delle insegne dei negozi"[10] (Ballerini 1978, 418). In his letters, Carnevali actually points out that he "learned English by continuous reading" and mentions his study of English grammar.[11] All the same, it is undeniable that the urban linguistic environment plays a role in his understanding of America—and consequently in his poetry. The expression "furnished room" is a semantic whole, rooted in the experience of the American metropolis. Quickly learned by the newcomer, it symbolizes a conglomerate of social and affective factors.

If "furnished rooms" symbolize emotional precariousness in the house, "free lunch counters" is the phrase that stands for the precarious eating habits of the migrant. In the *Autobiography*, Carnevali stated: "your free lunch counters saved my life, oh, New York!" (1967, 75). In "The Day of Summer," the lunchroom counters have a place in Carnevali's critique of food and culture as "altars of a little comfort, altars of a dyspeptic god gone crazy in America for lack of personality" where one may find all the foods brought to New York by immigrants ("Summer," ll. 207–8). Carnevali creates a Whitmanian list of the varieties of food on sale in the city streets, yet he also frames them within his critique of American multiculturalism. The image of the "dyspeptic god gone crazy" links food with culture and tradition only to underline the loss of value in accumulation. Referring again to Whitman, we may say that Carnevali sings "One's-self . . . a simple separate person" while showing diffidence toward "the word Democratic, the word En-Masse" ("One's-Self I Sing," ll. 1–2).

The people of the city are present in "The Day of Summer," but their language and accents create a hostile and chaotic environment:

Who threw these kids here among us, them and their fun
    and war, "GIMME!—GIMME!"
("The Day of Summer," ll. 173)

Work, milk, bread, clothes, potatoes, potatoes . . .
This is
The big
Beauty rumbling on.
Is this
The world's music forevermore?
This and the irrevocable peddlers
Who will come in an hour
To hurl loose:
"Pota-a-a-t-o-u-s, yeh-p-l-s, waa-ry meh-l-n"?
("The Day of Summer," ll. 44–54)

Here the poet reproduces the language of the streets, using phonetic spellings and punctuation to mark it as alien. Carnevali often used this tactic in his fiction when reproducing immigrant speech: in the short story "Bogeyman," a character exclaims "I gotta fon da dichonary book" (1919g, 22), while the unpublished "Lean Woman" story features an immigrant woman saying, "Mister, plaze, listun!"[12] American modernists often played with the dialects of minorities, either to expand their linguistic horizon or as a form of humor (North 1994, 9). Carnevali, who was conscious of being an outsider in the modernist milieu, appears to separate his inner speech from the dialectal reality that he witnesses and records: the former must appear in standard English. This approach is common among translingual authors, who often view the attainment of a particular standardized language as vital to their acceptance into the literary canon.

At the same time, "The Day of Summer" mocks journalistic language (he mentions "reading the *Evening Journal Sermon on Success*" right before having a nervous breakdown, l. 303) and that of a hostile literary marketplace:

> Oh, MAIL!
> Ah, beggars:
> "I-am-though-I-refrain-from-saying-it-better-than-you-in-
>   the-end. I-am-perfectly honest-evidently-nothing-up-my-
>   sleeves . . . It-is-out-of-my-bounteous-goodness-that-I-
>   like-you-a-little-in-spite-of . . ."
> ("The Day of Summer," ll. 79–81)

This prompts the poet to reflect on his "scanty rights to live" and "stuttering claim" to success. Reproductions of American language in long, irregular Whitmanian free verse are juxtaposed with short, even rhymed, lines that express the poet's inner world ("so we advance / at every chance / our stuttering claim and reference," ll. 84–86).

Carnevali's multiform verse enacts a separation of the poetic *I* and the linguistic environment, which goes against his immediate American references (Frost, Sandburg, and Oppenheim). So Sandburg, in a poem praised by Carnevali, writes of his amazement at the language forged in the great crucible of America:

> Stammer at the slang of this—
> Let us understand half of it.
> In the rolling mills and sheet mills,
> In the harr and boom of the blast fires,
> The smoke changes its shadow
> And men change their shadow
> A nigger, a wop, a bohunk changes
> ("Smoke and Steel," ll. 37–43)

Neutralizing its own racial slurs, Sandburg's poetry treats the working class with Whitmanian enthusiasm. One of Sandburg's very first poems,

"Happiness," asks "professors who teach the meaning of life" (l. 1) about what happiness is until one Sunday afternoon the poet sees "a crowd of Hungarians under the trees with their women and children and a keg of beer and an accordion" (l. 5). Migrants symbolize purity for "Carl the American," as Carnevali called him. Sandburg also cast a more inclusive look on Italian migrants than Carnevali did: his Chicago Italians are spontaneous and lively, quarreling children or street vendors. The poor and proud Italian matron of Sandburg's "Onion Days" grows in the long lines of the poem to attain the status of an American socialist heroine. Carnevali praised this inclusiveness in his review of Sandburg:

> And one may call him American only if one knows such solid American types as the workers and criminals he sings the language of—the forgotten, submerged world where the oldest essences of life are preserved and continually renovated. (E. Carnevali 1921a, 271)

Sandburg's view of migrants is uncomplicated and essentialist: migrants possess certain features that are inherent to their background, fulfilling a positive role in his idea of America. Carnevali's perception, on the other hand, is more nuanced and reveals how "the everyday culture of migrants cannot be regarded as a moment of securing tradition and identity," but rather as "the temporary results of processes" (Wolf 2012, 80). The Italian author may have expressed his fascination for the apparent inclusivity of American free verse in his essays, but he could never develop an uncomplicated and celebratory notion of assimilation such as Sandburg's. Moving between contrasting ideas of culture that threatened to flatten or annihilate his individuality, engaging with a language and style that were unfamiliar to him, he created poetry that foregrounds difference rather than inclusion.

In this sense, "The Day of Summer" is the strongest expression of a trend that began in his early poetry, especially in the 1919 poem "Procession of Beggars." The first poem of this group, "Last Day," focuses on Carnevali's inner world as he is "listening to the great appeal of the things that have gone / crazy—this drunkard, that laughter— / everywhere" (ll. 22–24). In the mismatch between the self and the urban environment, Carnevali mentions the "call" of the "dead eyes / in the dead faces / in the crowd" (ll. 25–27). The second poem of the group, "Marche Funèbre," is even more explicit in separating the poet and the crowd:

> The great corpse
> is the crowd.
> A whole day
> it takes
> to bury it.
> . . . .
> I'm here for . . .
> What am I here for?
> Oh, to wail
> a great
> good bye!

Carnevali dismisses the crowd as a faceless whole, associated with death. As he explains to an unnamed interlocutor that his role is only that of "wailing" a "great good bye," it becomes clear that he considers ironic detachment the only strategy to deal with a crowd that he does not believe he can redeem. The poetic *I* is not a Whitmanian synthesis with the spirit of America, but instead the only man alive in a crowd of "dead faces."

The fragment of "The Day of Spring" in Carnevali's Chicago notebooks starts with a similar image of the American everyman as dead or dying, crushed by the capitalist environment:

> The workingman
> sings
> sings himself to a sweet
> to a sad, a sweet death
> every morning—
> these days
> singing
> when he walks to his job.[13]

Similarly to "The Day of Summer," "The Day of Spring" seems to have been intended to criticize the alienating cityscape and its effect on humanity, using bleak irony: enjambments are used to counter the reader's expectations, as the "sweet" at the end of a line ultimately refers to death. "The Day of Summer" confirms this attitude toward the crowd, and the long lines and vivid images express Carnevali's incomprehension of the capitalist logic of the city:

This is the hour they go to their work
Eastward and westward—
Two processions, Silent.
("The Day of Summer," ll. 89–92)
Has the first of them
Found
Down there
Something for his happiness?
And has he telephoned or telegraphed to the others
That they are going,
Without looking around,
Without knowing one another,
ALL
T O G E T H ER
Eastward and westward?
("The Day of Summer," ll. 100–10)

The block capitals foreground the poet's puzzled reaction to the synchronicity of the crowd, expressing his own nonsynchronic attitude with respect to the city environment. The ironic suggestion that one of them might be directing the "procession" via telephone or telegraph sets the poet's priorities against the clockwork mechanisms of the city. Once again, Carnevali uses elements found in Sandburg and Whitman— rhetorical questions, the equation of the American crowd with a single entity moving eastward or westward with the sun—only to subvert them according to his own moral compass. The language of Sandburg and Whitman provided him with features for his stylistic inventory, influencing the formation of his poetic speech in his new language. On the other hand, there is no absolute mimetic relationship between Carnevali and his American models. He mentions Manhattan's "sacred crowds," but that is just an element of parody as it refers to the poet scouting the railway station for "Not-yet-known breasts and strange thighs" (ll. 245–46), reducing the celebration of the crowd to a search for sexual encounters. And when he evokes Whitman as predecessor: ("O city, there lived in you once, O Manhattan, a man WALT WHITMAN," l. 251) he does so in the past tense, referring to a poetic wholeness that he cannot bring back to life.

Short lines in "The Day of Summer" present the inner rhythm of the poet's self:

I am young,
Nice day,
I look
Straight ahead,
Staccato steps,
Stiff and cool,
I walk.
("The Day of Summer," ll. 157–63)

Lines like these progress the poetic narrative, recreating the "staccato steps" of the poet in the streets of New York—reflecting on the rhythm by means of rhythm itself. The poem accommodates external rhythms, but the inner rhythms of Carnevali's thoughts play a central role as they mediate between the poetic *I* and the "Street." They become more relevant as the poem gradually takes the form of a descent into insanity, expressed through fragmentation and obsessive repetition:

My youth is but a regret and a madness
A madness. . . . Jesus Christ! I am not old yet, never mind
    what I have told you, what I have been!
I have not irremediably committed myself, I am not lost—
For pity's sake
Let me go
Let me go free!
For pity's sake
Let me go
With my youth!
("The Day of Summer," ll. 128–36)

In her work on migrant narratives, Hron notes a pattern in the ways authors convey "anger, frustration, or anxiety" in their newly acquired language:

through exclamations, rhetorical questions, or repetitive declarative statements, or they may allude to psychological problems, such as trauma, confusion, or alienation, through repetition, fragmentation, or the use of ellipsis. (Hron 2009, 48)

These elements are apparent in "The Day of Summer," where repetitions and trauma vocabulary appear side by side with Carnevali's recordings of

the New York environment. Taken together, they represent the whole
of his urban experience.

As "The Day of Summer" ends, the prospect of a dangerous assimilation looms. As Carnevali decides to "walk with the marionettes" (l.
306), the poem concludes with an unsettling image of assimilation as
annihilation:

> I have a brain for everything,
> I shall dance their ragtime.
> Will someone whisper, sometime—
> "There is a man who dances
> With a strange embarrassment"?
> ("The Day of Summer," ll. 314–18)

As the typically American music plays ("*their* ragtime"), only the slightest
"embarrassment" is left. In the crowd, Carnevali does not find the same
totalizing vision as Whitman. Instead, his strong individuality is trapped
in a world of mere things. As Boelhower underlined, Carnevali's poetic
achievement was defined by his incapacity to redefine reality: "reality
wins; the transforming power of the inner self proves in the end to be
another American myth for the narrator" (1982, 143). Nonetheless, his
works—and their appearance in a magazine that claimed Whitman as
its artistic ancestor—represent an important effort to transform urban
reality via artistic expression. Carnevali's reception and re-elaboration
of American free verse was neither total nor painless, but rather a difficult adoption of foreign forms. The most notable result was "The Day
of Summer," in which elements of American models were used to offer
an unsettling display of migrant displacement.

Carnevali would come back to Whitmanian forms throughout his
career, even after falling ill in 1920 while living in Chicago. In fact,
one of Carnevali's most convincing attempts to come to terms with his
illness is in the form of Whitmanian free verse in the 1921 group of
poems "Neuriade" (also appearing in *Poetry*). This is a group of twelve
poems, most of them quite short; a few, like "Marche Funèbre," appeared
in earlier publications. Topics vary, yet there is a certain link to illness
and recovery—the title itself, "Neuriade," is formed by attaching the
Italian suffix *iade*, which distinguishes titles of epic poems (*Iliade, Eneide*),
to the root *neur*: a modern epic focusing on a modern obsession, the
psyche. Most of the poems are brief vignettes in long and colloquial lines

revolving around simple images, not unlike those Sandburg wrote at the time. For example, this is the entirety of the poem "Smoke":

> All the smoke of the cigarettes of dreamers went over to
> the sky, and formed that blue vault
> you see up there.

There are but few traces of the chaotic and multiform rhythms of "The Day of Summer," but some of the "Neuriade" poems still struggle with America and migrant individuality in Whitmanian forms. These poems refer to a time in which, as a reaction to his 1920 health crisis, Carnevali lived for some time in a shanty in the Indiana dunes near Lake Michigan. His subsequent description of this experience has been called "a deranged, hallucinated version of Walden" (Buonomo 2003, 58) as the poet apparently intended to redeem his life by getting back in touch with nature:

> I found a burnt-down shanty, shrouded in what seemed to be
> an old sail, and there I went to sleep. I slept utterly alone
> and unafraid. This night and the nights to come were bitterly
> cold and I froze but I rejoiced. I trembled, trembled with my
> illness and the cold, but I was happy. (1967, 191)

Carnevali in the 1930s recalled this moment of illusory hope that he might find balance in the United States. The 1921 poem from the "Neuriade" collection describing this experience, "Lake," conveys the same desire.[14] Unlike his years in Manhattan, on the Indiana dunes he turns his vision to nature, and "Lake" opens with a moment of Whitmanian celebration: "Sitting on a bench facing God's beautiful lake / A poem to God beautiful" ("Lake," ll. 1–2). Nature seems to make allegiance to America possible and to redeem both illness and cultural shock.

The poet links the natural environment with Chicago, where he found a more congenial atmosphere:

> Having risen out of your waters,
> In front of my great eyes now
> There is a mad blur of sunlight,
> And the City spread out before me calling from a great curve:
> "Come, enter, conquistador!"
> ("Lake," ll. 9–13)

The city's invitation is in enthusiastic, Whitmanian tones while he speaks of "my great eyes": it is a rare occurrence in Carnevali's poetry when he does not ironically downplay his achievements and personal appearance, choosing to celebrate himself instead. The Whitmanian tone is interspersed with European references as he describes himself bathing in the lake as a "fresh-water Neptune" (l. 24) while the "water rang little bells / trickling down / along [his] flesh" (ll. 25–27). The poet joins a pretechnological, mythical world through a Latin metaphor. His attempt to recover passes through an acceptance of nature and of the American landscape, but that does not eliminate the Old World references. At the same time, he underlines his own precarious health ("the love a poor sick body held . . . / a poor sick body gave it all to you," ll. 4–6), and "Lake" ultimately states that the search for stability is useless ("Words die in the fingers of a sick man," l. 30). Death—a theme in the collection, which also features an "Invocation to Death"—makes its appearance, but here it is another form of communion with nature: Carnevali "flirted with death" (l. 16) and "laughed at Death, as Death's brother, the devil, would" (l. 18). Nature mediates between the poet and Death as the poet tries to accept his own mortality.

Although quite short as a collection, "Neuriade" contains some of Carnevali's most sincere attempts at a Whitmanian celebration of America as well as his most evident disruptions of Whitmanian certainty. Facing sickness, Carnevali kept engaging with poetics, writing and discussing poetry as much as his condition allowed. The tradition of American free verse, and the negation of it, are still important features in his postcrisis poetry. The same American models were present in his mind even after his return to Italy. In the *Autobiography*, Sandburg appears at the end of a chapter about Carnevali's childhood:

> Goodbye, chestnut-trees of Cossato, if you are there no longer, goodbye, mushrooms and violets and strawberries, goodbye, little cakes of cheese, goodbye, small torrential rivers, goodbye, forests by the rivers—you probably have all gone, gone as all beautiful things go, not one lasts, as says great Carl. (1967, 30)

Here Carnevali is quoting a poem by Sandburg, "Autumn Movement," in which the opening line, "I cried over beautiful things knowing no beautiful thing lasts," precedes an image of the coming and going of seasons ("Autumn Movement," l. 1). In quoting Sandburg, the younger poet claims him as a colleague and companion, although this was no

longer the case. Sandburg is "great Carl," and Carnevali uses this familiarity to suggest his own place in American literary circles. Sandburg's
words, presumably written with the Illinois landscape in mind, resurface
in Carnevali's book, where he uses them to frame and comment on his
Italian childhood—creating one last short circuit between Italian roots
and the American tradition of free verse.

Carnevali's confrontation with American free verse was a long
process of reception and reelaboration. It started with the naive fascination of a self-taught twenty-year-old and transitioned into a style that
certifies how the assimilation into the new canon was never complete.
His deeply felt admiration was a necessary ingredient of the language
that Carnevali constructed to address and confront American literature.
He did not simply adopt American forms, but rather brought to them his
outsider's perspective, drawing on unfamiliarity and novelty to expand
their reach. Whitman and Sandburg were his models in addressing the
American "commonplace," but Carnevali drew on them to express his
own problematic transition: a search for something "splendid" and stable
that was lost in the instability of emigration.

3. Italian Echoes: Between Multilingual Influences and Complete Assimilation

Carnevali saw standard English as necessary for acceptance in American
literature: at the beginning of their collaboration, he wrote to Monroe
that he was "busy learning English and becoming less of an ignoramus."[15]
Yet, while working on the "Day of . . ." series of poems, he asked his
editor to retain his punctuation as written:

> commas, semi columns [sic], columns [sic] and dashes must be
> left where they are, as, by now, I have grown into a certain
> ortograph [sic] that is *my own* and not English, nor Italian,
> nor *correct* nor incorrect.[16]

While this comment concerns the more formal aspects of orthography,
it also contains Carnevali's acknowledgement that he considered his
language to be his own, neither English nor Italian.

Carnevali's poetry and fiction are written in a newcomer's English,
a linguistic medium used to penetrate American literature with a new
and uncompromising voice. This newcomer's English, however, always

appears to respect orthographical and syntactical conventions of American English, as seen in previous examples from this chapter. The occasional misspelling or uncertainty in a draft is usually corrected in successive versions: in terms of final product, there is no apparent strategy to deviate intentionally from the standards of the literary language that he read in *Poetry* and other magazines. Even when reporting the speech variants of other immigrants in his work (such as in the short stories "Bogeyman" and "Lean Woman"), their accents are reproduced via phonetic spelling that implies an English reader following generally established conventions: "Look AW-UT! Fer the eggs. Plaze!" ("Lean Woman").[17]

Notwithstanding, several Italian commentators have implied that Carnevali's English possessed certain Italian qualities. In 1925 Linati attempted to introduce him to the Italian public by speaking of a "lingua inglese irradiata da una vivacità tutta Latina, e quasi direi fiorentinesca"[18] (1925, 3), while Fink began his critical rediscovery of Carnevali by speaking of a "travestimento linguistico"[19] of Italian (1973, 86). Cacho Millet appears sure that "dietro al sedicente poeta americano c'era sempre la parola, l'istinto italiano"[20] (1981, 9), while Fracassa more recently advanced the hypothesis that Carnevali's poetic speech involved covering his native *langue* (in the Saussurean sense of underlying linguistic structure) with the "fonemi radicalmente alieni"[21] of another language's *parole* (2005, 143). This is one of the most compelling facts of translingual literary analysis: the temptation to see an author's native language always present beyond the superficial layer of the adopted language, filtering through the cracks.

Some "assimilated authors [working in a second language] seek by a sort of hypercorrection to make the linguistic traces of their origins disappear" (Casanova 2004, 255). However, this notion cannot be countered simply by setting "assimilated authors" in opposition with "dissimilated authors" who flaunt their cultural difference by creating their own hybrid version of the host language (Casanova 2004, 266). In fact, multiple shades of assimilation and a variety of translingual strategies are involved: translingual authors have in common the use of a second language to address new audiences, but their strategies vary as they face the "complex task of resisting, reformulating, or reproducing prescriptive literary and sociocultural models" (Hron 2009, 47). Each author's strategic choices depend on context and their particular experiences of bilingualism, which is never a smooth passage between two discrete entities but a continuum of competing elements.

There is another way of looking at Carnevali's American period, concentrating not on the steps that he took toward American literary English but on echoes of the Italian he left behind. Looking at the drafts and sketches in Carnevali's notebooks, it seems that he composed all his poetry and prose directly in English without passing through Italian—that his thoughts were "already" in English when he committed them to the page. In the notebooks that Carnevali left with his friend Mitchell Dawson in Chicago, drafts of poems and prose works (several of which were never published) are in English: the pages appear full of corrections, crossed-out words, afterthoughts and uncertainties, but the creative process seems to take place in English and tends to comply with common standards of syntax and grammar.[22] Carnevali chose English as his medium and adhered to its conventions with a newcomer's enthusiasm.

Why then have so many critics and commentators looked at his work as if it housed some discernible Italian element? Such claims are better understood in the light of a 1976 debate on the language of Mario Puzo's *Godfather*. At the time, a critic took phrases such as "she called herself Kay Adams" (with *to call* used like the Italian *chiamarsi*) as signs of linguistic alterity, wondering "how readers not familiar with this Italian expression [were] interpreting the passage" (Di Pietro 1977, 3). Other critics, Sollors reports, argued that "recipes for lasagna [were] generally available in American cookbooks," and "many languages (among them French and Russian) know the reflexive 'calling oneself' in the sense of 'being named'" (1986, 12). Puzo's appropriation of Italian linguistic elements does not prevent understanding on the American audience's part or damage the book's claim to a place in American literature. Nonetheless, a structure like "she called herself Kay Adams" can be easily superimposed over its Italian equivalent. It seems the result of a conscious choice, recognized by an informed reader as a nod to Italian without impairing the target audience's understanding. The same applies to Carnevali when he writes sentences such as "and as for spaghetti and ravioli, let me tell you once for all that parsley chopped fine and one small onion and . . ." (1920b, 32). The sentence structure does not pose difficulties for the American reader, nor does it deviate from the English norm. It is multilingual, but spaghetti was already a staple of American cuisine: a safe, nonpuzzling multilingual interference. A phrase such as "parsley chopped fine" works much like Puzo's "she called herself Kay Adams." While it hardly deviates from the English norm, the phrase reproduces an Italian structure (the colloquial Italian *prezzemolo tagliato fine*) rather than a more 'Anglo-Saxon' structure like "finely chopped parsley." The translingual origin of the sentence enacts Carnevali's cultural difference without impairing the American reader's comprehension.

Recent work on bilingualism concentrates on bilingual speakers' use of different linguistic tools depending on their life experiences as they "call upon different social *features* in a seamless and complex network of multiple semiotic signs, as they adapt their languaging to suit the immediate task" (Garcia and Li Wei 2014, 25). A bilingual is an individual who has the option to *choose* his or her every single word from more than one linguistic repertoire, and that horizon of creative possibility applies to authors who are bilingual, calling on them to make a choice with respect to their background and context. Translingual authors, even when they follow the standards of their adopted language to the letter—that is, to suit the task of being understood and accepted by the new audience—continuously make choices between the new words and the old. They can include words, phrases, or structures from the old repertoire when they feel that the most appropriate word is missing from the target language; therefore, some translingual authors code-switch in the space of their texts, with a very specific effect on the audience that may or may not be tempered by footnotes. Yet even their use of the target repertoire may not be devoid of influences and echoes from the old repertoire. Zabus coined the term *relexification* to describe the language of postcolonial literary works "using English vocabulary but indigenous structures and rhythms" (1991, 101). In this framework, the creations of authors like Chinua Achebe or Amos Tutuola become "palimpsests for, behind the scriptural authority of the target European language, the earlier, imperfectly erased remnants of the source language are still visible" (Zabus 1991, 106). Relexification and similar phenomena are part of the larger operation of bilingualism and the creative process of speech transformation. Such transformations must be seen within the context of both the expressive goals of the author and the specific relationship between the languages they use.

After all, languages are not closed, discrete systems—they are permeable and mutable, evolving as a result of mutual contact. Although nationalisms may wish them to be sites of cultural purity, languages borrow and adapt constantly from their close and distant neighbors. The resulting loan words, more or less incorporated into the fabric of the national speech, "open up the possibility that the foreign is lodged right in the mother tongue" (Yildiz 2012, 67). Considering the literary uses of words with foreign origins "helps to rethink writing practices . . . as critically postmonolingual projects" (Yildiz 2012, 69). English and Italian have a long history of traffic between them: reasons of cultural prestige have determined several exchanges over the centuries resulting in several English words that display their Italian origin more or less openly. For the purpose of this analysis, it is useful to remember the large number of English words with French origins, many of which share common Latin origins with Italian and may sound instinctively familiar to an Italian ear.

In approaching this new repertoire, Carnevali exploited such similarities and proximities between Italian and English, challenging the monolingual outlook of his texts by implying the presence of other idioms, rhythms, and systems of reference. These features are part of Carnevali's critique of American culture from within the forms and structures of American poetry. As seen in the previous section, passages like this involve the reuse of Whitmanian style to criticize Whitmanian celebrations of America:

> This and the irrevocable peddlers
> Who will come in an hour
> To hurl loose:
> "Pota-a-a-a-t-o-u-s, yeh-p-l-s, waa-ry meh-1-n?"
> Little apocalyptic faces . . .
> ("The Day of Summer," ll. 48–56)

Earlier in this chapter, I concentrated on the peddlers' speech and Carnevali's reproduction of spoken American English. Yet the passage can also be used to explore the impact of Italian on Carnevali's use of particular English words. The "world's music" involves the accents of American street vendors, which Carnevali records and reproduces alongside his judgments on them, expressed in adjectives such as "irrevocable" and "apocalyptic." The words are not un-English, but they are quite close to the Italian irrevocabili and apocalittiche by virtue of their common Latin origin. The history of the English language provides Carnevali with words that are part of a high register of English but are more familiar to him than many everyday English words because of the Latin or Greek root in common with Italian. The etymon becomes active and fertile for Carnevali, providing him with common ground in the translational operations that mark his passage from unfamiliarity to familiarity in English. At a stylistic level, this common ground expresses the reflections of the poetic *I* in contrast with the language of the American environment.

Carnevali's predilection for words with a common Italian/English root may be more or less intentional, dictated by choice or by an instinctive sense of familiarity. In both cases, such lexical choices express Carnevali's process of understanding, categorizing, and resisting America. In "The Day of Summer," the poet exclaims: "I was born for a sylvan century, may I claim to be left alone?" (l. 57). He casts the word "sylvan" against the "noise" of twentieth-century New York, evoking antiquated, poetic Italian (*silvano*): the juxtaposition makes its Latin root more evident in contrast to the environment. The word enters Carnevali's language, signifying a refusal to assimilate: it resurfaces in the late 1920s in a short story where he remembers a woman who "in New York, where the whirlwind of grime and dust tries to wrap her around, asks, as I did, for a little sylvan beauty" (1929b, 146–47). As Carnevali conforms to American style, he also employs the proximities of English and Italian to express differentiation. The text is no less "American" for this, yet it points to the author's Italian origins. By analyzing the Italian-English proximities in Carnevali's text, we better understand his ability to communicate an Italian point of view without trespassing the linguistic borders of English. He used this vocabulary to cast a judgment on America, conceptualizing the surrounding environment through metaphor or synthesizing his emotions in one word.

"The Day of Summer" dwells constantly on such linguistic proximities as the poetic *I* records the audible reality of Manhattan and then interprets it through words that have roots in common with Italian:

> But your faces are faces of rancor:
> . . . .
> Imbecility is an immense maw, and at noon
> It is hungry with a thousand crawling hungers.
> So that happy bewildered imbecile of a sun
> Looks bewildered at me,
> Wondering that I am so utterly disgusted
> (l. 194; ll. 200–4)

Carnevali's interpretation dwells on words that have immediate Italian counterparts and give an Italian flavor to his bitter attack on the existential void of Manhattan (*rancore, imbecillità, imbecille, disgustato*).

Carnevali transfigures the New York crowds using metaphors that largely rely on proximity: they are "grotesques walking / grotesques for no one to laugh at" ("Summer," ll. 95–96). The reference here is both to the grotesque as decorative art and to the ridiculous quality the poet spots in the crowd—a meaning especially pertinent to the Italian *grottesco*. "The Day of Summer" constantly plays with the juxtaposition of such judgements with the description of life in New York. The poet's profession of faith in the word relies on the proximities of Italian and English: "My malediction on the cowards who are afraid of *the word* (*the word* is a kind sweet child, a kind sweet child!)" ("Summer," l. 210). Carnevali uses the word "malediction," which is less common than *curse* but closer to the Italian *maledizione*, as the poet's judgment on the world becomes final, dividing it between those who believe in "*the word*" and those who do not. *The word* in question is English but linked to Italian by the etymon; perhaps in the poet's view the common root makes it more familiar and effective. The New York poems use words that have roots and sound in common with Italian to represent inner worlds. In "The Day of Summer," the poets are represented "Hesitating everywhere, hesitating fearfully" as they use their "delicate hands" and walk "unfrequented roads" ("Summer," ll. 211–13). In other earlier poems, more concentrated on the poet's inner world than on the poet-versus-America dialectic, the words that describe Carnevali's emotions and sensations often have an Italian equivalent ready at hand. "Drôlatique-Sérieux," from the "Splendid Commonplace" series, is a brief impression of sunbeams entering the poet's bedroom as he smokes a cigarette. The rays enter the room "with the glad fury / Of a victorious dagger wielded by an adventurous child" ("Drôlatique-Sérieux," ll. 2–3): the simile is obtained through an abundance of terms close to their Italian equivalents (*vittoriosa*, *daga*, *avventuroso*). At the end of the poem, as the smoke of his cigarette meets the sunbeams, he wonders whether this is "blasphemous" (*blasfemo*). At this stage, Carnevali tends to use the last line of his poems to summarize his impressions. At the end of the 1919 "Nocturne," the poetic *I* comments on the appearance of a small portion of the moon through the windowpanes: "It suffices." More Latinate than the Anglo-Saxon "enough," it is closer to the Italian *sufficiente* and enables the poet to confirm the poetic value of an everyday, mundane image. The same thing happens at the end of "When It Has Passed," where he sums up the poem's essence as "the remembrance" (l. 13)—close to the Italian *rimembranza*. At the end of "To the Poets," he likens their voice to "winds that purify and create"

(l. 11); "purify," close to the Italian *purificare*, is employed also in "The Day of Summer" to indicate the poet's desire of redemption from the pollution of the city: "Nevertheless I go to perform the ceremony / Of purification . . ." ("The Day of Summer," ll. 23–24).

The "Neuriade" collection, Carnevali's last poetic accomplishment in America, uses the proximities to describe his attempts to come to terms with illness on the shores of Lake Michigan. The description of the poet's inner world follows the patterns individuated in his New York poetry. He speaks of an "Old Accustomed Impudent Ghost" representing his troubled New York self, staring at him in defiance ("impudent," or *impudente*) from the mirror. The language of "Lake" also exemplifies some idiosyncratic features of Carnevali's English, as he uses English words as if they were their Italian equivalents, causing a slight shift of meaning in the process. He speaks of Lake Michigan "gilded in the morning" ("Lake," l. 22), using "gilded" as a direct translation of the Italian *dorato*, which means both "gilded" and, as in this case, "golden"; at the same time, he writes "Your absinthe / has intoxicated me" ("Lake," l. 7–8), and the poem's context makes it ambiguous whether Carnevali intended "intoxicated" or *intossicato*, "poisoned."

Carnevali's choice of words that are etymologically proximate often has a specific function in poetry. They appear within a rhythmic pattern that, as we have seen, aimed at aligning itself with certain styles of American free verse. Thus, they often stand out rhythmically with respect to the Anglo-Saxon words because of their length, which sets the poems further adrift from an already loose pattern:

> Heavy morning,
> With one friend gone
> And two loves ended,
> Heavy morning.
>
> Heavy morning,
> With all the dust
> Accumulated
> Over these books.
> ("Morning Song," ll. 1–8)

> At the bottom of the abyss of sleep
> A black cradle rocks.

Pain, slight, with *evanescent* fingers
Pushes it.
Under the cradle is earth,
To cover and stifle you.
("Sleep")

The way in which the first stanza is framed by repeating lines in a structure of four is reminiscent of folk music. When the Italianate word "accumulated" is present, it takes up a whole line in the loose four-five syllabic pattern. In the second example, the poet's tentative regularity almost creates iambic pentameters—a form so firmly established in English that even Whitman himself used it covertly in his poetry (Finch 2000, 32). A word such as *evanescent*, because of its length, resists assimilation into the everyday English of his poetry.

Proximate words, stemming from the most familiar parts of Carnevali's vocabulary, often appeared multiple times in different texts but performed the same functions. Carnevali's prose does not have the same need to synthesize the poet's view of the world around him in the short space of a line, investing single words with power by giving them a special place in his diction. Yet there are passages in his "Tales of a Hurried Man" where it is possible to find the same Italian-sounding adjectives that are in his poetry:

Opposite there tower the obese gas tanks, dolorous with rust, sick with blotches of grey paint, grotesquely solemn. (1920b, 28)

. . . witness the tranquillity of my feet as they step upon the carpet, witness the farina boiling. (1920b, 34)

Sweating in the summer like a degenerate's face. (1919g, 22)

. . . many do not know how tremendously, and maybe successfully, sacreligious [sic] skyscrapers are. (1920c, 55)

Words like "grotesquely," "tranquillity," "dolorous," and "degenerate" relate to Italian and in some cases are common in his poetry as well (grotesque, tremendous). Their closeness to Italian is signaled in different ways: in choosing the spelling "tranquillity" (closer to the Italian *tranquillità*) or by using *degenerate* as a noun (as in the Italian *degenerato*). They represent a component of Carnevali's attitude toward language: even in prose, where the performative and rhythmic quality of each word is less important, Carnevali relies on words that express closeness to Italian, signaling the specificity of his worldview within the English linguistic environment.

Carnevali's characteristic use of English reflects his bilingualism, but it is not a form of multilingualism. Here, two languages are involved within the same text, but not as two distinct entities. Even in purportedly monolingual texts, Carnevali's work suggests the presence of a double repertoire, drawing on the continuous creative choices of a bilingual author. Carnevali drew his favorite words from the areas of his linguistic repository that were more familiar, more easily assimilated, and more promptly reused (often with the Italian equivalent in mind, as in the case of the "gilded" lake quoted above).

In addition to using words influenced by his Italian background, Carnevali's American work sometimes presents explicit multilingual insertions from various languages (Italian, Latin, French, and German). I would contend, however, that this multilingualism is a particular case of the phenomenon outlined above. After all, bilingual authors, "with their access to the cultural background of two languages, can and do subconsciously switch between languages when searching for . . . *mots justes*" (Weston and Gardner-Chloros 2015, 197). Languages being far from separate, secluded repositories, this type of access includes the words that the bilingual's languages have borrowed from others—sometimes in unison, sometimes in discord:

> King of the triumphing mood, the iceman cracks easy puns
> 　　with a landlady of the dust!
> Kaiser of the lightness of the morning, the policeman,
> 　　swinging his stick, writes sacred hieroglyphs.
> ("The Day of Summer," ll. 174–75)

The German word "Kaiser" is a loan word in both English and Italian, known widely in the aftermath of World War I. The bilingual's repository of words may experience overlaps as well as proximities: Carnevali quite often used loan words that were not English but would be accepted in

English and had the same status in Italian. To this effect, Spanish loan
words appear in his poetry and prose:

> And the City spread out before me calling from a great curve:
> "Come, enter, conquistador!"
> ("Lake," ll. 12–13)

> I would like to meet the desperado who'd be so desperate
>   as to come around these quarters to steal!
> (E. Carnevali 1920b, 29)

The first example uses the word "conquistador" both for its historical
relevance in the American landscape and for its similarity with the
Italian *conquistatore*, "conquerer." The second example establishes an
etymological connection between the Spanish "desperado" (also a loan
word in American English), indicating a bandit, and the English "desperate," with faint echoes of the Italian *disperato*. Spanish loan words may
perform the same function as Italian words, also having some currency
in English. Carnevali also uses Latin to that effect: "the old paterfamilias
who whistle and wheeze and grunt and roar in a regular, rhythmical
continuous rage" (1920b, 37).

The French language has a special place in Carnevali's writing,
which seems appropriate considering his early instruction in French and
his quasi-religious admiration for Rimbaud. French is used partly because
of its penetration in the English language: for example, the structure "à
la," widely used in English, may be used to replicate the Italian *alla* in
phrases like "fierce men a la Cagliostro are out of fashion" (1920b, 32).
Carnevali also used French for poem titles such as "Drôlatique-Sérieux"
(1918), "Marche Funèbre" (1919), "Chanson de Blackboulé" (1919),
and "Aubade" (1920). Each poem's style and topic do not particularly
relate to French, but their French titles suggest Carnevali was using the
language to signal an international dimension and a certain prestige. In
at least one case, French poetic models enter his poetry in the form of
brief multilingual intrusions: the exclamation "(Sweet morning, *sœur de
charité!*)" evokes Rimbaud in "The Day of Summer" (164). The reference
is to Rimbaud's "Les Sœurs de charité," featuring a "jeune homme" who
seeks comfort from the ugliness of the world in a "sœur de charité" (ll.
9–12).[23] The quotation creates a hypertextual link between Carnevali's

own search for self-fulfillment in Manhattan and Rimbaud's quest, which acts as inspiration.

Italian words also appear in Carnevali's American works, although they are not particularly frequent or prominent. Many are Italian terms that were in common use in America:

> And as for spaghetti and ravioli, let me tell you once and
>   for all . . . (1920b, 32)

> Every locomotive that passes is a new image in the brain,
>   every fierce puff a different part of the same not unpleas-
>   ant sonata. (1920b, 35)

> Staccato steps,
> Stiff and cool,
> I walk.
> ("The Day of Summer," ll. 161–63)

These words are as acceptable as the other multilingual insertions in Carnevali's work: the loan words do not disorient the monolingual reader and relate to semantic fields usually associated with Italy: food and music. The case of the 1919 poem "Italian Song" is slightly different. This poem has the structure of a short folk song refrain, although Carnevali does not give any clue about a possible Italian source. The culture-specific word *jettatura* comes up in the second stanza:

> Until old age come, girl,
> Until the other man come,
> Until the jettatura get me,
> Until God see us:
> Until God see us. ("Italian Song," ll. 6–10)

The presence of the Neapolitan word for "evil eye" is the only indication of something "Italian." It is a brief experiment with the rhythms of folk songs and with themes stereotypically associated with Italy, such as love and passion.

Carnevali did not use multilingualism to express an uncompromising difference; rather, loan words from different languages appear linked to an Italian lexical repository that he could use safely in English: both the proximities and this use of multilingualism are signs of difference in conformity. In this light, Domenichelli's claim that Carnevali was trying to write "some *Ursprache*, where he could hear and speak and write the impossible poem in some unheard perfect language" (1998, 84), needs to be reframed. A term like *Ursprache* is inherently problematic to use. Walter Benjamin devised this transcendental essence of speech as pure possibility, underlying everyday speech, only glimpsed in translation: "all higher language is a translation of lower ones, until in ultimate clarity the word of God unfolds, which is the unity of this movement made up of language" (1996, 74). While Carnevali expressed his beliefs in the power of poetry to turn simple words into statements of truth, he did not do so in *Ursprache*, but rather in an English that sometimes revealed his Italian background and his knowledge of other languages. The translatability of languages accounts for fertile connections; however, their simultaneous involvement in the translingual text is the result of an interaction between actual sociocultural realities. Carnevali's use of English was not an effort toward a perfect language, but rather the artistic realization of bilingualism as a continuous flow of influences and sounds.

Moving within the spectrum of the two languages, he could simultaneously "make the English language disturbingly familiar for an Italian, and his own language disturbingly foreign for a native speaker—making evident the ultimate foreignness of all language to ourselves" (Ciribuco 2013, 48). Bhabha described the migrant's attempt to translate himself into the dominant language as "one void in the articulation of the social space—making present the opacity of language, its untranslatable residue" (1994, 166). As the foreign language, with its practical realization in the text, has been imposed as an "ill-fitting robe" over meaning,[24] the translator inhabits and exposes the space between languages:

> and it is from this foreign perspective that it becomes possible to inscribe the specific locality of cultural systems—their incommensurable differences—and through that apprehension of differences, to perform the act of cultural translation. (Bhabha 1994, 164).

Carnevali made use of his foreign perspective from the start of his career as a translingual writer, approaching English from the outside and enthusiastically at the same time. His speech originated from the specific localities of English and Italian, and in the attempt to bridge the difference and create his own speech he ended up with a language that highlights both connections and differences between them. This language is one of cultural translation, transcending linguistic and cultural spaces to express the poet's individuality amid established systems of meaning.

Carnevali claimed that his English "ortograph [sic]" was "[his] own and not English, nor Italian, nor correct nor incorrect." It is difficult to ascertain to what extent his use of the linguistic proximities, his reliance on words with a close Italian equivalent, was part of a deliberate project, and to what extent those words simply came to be frequent in his language because of their familiar quality. Whatever the degree of intentionality, Carnevali's use of language in America as a tool of cultural translation appears to result from a specific attitude toward the language of adoption—tending toward conformity without the preoccupation of hiding cultural difference.

Just like a bilingual is "*not* the sum of two complete and incomplete monolinguals" but rather a specific individual whose language depends on the "co-existence and constant interaction of the two languages" (Grosjean 2008, 13), Carnevali's approach to English was not simply an abandonment of Italian for English. From the point of view of the newcomer, even the most mundane words and phrases were new and unfamiliar, and a "commonplace" could appear "splendid" or threatening in the new language. In his poetry and criticism from the first years of his career, Carnevali appears both enthusiastic about the new expressive possibilities opened up by the new language and diffident of the literary debate that was unfolding in American letters. Subject to the continuous flow of contrasting influences and stimuli that come with bilingualism—the soundscape of the urban environment, stylistic and grammatical tenets, different versions of the American canon—he took refuge in an idea of free verse that could be simultaneously very American and substantially open. He gave a communicable, monolingual shape to his cultural displacement. Yet the style that he created speaks his difference and uniqueness in the approach toward English.

3

Representing Italy in America

During his years in America, Carnevali engaged both personally and professionally with a host of representations of Italy, Italian literature, and Italians in America. This chapter explores three aspects of Carnevali and his work in relationship to *italianità*: his simultaneous identification with and distance from other Italian immigrants; his role as an intermediary between American modernists and the Italian literary tradition; and his role as a proponent, critic, and translator of Italian modernism for American audiences.

Carnevali wrote his American works at a time when only a few "great beams of light" illuminated a diaspora without poets and storytellers (Marazzi 2011, 97). Marazzi cites some notable contemporaries of Carnevali, including novelist Bernardino Ciambelli, poet Arturo Giovannitti, and playwright and performer Eduardo Migliaccio, but not only was there no widespread consciousness of Italian-American literature being written at the time, but Carnevali was also quite disconnected from its pioneering stages. Indeed, Carnevali had an uneasy relationship with the Italian communities of New York and Chicago: he lived in close contact with them, but his writing shows that he found it quite difficult to identify with them. Carnevali's widespread use of the derogatory term *wop* is significant, as is his treatment of immigrants (Italians and others) in his early fiction. The point of view in these cases seems to be that of an author who writes in English for American reviews rather than that of a fellow migrant.

The following section focuses on Carnevali's use of the Italian literary canon in his American works, which is another important element of his reflections on *italianità* as well as a conceptual tool in his interaction with the American literati. English-speaking modernists such as Eliot and Pound were showing a renewed interest in elements of the Italian tradition (most notably Dante); Carnevali used his own discussion of the Italian canon to offer his own point of view on the modernity of the Italian tradition, which helped him define his place in American letters.

When it came to more recent Italian literature, Carnevali actively worked to promote and translate the Italian modernist authors. After he discovered the group of authors called *Vociani* (from the name of the Florentine magazine *La Voce*), he believed he had found a version of Italian literature that he admired. He started to correspond with Giovanni Papini (former editor of *La Voce*) and made several efforts to promote the group in the American reviews for which he wrote. These articles and translations are an interesting document of transnational contact between two versions of modernism as well as an indication of how Carnevali intended to use *italianità* on his own terms.

Carnevali's use of different signifiers of *italianità* communicates an uneasy relationship with his background: a complex pattern mixing feelings of belonging and feelings of removal that result in a very idiosyncratic use of Italian signifiers. However, at the same time, he made several genuine efforts to bring an image of Italy into the American debate. He made use of the cultural and linguistic elements that his background allowed him, but he did not use them as a given or as simple points of access to a culture that he accepted univocally. *Italianità*, this elusive umbrella term pointing to a history that is too wide to be covered extensively, yet can be accessed instantaneously by referring to a single key term or figure—like Dante—provided Carnevali with some very important tools for his assault on American letters.

1. Carnevali in Little Italy[1]

An important point of entry into Carnevali's complex relationship with *italianità* is his depiction of migrants and the immigrant experience in his poetry and fiction as well as in his *Autobiography*. Written long after his return to Italy, Carnevali's narrative of his encounters and relations with Italians in the United States offers several examples of the poet's contradictory and troubled process of identification with Italian Americans.

Emigrating in 1914, Carnevali joined the Italian community in New York, one of the most important in the city, growing from 145,000 people in 1900 to 391,000 in 1920 (Kessner 1977, 17). The majority of immigrants were "impoverished, illiterate southern Italian peasants" who came to America seeking "a livelihood as well as other decencies and comforts of life that their native country had denied them" (Casillo and Russo 2011, xxiii). In many respects, Carnevali's immigrant experience differed from that of his fellow migrants: for instance, he emigrated for personal rather than economic reasons. Similarly, while high levels of illiteracy were reported among Italian immigrants at the time of entry (Kessner 1977, 40), Carnevali had attended school until at least the age of sixteen.[2] It is true, however, that he was often unemployed or doing menial jobs, sharing his living situation with the most derelict of his compatriots in New York. The *Autobiography* that he wrote in English for the American public shows how Carnevali negotiated his identity case by case, moving between the American unknown and an Italian element he could not fully recognize as his own.

Carnevali visits Little Italy as soon as he climbs down from the ship, invited by one of his fellow travelers to visit his shop. Carnevali describes Mott Street, one of the area's main streets, as "sacred to filth and misery" (1967, 73). His companion's opinion is even harsher: "The whole Italian colony of Mott and Mulberry Streets, Oronxo[3] Marginati said, was not worth the price of the small amount of dynamite required to blow it up" (1967, 74). In this case, a migrant with relatively high social status looks down on the less fortunate migrants in the tenements. From the start, he sees the community as one of contradictions and inner conflict, far from being a site of recognition, belonging, and solidarity. Writing about a time when American political and social institutions often discriminated against Italians on a cultural or racial basis (Guglielmo 2003; Gardaphé 2010), Carnevali represents the immigrant community as a harsh environment with little solidarity and a certain tension between assimilation and individualism.

Carnevali the narrator is very attentive of the sounds and accents of this Italian America. Soon after arriving, he sees a bootblack and hears "the boss speaking to the little boy in the purest Neapolitan dialect" (1967, 74). Neapolitan speech is both familiar and alien to the north-erner Carnevali. It is a tangible sign of the local specificities of Italy, yet the author may only partially identify with it, as testified to by his comments on the Neapolitan song "Funiculì Funiculà" in the text: "Do not let the student of Italian letters be dismayed at these quotations. They are not Italian, they are Neapolitan" (E. Carnevali 1967, 43). In America, Carnevali finds a link with Neapolitan culture through a process that brings several distinct Italian elements into one setting. Carnevali's memoir finds him partially and temporarily negotiating such specificities yet also expresses his uneasiness with both the Italian community and the American mainstream. Italian speech, heard while walking the streets of New York for the first time, diminishes the universal quality of the city. Carnevali remembers thinking, while walking in the heart of Little Italy, "that this was no great city but a great village. It lacked the air, the smell, the noise, the atmosphere, of a metropolis" (1967, 74). In the Italian-speaking part of the city, the poet's expectations of cosmopolitanism are dashed amid the locality of Italian culture(s).

There is no uniform sense of community in the text, set in a merciless New York where every Italian must adapt or succumb. Carnevali's friends Missio and Morea abandon him, leaving him stranded and penniless. He recalls his jobs in Italian restaurants and shops with resentment and contempt. Carnevali reportedly lost a job at a grocery store for telling "the owner, a Sicilian" that he, Carnevali, had "more schooling than he" (1967, 84). He describes his colleagues at an Italian restaurant as "a bunch of unmitigated idiots" (1967, 77). In this environment, Italians exploit other Italians. Any form of cultural identification enters the American logic of profit, including restaurant owners who forbid Italian waitresses to sing while at work: "they had tried to stupefy that fine fire that was in the songs of the Italian girls" (1967, 77). In the meantime, Carnevali lives in a "rooming-house kept by Vincenzo Bevilacqua, a fat moron" with a "recently-imported little sister" (1967, 97). In the world of tenements described by Carnevali, where lives are regulated by the basic impulses of sex and hunger, human beings are "imported" like objects.

Carnevali's description of Italian migrants in Chicago, where he moved in 1919, follows the same pattern. His first employer there, Pasquale, is another example of the socially stratified, conflict-oriented emigrant community, in which a lack of mercy seems necessary to rise in the ranks. Pasquale is a Presbyterian minister—having abandoned his native Catholicism to integrate—and the editor of a newspaper called *The Citizen*. He is described as an "ugly brute" who "peppered his spaghetti, making it quite uneatable" and who "laughed himself sick" when he saw an Italian being hanged (1967, 155). This short portrait contributes to Carnevali's depiction of the Italian community in America as a merciless environment where contact with the home culture is easily lost in the name of violent, competitive assimilation. During his short time at *The*

Citizen, Carnevali wrote an article "against the Italian gangster element in America," which he claims almost got him killed, as his employer was "in league with bootleggers" (1967, 155). It is impossible to ascertain the degree of exaggeration in Carnevali's account. The episode is the only passage in which the author acknowledges the presence of the mafia in America. Although this issue was already central to contemporary representations of Italians in America, Carnevali only hints at the phenomenon as if it were a minor detail: in the economy of the text, even the most important sociocultural facts of the Italian presence in America are discussed only to the extent that they were a part of the author's struggle against displacement.[4]

The family circle is another big part of Carnevali's experience of Italy in America. There, his relationship with his brother Augusto changed:

> My brother was no longer the brute who had beaten me mercilessly, he was no longer my brother even, but my good old friend, my only comrade in this entire city, in this strange city that we no longer acknowledged, so full were we of Italy, our speech and our laughter so full of Italy . . . (1967, 85)

Distance and displacement help the poet reframe his relationship with his brother, not in terms of kinship but of shared predicament, as the two face the "strange" city together. Carnevali's marriage to Emilia (Emily) Valenza also indicates his incorporation into Italian-American society to some extent. Emily came from Piedmont, where Carnevali had spent part of his childhood; they were married in 1917. Their troubled marriage is described quite extensively in the *Autobiography*, including painful details such as Emily's abortion and cases of infidelity on both sides. They separated in 1919, when Carnevali moved to Chicago from New York. Carnevali's account of their relationship compares her background and lack of education with his own artistic aspirations. Emily appears disconnected from the literary world, which puzzles Carnevali: "she was so entirely ignorant that she wondered who Shakespeare was, and I told her that I had just met him in the street" (1967, 98). However, he portrays Emily as a person of great sensitivity who shared her husband's penchant for storytelling: "she could tell stories of her past in the Italian mountains very effectively, picturesquely, and vividly" (E. Carnevali 1967, 98).

Beyond his familial relationships, Carnevali's *Autobiography* explores the author's complex relationship to his own immigrant identity. The text absorbs different cultural stimuli, but the *Autobiography* is not a definitive statement on Italian America. Instead, we see Carnevali choosing how, or if, he identifies with his fellow migrants. In one episode of the narrative, he hides his nationality from his German landlady:

> There I passed for a Frenchman, because I had come to the conclusion that Italians were not well seen out of Italy. The enormous landlady used to call me "Frenchsiugno," and when I was behind in paying the rent she could mutter:

> "You will never pay me, nun, Frenchy, you devilish Frenchy" (1967, 88)

At this point, Carnevali had lived in the United States long enough to know that "not well seen" was in many cases a euphemism. Italians in America were subject to social and political discrimination, and Carnevali's attempt to pass as French was an attempt to escape the stereotypes projected on Italians. In all contexts, subjectivity is largely "shaped by the experience of social recognition" and "includes our sense of self in relation to others and to our various identifications," involving a "close connection between how society is organized, what social categories are available, and what subjectivities are possible in a particular historical time, place and situation" (Karpinski 2012, 22). Carnevali's *Autobiography* serves as a narration of his evolving subjectivity in America while discussing social categories, discrimination, and the constraints placed on Italian migrants. His strong sense of individuality made identifying with the Italian migrant community problematic. In this context, it is notable that Carnevali's rare moments of identification with Italy in the narrative reflect emotional connections rather than social ones.

Carnevali recalls traversing the streets of New York, looking for a job, and feeling overwhelmed by Italian memories: "I walked the streets often in a frenzy of hatred and sang an Italian song sometimes and stopped to cry" (1967, 75). The unnamed "Italian song" is a tangible sign of identity, serving as a catalyst for the author's nostalgia, triggered by displacement and frustration. Later, he links his early poetic aspirations with "that poor Italian who wept desperately in the streets of New York remembering Neapolitan songs" (1967, 85). The "poor Italian" of the anecdote is an ideal migrant who goes unnamed in the *Autobiography*, unlike many others Carnevali encountered. Looking back in the 1930s,

Carnevali relates a nostalgic moment that connects him to a sense of community. However, for him communion occurs at the ideal level and not in the concrete reality of Little Italy: "There were millions like me, millions, and if these millions had a voice it would be the voice of God" (E. Carnevali 1967, 85).

The *Autobiography* shows that Carnevali knew the stereotypes and cultural constraints associated with Italians in America; the text also testifies to his desire to escape them. As he entered American literary circles in 1918–1922, however, he could not avoid discussions about his nationality. Indeed, his American friends and colleagues were the first to raise the issue, and not only in reference to his translations and criticism. Several examples illustrate that the American milieu perceived Carnevali first as an Italian, and commented on his *italianità*.

Samuel Putnam, a translator and scholar who would later join the modernist crowds in Paris, wrote about Carnevali as "The Mad Wop" in 1922. In Putnam's eyes, Carnevali has true poetic gifts but is also the result of a sociocultural experiment of sorts: "take an immigrant boy, with a fine head . . . , and dump him into the murk and maelstrom which is our modern industrial civilization . . ." (1922, 9). He compares the purity of the "immigrant boy" to the chaotic stimuli of the American metropolis. Putnam attributes Carnevali's peculiar poetic achievements to cultural mismatch, an immigrant's attempt to make sense of America. In casting Carnevali as the "Mad Wop," Putnam presents a powerful vision of the Italian's groundbreaking otherness. The word "Wop" is used here in the figurative and poetic sense, much like Williams, who defined Carnevali as "the black poet, the empty man" in his *Others* editorial (1919, 4). Still, the use of a usually derogatory word aimed at Italian immigrants is a tangible sign of this alterity.

Another friend and editor, Ernest Walsh, also linked Carnevali's artistic accomplishments to his nationality: "he is an Italian just as a Frenchman is a Frenchman. A Frenchman is always theatrical when an Italian is dramatic. . . . Carnevali is not French" (1925, 327). An unpublished foreword to the *Autobiography*, written by Dorothy Dudley, linked Carnevali's peculiar "manner of intelligence" to primitive, non-Western sensitivity: "it is intellect which is sometimes called Mediterranean; yet it is found near and far; perhaps among Icelanders, probably among Africans; or to the Far East."[5] Poet and editor Robert McAlmon, who had worked with Williams in New York and established the Paris-based Contact Publishing Company in 1923 (publishing Carnevali's book in

1925), wrote in his memoir that Carnevali had "the violence of adolescence" but also "wit and irony, of the Latin order which one gets from the Italians" (1938, 152). These four different critics, in essays written after Carnevali's repatriation, referred to Carnevali as an outsider using four different labels ("Wop," "Italian," "Mediterranean," and "Latin") that have in common only their geographic nature and the purpose of marking Carnevali as interesting precisely by virtue of his foreign origin.

McAlmon also published "Fortuno Carraccioli," a parody of Carnevali's New York poems in 1931—long after Carnevali had ceased to be a constant presence in the New York literary milieu. The parody imitates Carnevali's long lines, confessional tones, and plain language. It also hints that Carraccioli/Carnevali may have had trouble interacting with other immigrants:

> Stopping at the corner saloon to have a beer,
> I see the young men old, the old men bitter,
> and they don't look at me as only a poor wop.
> They are Hunkies, Polacks, Russians,
> Fins, Kikes, Dagos, Greasers, and Swedes—
> all lousy foreigners themselves.
> (McAlmon, "Fortuno Carraccioli," ll. 27–32)

The parody does particularly well in identifying Carnevali's personal tensions as he walks the streets and faces the urban environment yet is constantly focused on his inner life. McAlmon's Carraccioli dislikes being considered "only a poor wop" and cannot engage in true conversation with migrants. The actual Carnevali in the years 1918–1922 appeared more interested in conversing with the American literati. It was in literary magazines that Carnevali responded to the constraints of ethnic prejudice (as a "Latin" or "wop") and addressed the many contradictions linked to his background.

Carnevali's responses to the different images and constraints applied to him (which failed to capture the impossible whole of *italianità*) are quite revealing of how he wanted to be seen as an Italian in America. Bhabha postulated that "to exist is to be called into being in relation to an otherness, its look or locus" (1994, 44). This should apply to contested spaces inside and outside of Bhabha's original postcolonial context, to all instances in which an individual is forcefully invested with the "artifice of identity" (Bhabha 1994, 44). This framework helps us escape from the "deadlock" of an identity-bound notion of multiculturalism, which conceives society as "a fusion of uniform cultural identities and of communities resulting from these identities" (Wolf 2012, 81). The revelatory notion that identity is a representational category—not an inherent or innate one—is crucial for a repositioning of the migrant author, unbound from the temptations of a stable cultural representation. The simplified category of "Italian," projected onto him by intellectuals and broader society alike, forced Carnevali to respond to its many constraints. Again in Bhabha's terms, Carnevali was compelled to "negotiate" his own identity in the host society and in the American debate within the field of the text. In this process, he referred to the contradictory processes of identification and denial that characterized his existence in America. In attempting to prove himself as an author, he also brought other elements into the picture relating to an Italian tradition that he was called on to confront. As he negotiated his right to exist in the literary milieu, Carnevali voiced his resistance to an unproblematic, essentialist view of identity.

No published work by Carnevali deals in its entirety with Italian immigrants in America, but there are elements of his published and unpublished work that address this topic. For example, the papers that he left with his Chicago friend Mitchell Dawson include a fragment of a manuscript for an unpublished short story. The fragment, which appears to be a very early draft, presents a character named Marcello, a headwaiter of the Rale Club in New York. Marcello shares some features of his background with the author: he hails from Asti, Piedmont, not far from Biella, where Carnevali spent part of his childhood. On the other hand, his physical description does not match Carnevali, who lacked Marcello's "fiercely beautiful black moustache."[6] In the narrative, Marcello was a dishwasher and waiter in London, Berlin, Paris, Calcutta, and Tokyo before becoming headwaiter at the Rale Club. The story insists on the fact that the hardships of emigration did not compromise Marcello's strength (as they did with the author): "but life couldn't put it over on Marcello—he'd washed too many dishes and he knew what people eat in the four corners of the world." Marcello had learned the languages of the countries where he had lived, "which he spoke equally fluently and equally badly"—as opposed to Carnevali's painstaking acquisition of literary English. Italian enters the story as Marcello thinks about his languages: "he could quizz [sic] and fool life in 6 different languages, per la Madonna!"[7] The insertion of the Italian exclamation signals an

imperfect English, learned just well enough to "quiz and fool life." On
the other hand, it demonstrates that language empowered the immigrant,
even though he could not meet literary standards.

The story features two other Italians working at the Rale Club:
Mr. Raggi, the manager, and "a poor little wop with crooked legs" who
works under Marcello's command. The fragment changes subjects abruptly
when Marcello and the "poor little wop" are about to interact—moving
to a flashback to Marcello's childhood in Piedmont—and then has no
conclusion. There is no sign left of the interaction between the tough,
successful immigrant and the newcomer, but the fragment seems to
anticipate the different layers of immigrant society later described in
Carnevali's *Autobiography*. Although this attempt at Italian-American
immigrant fiction remained unfinished, Carnevali did publish another
short story with immigrant characters in 1919 called "Bogey Man."
This short, autobiographical vignette, featured in the *Others* issue that
included Williams's celebration of Carnevali as "the black poet," is
particularly interesting with respect to Carnevali's relationship with his
fellow immigrants. The story takes place in Carnevali's tenement: as
he comes back home, a cleaning lady drops a broom, waking up and
angering his Polish neighbor.

> He took a book in his hands. Shook the book before my eyes,
> I gotta fon da dichonary book, see!
> Yes. . . . well. . . . what. . . . do you?
> See?
> Do you want to sell it? I don't want to buy it.
> Mabbe I no speak english. Listen . . .
> His big teeth appeared and disappeared, monstrously.
> (E. Carnevali 1919g, 22)

The presentation of the fellow immigrant is quite significant. Big,
monstrous teeth and, a few lines above, a "moustache like a threat" define
the man as dangerous and almost inhuman. The immigrant's language is
heavily marked at the grammatical and phonetic levels. This sets him
apart, not only from the society of native speakers, but also from the
other migrant, Carnevali: between the text and the paratext, the only
thing unequivocally marking the author of "Bogeyman" as non-American
is precisely his surname. His language, and the narrator's voice, are standard literary English, which he has acquired over the years. In contrast,

the other immigrant character's speech is in broken English, and the fact that he is holding a dictionary is no small detail:

> —I gotta fon da dichonary book. Mabbe you good . . . I
> no say you no good . . . mabbe. Hu make noise bump
> me. . . . I kick. . . . no can shleep. . . . I gib you fon
> da kick. . . . you no stand? I good, you no good, you no
> see, mabbe, I no say. . . .
> And then, with a last great push, with long-bursting
>   expansion:
> —I gib you fon da dichonary book.
> I understood at last that he wanted to throw it at me.
>   (1919g, 22)

The unnamed Pole has a dictionary, which should be an instrument of education, a tool for assimilation. Yet it figures here as tangible sign of his linguistic inadequacy, of the low status in which he is relegated. His linguistic frustration leads him to use the book as a threat.

The Pole's ineffective rage triggers Carnevali's partial identification with him: he thinks of the Pole as he walks down the streets, children pointing at him and calling him a bogeyman. Carnevali pins that down to his linguistic shortcomings, writing a poignant description of linguistic discrimination:

> They are all against you. All they who know english [sic].
> They enjoy knocking at your door, they who won't see how
> much you need your sleep, and you must get angry at yourself,
> because you know these creatures who go to vaudevilles and
> put on queer neckties on Sunday morning, you know they're
> awake making a noise which they have a right to make, being
> more beautiful than you, knowing english [sic]. (1919g, 23)

In these words Carnevali "shows by reflection that he understands profoundly the position of the linguistic outsider" (Viscusi 2006, 178), but he speaks from the viewpoint of the partially assimilated. He takes on the mantle of the poet of the commonplace, the one who managed to turn linguistic displacement into art and bring it into the arena of literary reviews like *Others*: "You could with some effort become a definite untruth, a pleasant one. You are an uncouth verity now" (E. Carnevali

1919g, 23). "Bogeyman" speaks of Carnevali's in-betweenness, his victorious struggle with the English language and his uneasiness with regard to other linguistically displaced persons—was he really so distant from that stage? Another 1919 unpublished short story, "Lean Woman,"[8] shows a similar dynamic, as the author-protagonist helps a woman open the door in the tenement building where they both live: this derelict woman's speech, like the Bogeyman's, is socially marked as broken English in contrast to Carnevali's narrator, who tends to Standard English. If the Bogeyman represents a migrant's rage against discrimination, the Lean Woman places herself in a subordinate position. While the narrator does little more than hold her things and light a match while she opens the door, she thanks him profusely ("Think ye, sor, think ye, Mister"), "as if she feared [he] take back a gift which [he has] given her."

Both Bogeyman and Lean Woman are immigrant types, hardly characterized in their ethnic specificities, cast by Carnevali in their roles to help him prove his point on the immigrant predicament—in this case, to speak against the immigrant fear of the unknown. At one point, he refrains from giving advice to the Lean Woman because she would "believe [he is] Jesus, and an already old misunderstanding would begin for [her]," while he admits: "I, who have read, know the reason of every religion and, therefore, know its final irrevocable death." In these two short depictions of non-Italian immigrants, Carnevali casts himself as a spiritual savior who would be able to redeem them from silence and inability. The two passages are ultimately about his achieved status as an immigrant writer.

In New York and Chicago, Carnevali seems more often intent on discussing the limits, boundaries, and quirks of his *italianità* in relation or opposition with the whole of America. The 1920 "Tale III" of the "Tales of a Hurried Man" has an almost nonexistent plot—Carnevali walks back home and cooks a meal—yet is a crucial occasion for him to discuss his predicament and criticize the imposed values of American life. Standing on the roof of his building, the author entertains thoughts of suicide as the ultimate artistic performance: "I could touch this intangible air if I sent my body whirling through it, in a spider's dance, to break over the flagstones. I would give a hundred persons at least the thrill of their lives" (1920b, 31). Instead, he decides to "walk down to [the] apartment and open the door with a Yale key, just like everybody." To him, conforming to the little everyday rituals of consumerist society equals giving up the search for poetic truth ("And they will not say that I have gone away from them to find the truth") and leads to Americanization: "they will admit that I am the most American of the Americans" (E. Carnevali 1920b, 31). This critique of American discourse prompts one of his few moments of total identification with the migrant community:

> I am an emigrant and I have left my home, I am homeless and I want a home. You look at me with evil eyes, with squinting eyes, you don't look at me, you sneer at me. I am emigrant, waiting, I know millions that are like me. (1920b, 31)

This statement assumes a different dimension when inserted in the larger context of the whole passage, which asserts the poet's individuality against the forced conformity of the host society. Existential displacement is somehow linked to the immigrant milieu, yet this reference to "millions" is an element of poetic imagery rather than a comment on the statistical reality of immigration.

Italian migrants appear in the story from a distance, blending into the very background as Carnevali walks home: "whitish and greenish the houses, the colors of the wives of the poor wops" (1920b, 28). The "wops" are part of the cityscape, and not recognizable characters with a voice of their own. The phrase "poor wops" carries a sense of detachment, as if their (economic, spiritual) poverty is something that the author can recognize but not share. The term "wops" itself is quite controversial: one would not expect an Italian-American writer to use a racially derogatory word to refer to his own community. The term is derogatory indeed, yet it situates the text within the context of immigrant discrimination while enabling the author to distance himself from the migrants he describes. Carnevali employed the word with a sympathetic and patronizing attitude toward his fellow migrants. It provided him with a name to define them while placing himself at a distance from the community.

"Tale III" uses irony to place Carnevali within an expanded and uncertain framework of *italianità*, where the author is the only Italian who speaks, and common frames of references are turned upside down. A kitchen scene offers the chance for a provocative use of Italian food:

> And as for spaghetti and ravioli, let me tell you once for all that parsley chopped fine and one small onion and . . . Yes, people do think that I am interesting! Characteristically an Italian, don't you know. And it's just what they want . . . the

local color, that attractive and light way of talking . . . and
those very extraordinary neckties . . . oh, perfectly charming!
(E. Carnevali 1920b, 32)

The first draft of what would later become "Tale III" linked the author's
identity with cooking, but in quite a different way:

My father was a born cook, and that's what I inherited. And
when the friends come you explain to them how the spaghetti
should be made, and there follows a conversation about Italy
and the canals of Venice. It is not true that there be nothing
but canals in Venice. You can *walk* all your way thru.[9]

In the draft, the passion for food is deeply rooted in identity, having been
"inherited" from a "born cook"—a translation of the Italian *un cuoco
nato*. Food has a transnational dimension in this account, prompting
what seems to be a session of questions about Italy from the author's
friends (not mentioned in the published story). On the contrary, in the
published story the author reacts when the image of *italianità* is projected
onto him. There, the narrating voice begins with the explanation of spaghetti, but suddenly interrupts itself to react to the stereotypical image.
Carnevali knew that a great part of his appeal in the New York milieu
derived from his being "characteristically" Italian.

In "Tale III," Carnevali reacts to the notion of a "characteristic"
Italian identity by addressing the symbols that American intellectuals
immediately associated with Italian culture: "And, anyway, Dante died
quite long ago, and there was a dash of Teuton blood in him, I bet!
Cagliostro is more the Latin. And today fierce men a la Cagliostro are
out of fashion" (E. Carnevali 1920b, 32). Rather than a disregard for
Dante, this passage seems to express Carnevali's refusal to be automati-
cally identified with him. He is willing to give up Dante, the established
and universally accessible symbol of Italian tradition, to the "Teutons."
On the other hand, he claims for himself a less canonical ancestor,
Cagliostro. An eighteenth-century adventurer and occultist, Cagliostro
epitomizes an Italian stereotype that had some currency in English-
speaking countries, where Italy was often imagined as a land of luxury,
paganism, and violence. This model of Anglo-Italian cultural relations
was "confected well in advance of the coming of most Italians to the
United States" yet was able to influence "the terms on which Italians

were first accepted into American society" (Connell 2010, 11). It dates back as far as the seventeenth century, when the changing geopolitical and religious situation made popular a cultural representation of Italy "as a land populated by wily and dangerous Machiavels," a "land of violence and sexuality not stabilized by the institutions of family and marriage" (Dasenbrock 1991, 2). Anglo-Saxon perceptions of Italy, alternating between fascination, fear, and diffidence, produced a fixed yet recyclable image. In literary circles, this image was projected onto Carnevali, who polemically embraced it in "Tale III" by redefining his Italian models (Cagliostro instead of Dante) and insisting on the symbols that separated Puritan America from pagan/Catholic Italy (food and sex):

> Alone with my wife, I have meals that are feasts. Anti-puritan meals. To the eternal glory of the magnificent eaters of my old land, Lorenzo de' Medici, Alessandro Borgia, Leone X, and Cornaro before he had got tired. Crunching a plant of dandelion under my teeth and devouring with my eyes the small space of my wife's breasts that she lets me see; eating a bleeding beefsteak . . . god! (1920b, 33)

Carnevali, responding to well-established prejudices about Italians in his own way, turns the ready-made image of the Italians as lascivious papists against its very inventors. He employs cultural discourses of food in his criticism of modern consumerism: "And if, in ten years, people will only chew foodstuff instead of eating, what the hell! We eat and laugh now, we eat and weep together, eh girl" (1920b, 33). The category of "foodstuff" relates to America (which is, for Carnevali, the land of the commonplace) while Italian food is associated with lust and vitality.

Italianità is not employed in the story as a preconceived, innate quality; rather, Carnevali's use of italianità responds to attributes that have been projected onto him. A preconceived and external image of Italy becomes a conceptual tool to be used against the American mainstream—not so much to defend group identity as to construe the author's individuality out of contrasting images. In "Tale III," the attack on America also makes use of the speech of Italian migrants:

> They are still singing the songs of the mountains—and a million Italians . . . well, they say "L'America, donne senza colore e frutta senza sapore"—America, women without

colour and fruits without taste. And maybe they are right.
(E. Carnevali 1920c, 56)

The saying expresses the migrant's reaction to the alienating and standardized American environment, setting "the song of the mountains" against
the modern city. Carnevali translates it into an American modernist
text, but in doing so he is not granting agency to the other migrants:
he is partially identifying with them, but as part of a multiform and
flexible Italian imagery that he uses to assert his own individuality in
the American text.

If we assume the typical first-generation ethnic writer to be a spokesperson for his community, driven by the need for a sort of "compulsive
representation" (Sollors 2008, 42) in order to defy stereotypes, then Carnevali falls out of the paradigm. Yet this is not to say that Carnevali never
challenged the stereotype in his writing. In this respect, he predates the
authors (Tusiani, Fante, and Di Donato) that Tamburri included in the
"stage one" of the "hyphenated writer" when an immigrant intellectual
"not only questions his/her origins, but . . . is indeed bent on disproving
the suspicions and prejudices of the dominant culture" (1991, 39). Just
as Tamburri at the end of his seminal essay problematized the notion of
the hyphen itself and the ideological gap it denotes, Carnevali challenges
the idea that an "ethnic" writer must relate to the host community and
migrant community as two fixed concepts already replete with signifiers
of identity. His identification with Italy and Italians was a troubled and
contradictory one, but he was far from approving of the discrimination
Italians encountered in the United States.

Although there were few English-language literary spokespeople
for Italians in America at this time, there was a very active Italian-
language press that campaigned vehemently against discrimination and
"sought to justify Italian worthiness as a civilized race," something it
accomplished in Italian circles "by focusing on *italianità*, or a celebration
of all things Italian" (Vellon 2014, 15). Carnevali was probably aware of
this; however, in English-language literary reviews he refused to defend
the honor of his compatriots. The reasons he gives are quite consistent
with his agenda: "I could have written a tremendously happy treatise
to show why the wops break one and every law of the United States"
except that "they don't—and it wouldn't have sufficed—and reform is
reform and I chose revolution—I quit" (E. Carnevali 1920c, 54). For
Carnevali, then, it was not a matter of his superiority as much as it was

his view that the poet's mission (of writing the "splendid commonplace" and redeeming everyday life from its brutality) was incompatible with the role of ethnic spokesperson.

Perhaps because it occurred within his chosen field of literature, Carnevali did rise to the defense of the Italian community on at least one occasion. In 1919, T. A. Daly, a columnist and poet, published *McAroni Ballad and Other Poems*, a supposedly humorous collection of poems written in an English that imitated the speech of Italian immigrants. Carnevali wrote a review of the collection for *Poetry*, starting with a polemical note imagining that all the Italian immigrants should "throw their pick-axes in the air and dance a tarantella" and sing the *Star-Spangled Banner*, because they "have at last their laureate poet: T. A. Daly" (1920d, 278). Drawing on expertise that Daly did not possess, he notes that "the dialect is untrue, the names are impossibilities (Scalabrarta, Scalabrella, Gessapalena)" and denounces the "shameful and shameless lack of knowledge of even the most obvious facts concerning Italian."

A stereotype is not just a distorted depiction; it is also the stereotyping group's attempt to control the unfamiliar and create an Other, which is "always constructed as an object for the benefit of the subject who stands in need of an objectified Other in order to achieve a masterly self-definition" (Pickering 2001, 168). The Other is constructed independently from its real-life existence (as Pickering remarks, "the location of the Other is primarily in language") to be ridiculed or patronized. As an Italian working within the mainstream intelligentsia, Carnevali could expose the language of the stereotype: a language full of "impossibilities," constructed to sound alien to the target audience, but not necessarily grounded in the experience of the stereotyped community.

Although he sided with the Italian immigrants against Daly, nevertheless Carnevali remarked on their ingenuousness:

> O naiveté of my Sicilians and Calabresi! . . . And how scared and frightened he would be should he know what tremendous things your purity and naiveté are, in this country of grey and moving pictures!—should he know what your smile is, your tremendous smile, in America! (E. Carnevali 1920d, 279)

From his antiestablishment position, the innocence of the Italians is to be defended against discrimination. Yet, despite his positive intent, the depiction of migrants as primitive and pure also denotes, to a degree, a lack of interest in their voice. Even in his defense of Italian immigrants, Carnevali did not see himself as a spokesperson for the Italian community. Although Carnevali might decry the mistreatment of Italians in America, he also had little desire to participate in the traditional culture they brought with them across the ocean. He continued to hold himself apart from other Italian-Americans even when arguing in their defense.

Carnevali is now part of the Italian-American canon, although he may never have been willing to engage with Italian-American culture in the traditional, canon-building sense. He knew other Italian-American authors well enough to cast judgement on them: in a 1919 letter, discussing his project for a magazine, Carnevali made his own list of "ciò che c'è di buono in America,"[10] including various American authors (Sandburg, W. C. Williams, Frost, T. S. Eliot), but "né Giovannitti né Ruotolo" (E. Carnevali 1981, 85–86). Carnevali engaged almost exclusively with American literature and treated *italianità* as a constructible, shape-shifting identity that could include his uneasy relationship with the Italian immigrant community as well as his polemical reuse of Italian tradition(s). He worked and reworked the notion of culture as a unitary entity, demonstrating that the artist's individuality necessarily arises from personal reelaboration of different cultural constraints. As he increasingly engaged with American modernist poetry, the representation of a multiform *italianità* remained a constant of his works.

2. Carnevali and Dante: Tradition and the Individual Italian

In his influential 1919 essay "Tradition and the Individual Talent," T. S. Eliot claimed that the historical sense is "nearly indispensable to any one who would continue to be a poet beyond his twenty-fifth year" and that it "involves a perception, not only of the pastness of the past, but of its presence" (1964, 4). The modernist search for a stable tradition existed alongside the avant-garde desire for rupture, often propagating in waves along the same forums. As Carnevali entered the modernist debate, his relationship with the Italian literary tradition became more focused, as he was often called on to discuss Italian literature in the pages of *Poetry*. This also provided him with a chance to redefine himself in relation to his background as he responded to the image of Italian tradition (and of Dante in particular) that modernist authors had.

While few would deny that Dante occupies a central role in the Italian literary canon, transnational authors like Carnevali challenge and redefine the idea itself of a national canon. This concept has been traditionally seen under a straightforward generational and ethnic/linguistic lens, summarized in Bloom's famous exploration of the Anglophone canon through the idea of the "anxiety of influence." This idea is based on a notion of poetic tradition as a series of understandings and rewritings of the past, with a definite dialectic component as every strong poet contributes to history by responding to his predecessors:

> For the poet is condemned to learn his profoundest yearnings through an awareness of other selves. The poem is within him, yet he experiences the shame and splendor of being found by poems—great poems—outside him. (Bloom 1997, 26)

Bloom's dialectic view of the canon may account for differentiation within continuity, ensured by the phenomenon of identification with and revolt against the literary "fathers." More recently, comparative literature scholars found this kind of model too focused on national communities, at risk of creating an image of "literature as agonistic warzones" (Prendergast 2004, 7).

A literary canon comes into existence a supra-individual entity, where individual contributions compete dialectically with each other. However, far from being a homogeneous, mononational (or monolingual) flow, a canon is the result of a continuous operation of rewriting of literary history by authors and scholars alike, each of them assuming his or her view of literature as his or her own, each of them drawing from various sources across time and space in a process that is never univocal or circumscribed. Modernist authors like Pound, Eliot, and Joyce, with their (very different) cosmopolitan approaches, "massive number of cross-national influences[,] . . . and appropriations" were crucial in subverting "the usual dynastic narratives of compatriot X begetting compatriot Y begetting compatriot Z" (Ramazani 2009, 25). Carnevali experienced this transnational outlook from the peculiar point of view of one of the national traditions that his modernists colleagues preferred. Modernist Anglophone authors had strong links with Italy, concentrating on both contemporary Italian culture and its artistic tradition: "for them, Italy was both present and past, both a living force and an emblem of the past" (Dasenbrock 1991, 104). Carnevali, the Italian among them, reacted to the modernist affinity with Italy in a way that affirmed his own artistic agenda.

As noted above, Carnevali used his polemical reminder to the American literati that "Dante died quite a long time ago" to express his desire to reconfigure *italianità* on his own terms. Indeed, Dante figured prominently among the cultural references he brought to his criticism. The 1921 essay "The Book of Job Junior" mentions Dante "chased like a homeless dog from one town to another" building his vision of hell and calling Italy "not a city woman / but a whore" (2006, 12). This rewriting of Dante's exile, together with the translation of his line "non donna di province, ma bordello!" (*Purgatorio* VI, l. 78), enabled Carnevali to criticize current aesthetic tendencies, reframing the image to complement his own aesthetic preoccupations. The translation is also quite free and idiosyncratic: the original "donna" (*lady/ruler* in the medieval sense of the world) is translated as "woman," as it would be in the case of the modern Italian "donna." Carnevali freely translated the quotation, a part of his cultural background since his national education, and adapted it to express his own meaning.

When Carnevali was asked by the *Poetry* editors to write an essay on Dante for the sixth centenary of his death in 1921, he wrote a piece that expressed both the importance of the founding father of Italian literature and the problems posed by modern imitations and references. Carnevali reminds the reader that on that important Dante anniversary, "the whole world is thinking of him," while his spirit "seems to be questioning the changes of six centuries" (1921b, 323). He is preoccupied with Dante's distance from the present time and the questions of identity posed by such distance. He speaks of Dante as an "aristocrat and monarchist," although he acknowledges that "he was of too immense stature not to have deeply humane sympathies" (1921b, 323). While answering to the modern mind-set first—prompting him to identify Dante as "aristocrat and monarchist"—he reframes the founding father within reassuring ideological boundaries as he writes of Dante's "humane sympathies." When he underlines that "his work was not for the elect" (E. Carnevali 1921b, 323), it is interesting that he used the most immediate translation available of the Italian *eletto* ("elected" but also "anointed" or, by extension, "superior"), translating Italian categories for the English-speaking public. Given Carnevali's democratic, Whitmanian view of the role of the artist, his preoccupation lies in making sense of the distance in space as well as time between Dante and his readers, justifying Dante's relevance to the present time, reusing him as reference in his discussion of modernity.

In Carnevali's modern review of the Italian tradition, he goes as far as appealing to contemporary debates to explain Dante's relation to fellow medieval authors Petrarch and Boccaccio (often taken together with Dante in a triumvirate of founding fathers of Italian literature). He reframes them in accordance with his own view of present-day literature, taking Boccaccio to represent every "artist who works to entertain and amuse his public" (1921b, 323). Petrarch is portrayed as more focused on the inner world—"in whose trail a thousand outcasts, egocentrics, morphinomaniacs, came" (E. Carnevali 1921b, 323). Dante, finally, "embodies the greatest tradition—that of those who through literature judge men and the times" (E. Carnevali 1921b, 324).

Carnevali's judgements do not correspond to an organic, critical sense of Italian literature as much as to his own desire to position himself with respect to it. The essay articulates a pattern of distancing and appropriation: Carnevali insists on the fact that "Today his ethics are dead," but at the same time they constitute "the skeleton around which the beautiful immortal flesh of Dante's words was cast" (1921b, 324). Carnevali construes the sound of his poetry as "immortal," with the sound component constituting an element of continuing and reaffirmed presence, as the words can be quoted and read aloud. Carnevali signals his national identification by claiming the privilege of reading an untranslated Dante, whose "magical beauty" may be appreciated only by an Italian, "and a good Italian." Carnevali assumes the stance, in the American milieu, of the repository of the *Commedia*'s "magical beauty." He does not provide quotations in the essay, translated or untranslated: the American reader must necessarily take him at his word.

Carnevali gives Dante credit for having written "in what was called *il volgare*, the language spoken by the *volgo*, the people" (1921b, 323). He comments, almost in Whitmanesque tones, that this "points out again that all great things have their foundations in the *volgo*, as all buildings in the earth" (E. Carnevali 1921b, 323). Dante's desire to provide Italy with a national, literarily dignified language articulated itself in his poetry and in the treatise *De Vulgari Eloquentia* ("On Eloquence in the vernacular"), which would be taken as a model "much later by writers who found themselves in a structurally similar position" (Casanova 2004, 55). Carnevali's consideration of the Italian tradition ultimately leads him to express his views on the popular, everyday roots of art. His etymological reading, referring to the origin of *volgare* as relative to the *volgo*/people, bends the rule of philology to serve his own democratic view of art.

Given Carnevali's position within the modernist milieu, one remark stands out: "We are waiting for the poet who will give us a *Divina Commedia* of our own times," he writes, warning that what "we expect" would necessarily be drastically different (E. Carnevali 1921b, 325). The passage does not discuss modernism explicitly, but it is written with the awareness that Dante was being "read (and misread) in a variety of ways by the great modernists" (McDougal 1985, x) in a search for tradition that combined philology with criticism of modern life. A young Ezra Pound constantly referred to medieval Provence and Italy in pursuit of a tradition that would help him redeem the present:

> And yet I know, how that the souls of all men great
> At times pass through us,
> And we are melted into them, and are not
> Save reflexions of their souls.
> Thus am I Dante for a space and am
> One François Villon, ballad-lord and thief.
> ("Histrion," ll. 2–7)

Pound's early poetry expresses a troubled identification with literary models like Dante, Villon, and the troubadours; and a nostalgia for a greatness that he attributed to the past and attempted to re-create in the present. He engaged with the texts through translation, including a translation of Guido Cavalcanti's poetry, which he filled with "archaic neologisms" (Venuti 2008, 171)—that is, a modern English filled with archaisms. Pound established an intimate dialogue with the Italian Middle Ages, which served not only to illustrate Cavalcanti's poetry to readers but also to provide material for his original work, setting the standards for modernist translation as a "comprehensive textual strategy for negotiating between the demands of transmission and transformation, between the authority of tradition and the demands of innovation" (Yao 2002, 22). Bits—untranslated and translated—of Italian medieval poetry appeared in poetry by Pound and Eliot as Carnevali was writing, and it was in this context that he wrote that he was still "waiting" for a *Divina Commedia* of his time from the point of view of an Italian outsider.

Carnevali's arguments about the difficulties of writing a *Commedia* of the twentieth century are particularly interesting, emphasizing both the vastness of Dante's work and the lack of humanity that he saw in his time. In the twentieth century, he argues, "Hell" is on Earth: "A hell more terrific than the hell of Dante is the hell of modern warfare" (E. Carnevali 1921b, 325). Carnevali insists on the "real" hellish experience of an overpopulated, gray, and deforested world perpetually at war. His article presents a critique of capitalism as antihumanism that perhaps would have pleased Pound:

> And the makers of these are business men who do not see, and workers whom a whirlwind sweeps into this modern tremendous factory, and leaves there like fledglings caught in the blast of an immense furnace. Out of this factory the human soul comes crushed—out of this factory of neurosis, the modern world. (E. Carnevali 1921b, 325)

The passage alludes to industrial alienation and psychological sickness, two themes that are typical of modernism and reflected in many works that showed the effect of the changing economic and social conditions on the human experience of the world; Carnevali was not alone in his preoccupation with the "factory" that "crushed" the human soul. In his comments, Carnevali does not mention various modernist attempts to write a *Commedia* of their days, of which he may have at least heard (*The Waste Land* was soon to be published, and some *Cantos* had come out in drafted versions). He seems to ignore them yet at the same time to speak to them as he defines the most important difficulty they faced: a world that had grown unexpectedly huge and difficult to grasp with the all-encompassing look of major literature. While "Dante's conception of his narrow world was centered around two main hypotheses—that of the absolute monarchy and that of the Roman Catholic power," nowadays a poet was facing the challenge of "gather[ing] together in his thought a world which facility of transportation, and science in general, have made enormous" (E. Carnevali 1921b, 326). It is highly unlikely that he did not know that Pound was attempting some sort of *Divina Commedia* for their time, and these words may hint exactly at that—the difficulty of making sense of this enormous world, resulting actually in the entangled references and multiform language of the *Cantos*.

The reference is not direct, but the description of the challenge faced by Pound is poignant. It seems that Carnevali did not hold Pound in high esteem at the time: in 1920, he wrote a review of the latter's collection of poetry and essays *Pavannes and Divisions* (1918). Carnevali

voices his "Irritation" (the title of the essay) at Pound's status as a leading modernist intellectual:

> A faith in art which consists of a few don'ts shouted at some
> imaginary and improbable followers; of repetitions of phrases
> by old and ancient masters, duly stripped of their original
> glamour, as all repetitions are. (E. Carnevali 1920a, 212)

The reference to a "few don'ts" alludes to Pound's 1913 essay "A Few
Don'ts by an Imagiste," which outlines advice for poets who wanted to
achieve that polished and precise verse and also includes indications
of which traditional models to seek and which to avoid. Carnevali
particularly criticizes the sterility of Pound's claim to tradition; he does
not question Pound's ideas but rather accuses him of expressing "coldly
and precisely" the same things that "were screamed without precision,
and with blind illogical heat, by Blake, by Shelley, by Nietzsche, by
Rimbaud" (1920a, 219). Domenichelli explained Carnevali's criticism
of Pound as an attack on a "series of masks (Pound's idea of the poetic
persona), a series of *poses*" coming from a man who "seems to have lived
burning the candle at both ends," a "hurried man" with "no time for
paraphrase, lies, masks, and inauthenticity" (1998, 86). Carnevali's "Irritation," in fact, sets them in contrast on such terms: Carnevali wanted
to present himself as a "hurried man," while Pound's early poetry takes
much of its force from "masks." It is true that Carnevali had adopted
a series of masks of his own when transitioning into English—that of
the post-Whitmanian bard of the "commonplace," but also those of the
nineteenth-century artistic personalities who based their work on the
prominence of emotion and irrationality (such as Blake or Rimbaud,
mentioned in the passage quoted above). His gaze, however, was fixed
on urban reality because of the urgency of the migrant predicament,
and his own use of a different language was a migrant's matter of life
and death—a plea for acceptance into American literature rather than a
philologist's attempt to bring Italian elements into American literature.

Carnevali criticized Pound's erudite, translational interest in the
European past as sterile nostalgia, a "longing for the times of Chivalry and
the beauty that was Greece" (1920a, 218); he even used his own Italian
migrant experience to affirm this point. Lamenting the "tangled[ness]
and twisted[ness]" of Pound's aristocratic art, he contrasted it with the
"exquisiteness" of "an Italian mother [he] saw in Taylor Street biting

in a sweet frenzy the mouth of her sloppy child" (E. Carnevali 1920a, 216). Carnevali countered what he took to be Pound's "aristocracy" by construing a sentimental image of immigrant bonding, once again reaffirming his status as an outsider within modernism.

As an outsider at a time in which "virtually all the major modernist writers in English [were] trying to write the *Commedia* of the twentieth century" (Dasenbrock 1991, 209), Carnevali raised the issue of the validity of the uses of tradition while attempting to figure out his own literary ancestry. Essays like "Dante—And Today" and "Irritation" penetrated the discourse of modernist reuse of the Italian past from a unique perspective for American readers, voicing possible Italian doubts on the "*Commedia* of the twentieth century." From the point of view of the Italian presence in America, Carnevali's essays enact the dichotomy between Italy as a source of cheap labor in the American metropolis and as the birthplace of some of the crucial figures in Western culture. Carnevali does not intend to solve the dichotomy, but rather to expose and explode it, flaunting an *italianità* that exists only in the peculiarity of his persona.

3. "Something of Govoni in Frost": Translating Italian Modernism

If Carnevali's American writings denote a troubled and complex identification with both the Italian immigrant community and Italian tradition, there was a field in which he was very vocal about his *italianità*: the translation of Italian modernist authors. Carnevali translated short pieces from different authors for a "Five Years of Italian Poetry (1910–1915)" collection published in January 1919 in *Poetry*. He translated an essay by Papini for *The Little Review* in June 1919 and a short story by Papini ("Congedo"/"Leavetaking") for *Others* in July 1919. There are other unpublished translations in the archives, including a long poem by Palazzeschi ("L'incendiario"/"The Incendiary") and fiction from Papini ("Mezz'ora"/"Half Hour"). The texts came mainly from the Florentine review *La Voce*, of which Carnevali was a self-declared disciple—for which reason he started an epistolary relationship with Papini. Carnevali employed the translation of Italian authors in the construction of his career in America while redefining his own links with Italy.

Translation scholars agree that translations are inseparable from their context and goal: they "always come into being within a certain cultural environment and are designed to meet certain needs of, and/or occupy certain 'slots' in it" (Toury 1995, 12). Carnevali's work on the Italian modernists did not produce macroscopic effects on the receiving end; this work did not start recognizable trends or introduce stylistic models into America. He did, however, intend to occupy a certain "slot"—more precisely, the space for confrontation that Carnevali saw between Italian and American literary modernisms. In this transnational network that he sought to create, he would become a mediator between Italy and America—a project that involved the creation of a transnational literary magazine, *New Moon*. The project may not have succeeded, but its scope and goals make it worthy of investigation now as a transnational enterprise that, if successful, might have established deeper, ramified Italian-American literary connections.

Carnevali's career as a translator began in 1918 when he worked for Joel Elias Spingarn, a New York–based scholar and activist with an interest in all things Italian. Spingarn hired Carnevali as his secretary, also asking him to translate Croce's *Breviario di Estetica*. The young translator's work progressed slowly and with difficulty. In a June 1918 letter, Carnevali appealed to his employer for patience, explaining that he was not able to complete the translation before the deadline. The translation was never published and is now lost, although Carnevali apparently finished it, as he wrote to Croce himself: "Ho tradotto, male, per il Sig. J. E. Spingarn, il suo Breviario di Estetica . . ."[11] (E. Carnevali 1981, 61). The relationship between Spingarn and Carnevali soon deteriorated: Edward Dahlberg, in a short memoir on Carnevali, implied that he was fired for stealing books from his employer.[12] Dahlberg's allegations are now impossible to prove, but another element stands out in this account: Spingarn was known as a cultural mediator, an important figure in introducing Italian authors such as Croce and Vico in America. Carnevali pursued the same path, but not together with Spingarn. That year, he found issues of the magazine *La Voce* in the New York Public Library, which inspired him to reconsider his relationship with Italian culture.

Carnevali wrote to Croce in August 1918: "nella Public Library ho scoperto tutti i numeri della Voce, e ciò mi ha dato una gran fame di cose italiane"[13] (E. Carnevali 1981, 62). Published in Florence, *La Voce* would become Carnevali's strongest Italian reference and his main source on the timid emergence of literary modernism in Italy. It is important to remember, when speaking of an Italian "modernism," that the term has been only retrospectively applied to diverse, isolated cultural phenomena dealing with the impact of modernity in Italy (Somigli and Moroni 2004, 4). In this atmosphere, the Florentine magazine had a remarkably international inclination with respect to other Italian reviews. Its founders (Papini, Prezzolini, and Soffici) were influenced by their own experience of the transnational avant-garde of Paris and expressed their desire for a general renovation of Italian culture.[14] From the first issue, the *Vociani* promoted the diffusion of a cosmopolitan culture that would enrich Italy without making it forsake its own tradition:

> Si tratta di ridare all'Italia non soltanto il contatto colla cultura europea ma anche la coscienza storica della cultura sua, ch'è pur tanta parte della cultura europea. Io mi contento di poco: Nazionalisti no, ma Italiani sì![15] (Papini 1908, 1)

La Voce, as Prezzolini and Papini intended it, was relatively short-lived: the group broke up shortly after the beginning of World War I over the magazine's politicization. Another editor, Giuseppe De Robertis, turned *La Voce* into a purely literary review before it finally closed down in 1916. In 1918, Carnevali became an enthusiastic admirer of an editorial project that had been dead for two years. It may have been a belated discovery, but it put him in contact with a version of Italian culture that responded to his needs: an Italian culture that engaged with the modern world, where ethical and aesthetic innovation went hand in hand. Carnevali asked Croce, with candid enthusiasm, to send him the addresses of the *Vociani* Papini, Prezzolini, Slataper (who had died three years earlier), Soffici, and Palazzeschi (1981, 62–63). He corresponded with Papini for about a year, and Papini quickly became his most important Italian contact.

Carnevali's letters to Papini express his will to become the translator of the *Vociani* as well as the mediator between Italian and American modernisms. In February 1919, Carnevali enthusiastically mentions an essay that he intends to write on Papini, as well as his proposed anthology of translated Italian poets:

> Questo sarà buona réclame per lei—e se qualcuno (forse avrò il tempo di farlo io stesso) tradurrà i suoi libri per una casa editrice americana, avrò l'onore di dirle che sono stato io più o meno ad invogliare il pubblico (il)letterario americano[16] (E. Carnevali 1981, 67)

The young expatriate insists on his role as a cultural mediator, asserting that American readers "devono conoscere Palazzeschi, Govoni, Jahier e Soffici. E se non lo faccio io nessuno lo farà"[17] (1981, 68). Carnevali attempts to capitalize on his position as an Italian in New York, carving for himself a niche as translator and editor. He tells Papini of his incumbent position as assistant editor of *Poetry*, asking the Italian author for help in giving *Poetry* an international dimension.[18] At the same time, Carnevali sends Papini lists of prospective subscribers for the latter's new magazine *La Vraie Italie*.[19] Carnevali's interest seems to lie, at this point, in the creation of an international network, to be fueled by his translations. His letters to Papini refer continuously to his efforts to disseminate the *Vociani* in America. In May 1919, he expresses his intention to translate Papini's autobiographical novel *Un uomo finito* (1912). Carnevali also laments that "un professoruccio italianescante"[20] has blocked publication of his essay on Papini for *The Dial* (1981, 73). In another May 1919 letter, he confirmed that "piccoli disordinati e wretched magazines son tutti pronti e contentissimi d'accettare traduzioni"[21] (1981, 74). In the meantime, in August 1919 Carnevali starts mentioning his plans for a magazine of his own (1981, 85), inspired by *La Voce*, to be published in America under the title *New Moon*. Carnevali intended the magazine to have an international dimension ("Avremo uno 'scambio' con quei giornali Italiani e Francesi che ci interesseranno"[22] [1981, 86]) and to feature Italian contributions translated into English.

This ambitious project, remarkably transnational even by modernist standards, never saw the light of day because of Carnevali's illness. However, all of Carnevali's translations are testament to the young author's will to bring the two sides of the Atlantic in contact by communicating to the American public an idea of Italy that he could identify with. The criticism that accompanies Carnevali's translations is an enthusiastic and idiosyncratic account of contemporary Italian literature tailored to his tastes and to the American literary public.

La Voce had not been very prominent among American critics during its life span.[23] Carnevali's 1919 article was advertised on *Poetry*'s first page as "Five Years of Italian Poetry," purporting to be a general treatment of the whole Italian contemporary debate. The introductory essay to "Five Years" starts by relegating Carducci and Pascoli to the past, while quickly dismissing D'Annunzio in virtue of his having "reached the appreciation of fat American reviews" (1919a, 209). This comment confirms, with more polemic strength, Carnevali's public renunciation of Carducci and D'Annunzio (Monroe 1918). He then tackles the issue of another Italian movement that had received international attention in recent years: Futurism. The Futurists had traveled for years "through the major capitals of Europe, creating astonishment and winning important allies but also inciting vehement reactions" (Levenson 2011, 47). Carnevali's response to Futurism's international dimension draws from *La Voce*'s Prezzolini:

> Marinetti is more grandiloquent, more obvious, and writes noisier classical bombast than any cheap *passatista*.[24] That's why they hear him around the world. But Prezzolini, lovable critic, full of strength and cleanness, has fixed him and his gang, in the only intelligent articles on futurism that have appeared in Italian magazines, where pigheaded professors have waged war against it, and nasty ignorant youths have defended it. (E. Carnevali 1919a, 213)

Carnevali chooses the middle path between avant-garde rupture and stubborn defense of Italy's glorious past. Carnevali's critical stance is made explicit by the reference to Prezzolini and by his choice of authors to translate, reflecting his admiration of *La Voce* (and its sister publication, *Lacerba*) and his desire to present Florentine modernism as something apart from both "pigheaded professors" and "nasty ignorant youths."

Carnevali presents the poets in brief biographical vignettes, using the little information he could draw from the magazines themselves. The tone is colloquial, almost intimate, as he describes Slataper as "a big, hard, and clean boy" from the Carso mountains (1919a, 210). He praises Papini: "more than a warrior or a martyr has Papini given his life to his country, his people" (1919a, 210). There is perhaps an echo of Carnevali's reflections of his own transnational experiences as he discusses Soffici's Parisian avant-garde encounters as he "fights his way through French influences to a broken jagged sort of poetry (words at liberty, and lyric simultaneities)" (1919a, 211). Di Giacomo, on the other hand, is puzzlingly identified as "the national poet" by virtue of his having "been acknowledged by Croce" (1919a, 210). In Italy, Di Giacomo was never considered much of a "national" poet. He wrote mainly in Neapolitan dialect at a time in which dialectal poets were generally excluded from the mainstream literary debate. Carnevali's apparent misstep may be ironic, as he explains Di Giacomo's poetry by relying on established stereotypes ("short stories and poems of the irremediable sadness and the irrational tragedy of the old Naples"). Carnevali attributes to Di Giacomo "a tenderness that is real in Italy because of the climate, etc.; and would be sentimentality in America" (1919a, 210), possibly catering to American stereotypes of Italian sentimentality, creating a ready-made image for the benefit of the receiving culture.

Anglophone terms of comparison make their way into the essay, appealing to the readership's point of view. Writing about uninspired and mannerist imitators of Carducci and D'Annunzio, Carnevali calls them "the Mackaye type and the Woodberry type of poet" (1919a, 209), referring probably to American poets Percy MacKaye and George Edward Woodberry. Carnevali defines Rebora's style as "imagism," a term that likely was still circulating in American criticism but had no equivalent in Italy as a movement. Govoni's poetry is described as "the most musical, most humane free verse," describing "the luridist [sic], obscenest facts in the life of an old Italian city" in a "delicate" voice (1919a, 210). Carnevali states that there is "something of Frost in him—or, I should rather say, something of Govoni in Frost" (1919a, 210). In all likelihood, Govoni and Frost did not know each other, let alone take inspiration from each other's work. Carnevali can compare them because, unlike his audience, he treats both languages as his own: his acknowledgment of "something of Frost" in Govoni, and of "something of Govoni in Frost," is an attempt at a synchronic approach to Italian and American literature, taking each poet in turn as a familiar reference. At this point, Carnevali sees no clear-cut distinction between the familiar and the unfamiliar: he participates in American literature as an outsider, gains his knowledge of the *Vociani* in America, and engages with them by presenting their work to the American public. The essay expresses Carnevali's translational attitude as a desire to bridge a gap between different declinations of modernism, each vignette also revealing ideas and images of Italian literature that he wanted America to see.

Carnevali's article, intended to be a comprehensive look on Italian poetry of the time, revolves around a few authors and some relevant themes represented through a small number of texts. His translations from Scipio Slataper's 1912 autobiographical novel *Il mio Carso* (*My Karst*), for example, are very brief excerpts, only three paragraphs and two isolated sentences. The results appear indeed closer to poetry than prose:

I love the rain heavy and violent . . .
It comes down tearing off the weak leaves . . .
(E. Carnevali 1919a, 218)

Through the translated poems, Carnevali highlights particular
themes that readers may interpret as reflecting current Italian interests,
such as the representation of Italian countryside, World War I, and the
type of young restlessness captured by Futurists.

In addition to Slataper's images from the rural northeast, Carnevali
includes poems from Saba and Govoni depicting Italian country life.
The choice of Saba's "Il maiale" ("The Pig"), a 1912 poem that Saba
would later exclude from his *Canzoniere* once he became a nationally
famous poet, is puzzling. "Il maiale" would hardly be a choice nowadays
for representing Saba in an anthology, yet Carnevali responded to it
and decided to translate it. More precisely, he did not translate the first
half of the poem, in which Saba depicted a pig that eats contentedly,
unaware of his fate, but rather cut directly to the moment in which the
compassionate poet imagines the innocent creature being butchered:

Ma io, se riguardando in lui mi metto,
io sento nelle sue carni il coltello,
sento quell'urlo, quella spaventosa
querela . . .
("Il Maiale" 12–15)

But if, while looking, I put myself in his place,
I feel down in his flesh the pain of the knife,
hear that scream
that fearful quarrel.
(E. Carnevali 1919a, 218)

Carnevali's version turns a reflection on the ambiguities of an apparently serene country life into a climax of tormented compassion. On the
other hand, he keeps the titular "Happiness" of Govoni's "Felicità." This
depiction of country life lacks any conflict, as the poet walks around
the countryside in a good mood ("I don't know why, / but I'm happy
this morning," 214) and then lists all the possible images that may be
responsible for this sudden happiness: whether the "rondinini" ("little

swallows") or the "maialino" ("little hog"), the poet's mother feeding the animals, or "the wife of the cowherd" taking "rosy crosses of bread" out of the oven. Bucolic images accumulate in the poem, presenting themselves in translation as depiction of a timeless, uncomplicated lifestyle in the Italian countryside.

Carnevali also translates more problematic texts addressing World War I, such as Palazzeschi's "Le due rose" ("The Two Roses" of the title being a white pillow and a red wound) and Jahier's short prose piece "Reservists" ("Richiamati").

Palazzeschi was one of Carnevali's preferred sources for translations, and two of the poems he chose to translate (one published with the rest, the other left unpublished) illustrate the possible reasons. The two poems, "L'indifferente" and "L'incendiario," express a refusal of conventions and institutions in a strong, polemical language that Carnevali often used in his own material. "L'indifferente" expresses detachment from family, a theme that must have resonated with Carnevali:

> Io sono tuo padre.
> Ah sì? . . .
> Io sono tua madre.
> Ah sì? . . .
> Questo è tuo fratello.
> Ah sì? . . .
> Quella è tua sorella.
> Ah sì? . . .
> (Palazzeschi, "L'indifferente") . . .

> I am your father.
> Is that so?
> I am your mother.
> Is that so?
> This is your brother.
> Is that so?
> That is your sister.
> Is that so?
> (E. Carnevali 1919a, 217)

Palazzeschi's sharp, declarative free verse lines fit Carnevali's style, and he probably responded to the sense of uprootedness expressed by Palazzeschi, linking it to his own abandonment of family.

Carnevali's unpublished translation of Palazzeschi's "L'incendiario" ("The incendiary")[25] also shows his interest for Palazzeschi as author of antibourgeois poetry. The poem belongs to Palazzeschi's futurist period, which Carnevali obscured by eliminating Palazzeschi's original dedication to Marinetti, "anima della nostra fiamma."[26] Set in an atmosphere of general political and artistic unrest, "L'incendiario" presents an arsonist brought, in a cage, in front of the crowd—as a metaphor of the relationship between poetry and social and cultural unrest at the time. The first part of the poem is made up of the bystanders' dialogue, and Carnevali worked on its dialogic structure, using colloquial English to convey the hypocritical façade of law-abiding citizens:

> — Ma la sua famiglia?
> — Chi sa da che parte di mondo è venuto!
> — Questa robaccia non à mica famiglia!
> — Sicuro, è roba allo sbaraglio!
> — Se venisse dall'inferno?
> — Povero diavolaccio!
> — Avreste anche compassione?
> Se v'avesse bruciata la casa
> non direste così.
> — La vostra l'à bruciata?
> — Se non l'à bruciata
> poco c'è corso.
> ("L'incendiario," ll. 24–35)

> — What about his family?
> — Who knows from what part of the world he is!
> — That sort of filth hasn't any
> — Sure, he's a hobo!
> — And if he came from hell?
> — Poor old devil!
> — And you would pity him?
> Had he burnt your house
> you wouldn't talk like that.
> — Was it yours, he burnt?
> — If he didn't really burn it, he almost did.
> ["The Incendiary," typescript][27]

The translation reframes the original's tone in contemporary American society, responding to Carnevali's own interest in the theme of the outsider. He translated "Questa robaccia (*bad stuff/ bad sort*)" with "that sort of filth," making the crowd even more violent in its rejection of the arsonist. His translation of Palazzeschi's "roba allo sbaraglio"—literally a "wayward sort"—into "hobo" reframes the poem more precisely into the American social landscape. The poem changes with the sudden apparition of a Poet, who declares his admiration for the arsonist:

> Quando tu bruci
> Tu non sei più l'uomo
> Il Dio tu sei!
> ("L'incendiario," ll. 157–59)

> When you burn
> You're no more the man
> The God you are!
> ("The Incendiary," typescript)

The texts translated by Carnevali responded to his interests as well as to his desire to present an uncompromising image of contemporary Italy. The small anthology "Five Years of Italian Poetry" encompassed, in its rather short span, discussions of World War I and political unrest as well as the representation of rural Italy. The way in which Carnevali handled the texts, giving them new life in the American magazine, testifies to his desire to connect with the experience of Italian modernism.

The language that Carnevali used to achieve his goal of making Italian modernism his own is particularly interesting. The challenge of translating into a second language always requires a very specific set of skills:

> In translating from a second language, the main difficulty is in comprehending the source text. . . . In translating into a second language, comprehension of the source text is the easier aspect; the real difficulty is in producing a target text in a language in which composition does not come naturally. (Campbell 1998, 57)

The ability to translate into the second language depends, generally speaking, on the translator's competence in the target language; in particular, textual competence (i.e., the ability to produce natural-looking texts) is crucial. Carnevali's textual competence in English had developed rapidly and tended toward linguistic assimilation: there are no grammatical or syntactical mistakes in Carnevali's translations. On the other hand, his attitude toward language, and toward the American literary milieu, was not one of compromise: Carnevali believed in the strength of his own speech, a language that was English and at the same time depended on his Italian background. Furthermore, his ideal of translation was linked to his idea of poetry as a calling: in a review of translations from Chinese, Indian, and Persian poetry, he remarked that "mere scribblers ought to leave the poets of other nations alone" because "only a poet, and a good one, may translate adequately the work of another poet" (E. Carnevali 1922b, 348).

Much of the translation debate of the last few decades has been influenced by Venuti's distinction between a domesticating translation—made by giving preference to structural and cultural elements of the target culture—and a foreignizing one, which brings the reader as close as possible to the experience of reading the source language. A foreignizing translation "restrain[s] the ethnocentric violence of translation" and counters hegemonic tendencies hidden behind the "illusion of transparency" of domesticating translations (Venuti 2008, 16). Based on his linguistic competence, his poetic ideal, and his admiration for the source, Carnevali produced translations that sound decidedly foreign, and the result was not easy on American readers unacquainted with Italian.

Carnevali's translations exhibit some idiosyncratic choices, especially in word order and at the lexical level. The very title of his translation of Palazzeschi's "L'incendiario" ("Incendiary") is a word that sounds very much like the Italian title, but is usually an adjective in English; "arsonist" would be the more usual translation. Also, keeping as close as possible to the Italian, Carnevali uses English words with etymological closeness, of the same kind that punctuate his original poetry from the time:

Quegl'insetti immondi e poltroni,
sono lividi di malefica astuzia
("L'Incendiario," ll. 124–25)

those putrid lazy insects
are livid with malignant shrewdness.
("The Incendiary," typescript)

The choice has its strengths: Carnevali's translations appear awkward and convoluted at times, but they also transmit the uncompromising specificity of the language. In translation, Carnevali provides Palazzeschi's polemical, violent free verse with an added layer of linguistic violence, facilitating as little as possible the American reader's comprehension.

In its painstaking fidelity, Carnevali's translations sometimes appear closer to a "crib," a literal translation in need of further work, rather than an accomplished text. His work on Papini provides a chance to test this hypothesis, as the translation of one piece by this author, "Mezz'ora" ("Half Hour"), survives both as a manuscript in Carnevali's notebook and in typescript. A combined analysis of notebook and typescript makes it possible to advance the hypothesis that much of his first word-for-word rendering of the text made it to the final version, while he nevertheless rethought some of his choices and amended the most obvious misunderstandings. The notebook version was likely a very early effort to translate the text, as testified by the many words that are crossed out or added on the margins and by the blanks where he did not have an English equivalent ready:

> Una città senza case—nient'altro che sotterranei e botole . . .
> (Papini 1920, 96)

> A city without houses—nothing but basements and (botole) . . .
> ("Half Hour," notebook)[28]

> . . . una poesia più vicina e più intelligibile del fiocco di seta vaporosa che da una grondaia all'altra—via lattea del giorno—taglia come un ponte di bianchezza il fiume fusciacca del cielo . . . (Papini 1920, 96)

> . . . a poetry nearer and more intelligible of the flake of vaporous silk which from one eave to the other—milky way of the day—cuts like a bridge of whiteness the (fusciacca) river of the sky . . . ("Half Hour," notebook)

These are the most evident indications that Carnevali's word-for-word translation style derived primarily from an almost impromptu approach to the unfamiliar target language, drawing heavily on the more accustomed Italian text. Not only some words are left untranslated, but a grammatical mistake ("del" in "più intelligibile del fiocco" treated as a possessive instead of a comparative) also underlines that the translation is initially born of a word-for-word method. This approach is later corrected in the typescript, which appears ready to be sent to a magazine for publication (bearing Carnevali's New York address at the top): there, "more intelligible of the flake" becomes "more intelligible than the flake." The typescript presents, in many cases, a further step away from Italian and toward English:

> "Regnare sopra un paese di questo genere, in un tempo così scientifico!" (Papini 1920, 97)

> "To reign over a country of this kind in a times so scientific!" ("Half Hour," notebook)

> "To reign over a country of this kind, in such scientific a time!" ("Half Hour," typescript)[29]

> ". . . ragionevolezza di questi ultimi confini . . ." (Papini 1920, 97)

> ". . . reasonability of these last confines . . ." ("Half Hour," notebook)

> ". . . reasonableness of these extreme boundaries . . ." ("Half Hour," typescript)

The second excerpt in particular shows how Carnevali worked from the Italian "confini" toward "boundaries," passing through "confines," which is more Italian-sounding but less apt in meaning. The most relevant aspect of this analysis is that, in spite of evidence of progressive passage from a word-for-word reading to an edited typescript, the typescript still contains Italianate expressions and word-for-word renditions:

> . . . questa piazza-trapezio dove non si metton bandiere che per l'assassinio del re. (Papini 1920, 95)

> . . . this trapezium square where they hang out flags only on the assassination of the king. ("Half Hour," typescript)

Carnevali's typescripts, ready to be sent to editors, presented many signs of Italianate language even after the most idiosyncratic elements had been amended. He may have encountered difficulties with English in a task that required native-like competence, but he also willingly retained some Italianate forms, probably to preserve the style and rhythm of the authors he admired.

The most evident marker of Carnevali's closeness to the Italian source is the word order. Inversions of verb and subject are usually the result of the translator's following of the original Italian—where such inversions are more easily tolerated. Carnevali's awkward "There on my bench *where was born / my book*, as for a benediction" depends on his adherence to Palazzeschi's "Là sopra il mio banco *ove nacque, / il mio libro*, come per benedizione" ("L'incendiario," ll. 193–94). In the translation of Jahier, this leads to a translation that has, much more than the original, the tone of oral speech. That is due to the presence of sentences with no verb, a practice that is common in Italian but usually relegated to oral speech in English: "But he was a reservist. Aged. Many things are already irremediable" (E. Carnevali 1919a, 217). Sometimes the Italian word order leads to poetic effect: Slataper's "Amo la piova pesa e violenta" (1920, 33) is rendered, in Italian fashion, as "I love the rain heavy and violent" (E. Carnevali 1919a, 218). The lady in Jahier's "Richiamati" is compared to "Italy over the buildings of the exposition" (E. Carnevali 1919a, 216)—that is, a statue of the traditional feminine personification of Italy towering over the buildings of an international exposition. In this case, the lack of contextual explanation may even prejudice the reader's understanding of the text. The source text did not require contextual explanations in Italian; Carnevali did not believe it necessary to provide a context for his translation or rearrange the word order so that American readers would understand more easily.

Carnevali's 1919 translation of Papini's "Congedo" renders the source's accumulation of lyrical images with painstaking fidelity, almost prejudicing the audience's comprehension:

Notti di seta nera con accompagnamento di fiumi e di gelosie napoletane. (Papini 1920, 101)

Blacksilk nights with accompaniment of rivers and neopolitan [sic] jealousies. (Papini 1919, 20)

Sopra le terrazze che danno sui prati gli occhi dei bambini si specchiano nei giaggiòli e monta l'odore borghese delle rose di velluto rosso. (Papini 1920, 101)

Over the terraces facing the fields the eyes of children are reflected in the irises and the bourgeois odor of red-velvet roses is arising. (Papini 1919, 20)

The source accumulates images and similes to set the mood of the story (the narrator bidding farewell to a woman); the target text hardly attempts to arrange them and make them accessible to the target audience. Carnevali employed nouns and adjectives with an etymologic kinship with Italian ("accompaniment,") even when more common English words would have been available (e.g., *fragrance* or *smell* for "odor"). This happens even when there is a risk of confusion—as in the case of "irises," which are unmistakably flowers in Italian, while the context ("the eyes of the children are reflected in the irises") makes the reader wonder whether the phrase is about flowers or the human eye.

It seems apparent that the closeness of Carnevali's translations to their source material depended on the linguistic resources he had at his disposal at the time of translation. There may also be purely literary reasons, such as his admiration for the authors he was translating and his desire to bring their work to the American public in its purest form. Given his esteem for Papini, it is no wonder that he often impersonated his model both in translations and in his critical work. Carnevali's essay on Papini—refused by the aforementioned "professoruccio" and eventually published in *The Modern Review* in 1922—is an example of this mimetic tendency. It opens by describing Papini's (and Carnevali's) native Tuscany with words translated from Papini's autobiography *Un uomo finito*:

Born in 1881 in Tuscany—sky so beautiful even when it is ugly, twisted pallor of the olive trees, black spears of cypresses . . . (E. Carnevali 1922a, 11)

Intendo questo cielo cosi bello anche quand'è brutto, questo pallore contorto d'olivi, queste lancie [sic] nere dei cipressi . . . (Papini 1913, 276)

Carnevali appropriates a whole sentence without indicating that it is a translation: Cacho Millet commented that Carnevali could not describe his own native Tuscany without borrowing his idol's words (1981, 33). Carnevali attempted to appropriate an image of Tuscany (and of Italy) by turning the words of his favorite Italian writer into his new language of English.

In "My Home" (draft of "Tale III"), Carnevali acknowledges Papini's stylistic influence:

> And I have told myself that I write like Papini; whenever I write there is, especially these last days, Charles-Louis Philippe in the way; and Soffici, sitting serenely in the back of my head keeps whispering, "You damn fool, you liar, you damn fool."[30]

The texts date from 1919, the time when he and Papini were corresponding and Carnevali was translating his work. This passage, which was eventually excised from the published "Tale III," expresses Carnevali's doubts about his capacity to live up to his influences. It may also point to the impact of Papini's short prose, some of which he was translating at the time, on his "Tales of a Hurried Man." At the same time, the *Vociani* influence is always inserted in a framework of international influences: after mentioning Papini, "My Home" discusses Charles-Louis Philippe, Hugo, Rimbaud, Longfellow, and Poe in the space of a few lines.

While Carnevali often translates Papini's critical opinions in his essays, there are also lines in his poetry that perhaps echo Papini's autobiographical novel *Un uomo finito*, a favorite of his at the time. Describing his years as a young writer, in the novel Papini speaks of his disdain for the crowds of the city as composed of mere shadows, "burattini pretensiosi del mio teatro interiore"[31] (1913, 78). In "The Day of Summer," as Carnevali tries to focus on his inner world by refusing to acknowledge the crowd of Manhattan, he finally gives in: "I will walk with the marionettes / . . . I'll go talk to them / Now I'm dumb enough" (ll. 306–9). Similarly, Papini remembers "quando . . . si guardava la città distesa vigliaccamente sulle sponde del fiume lento e si diceva: sarai nostra"[32] (1913, 65); Carnevali's "Lake" describes Chicago "spread out before me calling from a great curve / 'Come, enter, conquistador!'" (ll. 12–13). Finally, as Papini concludes his book by stating, "ma oggi io mi sento di appiccare un incendio da non potersi più spengere e che dia fuoco al mondo"[33] (1913, 291), the 1967 version of Carnevali's speech at Lola Ridge's ends with the line "Quench my fire or I shall set fire to the world" (1967, 148).

Carnevali's *Autobiography* presents several passages that may be traced back to Papini's *Un uomo finito*, which some commentators have seen as an important source of inspiration for him: "the intertextual model for his own narrative strategy" (Boelhower 1982, 145). The *Autobiography* does not have an actual, solid narrative strategy, being a collection of fragments—but several passages in it appear to be translated from Papini's autobiography. Papini wrote, "mi gettai a capofitto in tutte le letture che mi suggerivano le mie pullulanti curiosità"[34] (Papini 1913, 16); a freshly immigrated Carnevali "dived fearlessly into George Bernard Shaw" (1967, 92). Thus a young Papini: "così feci, una bigia mattina d'inverno, il mio sposalizio con la gloria"[35] (1913, 33); Carnevali seems to reverse this ironically when he defines emigration as his "great marriage with misery, and the offspring of this match was hunger" (1967, 95). The phenomenon takes on an meta-textual dimension: Papini illustrates his passion for books by writing, "piansi sopra una semplice e nuda vita di Mazzini"[36] (1913, 152), and Carnevali reports weeping "tears of fire" over a chapter of Papini (E. Carnevali 1967, 166). Carnevali consciously impersonates Papini in his work,[37] taking phrases from *Un uomo finito*—a book that he would have liked to translate—to construct his own persona. This move from translation to imitation is certainly not new in literature: boundaries between the two were considerably thinner in the Middle Ages or the Renaissance, where "the author's text was assumed to be predicated upon pre-established models" and translation was akin to literary imitation, a practice "through which the author could establish a unique identity" (Hokenson and Munson 2007, 38). In Carnevali's case, this relates to his way of managing the linguistic resources at his disposal, not only drawing from Papini but also combining the echoes of Papini in a new linguistic context, using phrases and words that he had absorbed from his background to influence his new environment.

In 1920, probably because of the first manifestations of his illness, Carnevali appeared less certain of his projects: "E forse non tradurrò l'Uomo Finito. Perchè prometto sempre?"[38] (1981, 103–4). Contacts between Papini and Carnevali gradually ceased, possibly because of arguments between the two: "Non s'arrabbi più con me. Se sono stato impudente me ne pento amaramente"[39] (E. Carnevali 1981, 105). Carnevali ended up alone and isolated, disconnected from the Italian as well as the American milieu. He kept on translating sporadically, even from his sickbed. He translated, for example, a short story by Carlo Linati, "L'ultima moglie di Barbablu," for the magazine *This Quarter* in 1925. More importantly, he translated some of Pound's *Cantos*—an enterprise I discuss in chapter 5.

As for Carnevali's *Vociani* translations, they were largely forgotten. They were rediscovered decades later by one of the editors of *La Voce* itself, Giuseppe Prezzolini, in his 1963 book *I trapiantati*. Prezzolini, who had moved to New York in 1929 to teach Italian at Columbia University, researched Carnevali out of curiosity for this "nostro fratello sconosciuto, di noi della *Voce*, dico in America"[40] (1963, 288). Prezzolini praised his critical appreciation of *La Voce*, stating that Carnevali's essay was "più penetrante di molti professori" especially in relation to the time, in which "si trattava di scoprire dei valori e non di condividerli e approfondirli"[41] (Prezzolini 1963, 291). Considering Carnevali's distance from Italy at the time, Prezzolini seems surprised by Carnevali's familiarity with the *Vociani* authors. He concludes the essay with a note of pity for this man who "sotto tanti aspetti avrebbe potuto 'parlare con me' "[42] (1963, 293). Prezzolini regrets this might-have-been: an intellectual conversation between Florentine and American modernists.

Today we know that such a conversation was indeed attempted through Carnevali's repeated contacts with Papini, although their correspondence was interrupted by Carnevali's illness and a possible falling out between the two. Carnevali's translational enterprise, intended to present his personal view of the contemporary Italian debate and establish his role as cultural mediator, had only limited resonance. At any rate, it now stands as an enthusiastic and passionate attempt at a transnational connection made by one of the few men who at the time could see "something of Govoni in Frost" and who struggled to create a language with which he could communicate his experience of Italian literature without compromise to the American public.

Carnevali's relationship to *italianità* includes a complex knot of feelings of belonging, intertextual relations, a modernist idea of tradition, and the managing of linguistic resources—all in continuous tension with the need to introduce himself as a poet with his own agenda, and the desire to be regarded as a transnational mediator between Italian and American modernisms. It includes missed opportunities and the writer's stubborn insistence on showing only the side of Italy that he liked, not what Americans expected of him. Carnevali's complex relationship with *italianità*, in all its contradictions, is a document of the many contrasting ways in which a translingual writer can deal with his or her cultural heritage—hiding it or flaunting it, but in any case painting a necessarily personal picture of a landscape that otherwise would be impossible to paint.

4

A Language for Bazzano

An Italian American Returns Home

In February 1920, a series of traumatic events unfolded in Carnevali's life. One of these was a troubled relationship with Annie Glick, a woman Carnevali met in Chicago. Her rejection of him caused Carnevali severe distress: "Annie, you had no pity for me. You scoffed at my misery and my poverty . . ." (E. Carnevali 1967, 164). At this time, he started showing signs of paranoid and neurotic behavior culminating in an episode in which he believed for some time that he was "the First God, the Only God" (1967, 176). In the aftermath of this, he moved from one hospital to another in Illinois and Minnesota, later spending time alone in the Indiana dunes in the summer of 1920, hoping for spiritual as well as physical recovery. The initial diagnosis was syphilis, as he wrote to his friend Mitchell Dawson.[1] In this period of crisis, Carnevali relied on the help of Chicago friends, such as Dawson, Harriet Monroe, and Sherwood Anderson.

This new phase of his life did not altogether prevent him from writing. Although he was no longer the assistant editor of *Poetry*, almost every issue between October 1920 and April 1921 features at least one article by Carnevali, mostly critical essays. Yet his health strongly affected his chances of making the impact that he hoped to have on American literature. In 1922, Carnevali was diagnosed with encephalitis lethargica, a disease that affects the nervous system. He was repatriated to Italy, where he spent the last twenty years of his life—mostly in the town of Bazzano, near Bologna. In spite of his sickness, he continued to write—in English, the language in which he had become a poet.

133

This chapter explores Carnevali's writing in the 1920s, from the crises of mental and physical health that led to his return to Italy in 1922 to his work in Bazzano, where he encountered both familiar customs and an emerging Fascist state. The works from the late 1920s are ideal for analyzing the evolution of translingual writing in a changing context. They are evidently the product of an upset mind, and the poet was well aware of his fading relevance on the literary scene; however, he tried until the end to make art out of his suffering.

The first part of the chapter deals with Carnevali's literary account of the illness itself, especially the chapters of the *Autobiography* dealing with the 1920 psychotic episode and its aftermath. These passages were written several years after the incident, and they represent the author's attempt at explaining his illness while keeping its narration in literary form. The degree of intertextuality and stylistic purpose is still high, with the author explaining the crisis through a myth of the mad artist, centered on Rimbaud. The chapter then moves on to Carnevali's first years in Italy and its key concern for those years: keeping his place in the literary world while battling encephalitis. Writing in English from Italy, Carnevali proved himself a keen observer of the Italian reality that surrounded him, documenting the life of a provincial town during the rise of Fascism. In the third part, the focus is especially on the linguistic aspects of Carnevali's Bazzano works as his English continued to evolve, opening a new chapter in the story of his developing language. In America, he had accessed English as an outsider, moving in rhythmic and lexical proximities between Italian and English but always staying safely within linguistic norms. In Italy, context played a greater part. Carnevali's "Bazzano language" is proof that translingual writing, linked as it is to the naturally fluid development of language throughout the life of a bilingual, is a process of continuous evolution.

1. Carnevali's Godhead: Turning Mental Distress and Displacement into Literature

Modernism is often linked with developments in psychology and psychoanalysis:

> [B]oth psychiatric medicine and the creative arts during the
> late nineteenth and early twentieth centuries were marked by

a massive "turn inward" and a thoroughgoing psychologization of their methods, subjects, and intentions. During these years, artists, philosophers and scientists probed beneath the surface reality of reason in order to uncover deeper irrational or nonrational levels of human experience and cognition. (Micale 2003, 2)

Modernist authors, such as Woolf, Kafka, and Beckett, investigated the issue of distress and mental illness in their works; and yet rarely did mental distress occupy such a central position in the work of an author as in Carnevali's later writings. Illness is the raison d'être for these texts, which testify to Carnevali's will to overcome and transfigure sickness by giving it a literary dimension while continuing his aesthetic and intellectual development as much as possible.

In the early months of 1920, Carnevali suffered a psychological incident that would have a great impact on his subsequent life and writing. On the night in question, he experienced a form of detachment from reality in which he appears to have walked through the streets of Chicago in a state of delirium. In their study of migration and psychosis, Grinberg and Grinberg underlined that "a depressive or borderline or delayed psychotic state" may appear in migrants even years after emigrating and after "an apparently conflict-free period" (1989, 145). Carnevali's experience seems to conform to these observations. As he describes the episode in his *Autobiography*, the crisis affected his comprehension of the surrounding reality:

> Out in the snow again I said out loud: now that corner is going to stop being a corner, that lamp-post cease being a lamp-post, that gutter no longer run with its burden of dirty water, because the beloved list of understandable things has been inadvertently destroyed, because in this immaculate sky-piece a screw has been loosened, a nut has gone daffy, has gone cuckoo, and the whole machine of reality has jumped the switch. (E. Carnevali 1967, 177)

As is the case in Carnevali's narration, the migrant who experiences such a dissociation between inner and outer world "feels locked into a world of bizarre objects from which he cannot escape since he lacks the consciousness that would provide the key to escape" (Grinberg and

Grinberg 1989, 139). Carnevali's encounter causes him to question his perceptions, much as other migrant victims of psychosis expressed their sense of losing contact with their surrounding reality.

This is the last description of an American city in the *Autobiography*. This environment was the setting of Carnevali's struggle to adapt and preserve his identity: in the crisis, lampposts and street corners lose their ontological status to become something else beyond the poet's grasp. The language of the American metropolis becomes, for the last time, a useful tool for interpreting and describing reality. The number of local idioms that he chose to use in the passage is remarkable: in writing that "a screw has been loosened" and "a nut has gone daffy, has gone cuckoo," he is showing his prowess with the linguistic tools that he has picked up along his journey—while describing a split between himself and the linguistic landscape. When the new language of America falls short, and it becomes "impossible for [him] ever to grasp reality again" (1967, 177), Carnevali finds a paradoxical response: going beyond human language.

Written more than a decade after the incident, the *Autobiography* construes the crisis, and Carnevali's delusional transformation into "the First God," as a turning point: in the narration, illness becomes a central feature of Carnevali's life, as he gives aesthetic significance to neurosis and panic. The god that he claims to represent is a broken, miserable creature: "I believed absolutely now that I was the Only God. But no god was ever humbler than I, and no god ever made worse blunders" (1967, 176). There is an ironic undertone, as Carnevali is aware at the time of writing that his claim to be a god had been a psychotic episode—that he had been, in his own words, "an utter fool" (1967, 179). Focusing on the autobiographical narration, the crisis may be analyzed from different points of view. As Buonomo underlined, "the actual, frighteningly 'concrete' diseases he contracted in Chicago . . . lose nearly all physical connotations in the narrative and become a malady of the body, the mind, the soul" (2003, 57). Carnevali's suffering has both a clinical and psychological dimension, not to be underestimated. There are also, however, cultural and artistic angles to explore, considering both Carnevali's artistic agenda and the "historical and geographical specificity" of mental health, "a specificity that characterises all kinds of experience but perhaps none so emphatically as madness" (Valentine 2003, 96). Our understanding of mental distress evolves in time and space, so that some mental illnesses seem to be more linked than others to specific cultural contexts. Carnevali's crisis as told in the *Autobiography* appears related to other episodes observed in migrant contexts as well as to a peculiar nineteenth-century idea of the poet as a mad genius.

The myth of the poet as mad genius postulates the existence of exceptional beings who are at risk of being driven mad by the discrepancy between their own greatness and vile reality. In the nineteenth century, it represented a poetic reaction to the challenges of modern world's materialism:

> One way to meet the challenge was to deny that literature has a truth function or, alternatively, to declare that the epistemological function of literature is situated on a level beyond reason—reason as defined by positivist rationality. (Thiher 1999, 206)

Carnevali had already shown interest in this myth in the years before the crisis, but the crisis appears to have exacerbated it: in the narration, he depicts himself "walking the centuries, looking for [his] face." The search leaves him certain that he "belonged to the nineteenth century more than to any other," perhaps "entirely, insanely to the nineteenth century" (E. Carnevali 1967, 176). His nineteenth century is made up of figures he calls "masks"—Verlaine, Rimbaud, Schumann, Carducci, Leopardi, Nietzsche, and others. These men, who have little in common, are conjured all together in the text for the fact that they were "all more or less crazy, all more or less sick," providing Carnevali with a canonical, literary framework with which he could justify his fascination with the irrational. The episode may have a clinical dimension, but this reframing on Carnevali's part is hardly a surprise in the context of his previous writing.

It is very appropriate that, in compiling the *Autobiography*, Boyle (without warning the reader) interspersed the episode of the crisis with fragments from a 1919 short story, "Dancing as an Art," which contained all the motifs of the crisis: preoccupation with fading youth, dreams of achieving aesthetic perfection, and a broken self as a result. In 1919, twenty-two-year-old Carnevali wrote about a thirty-year-old version of himself meeting the mysterious Mr. Snake, who seems to be the personification of dancing, and of harmony itself:

> I enjoyed his dancing and was very much interested in it.
> —Mr. Snake, I think I want to learn how to dance.

—My dear man, dancing is art, every art—art.
—That doesn't make much of a difference to me.
—It made all the difference in the world to me. (1919f, 26)

The narrator then attempts to dance, following Mr. Snake's example, but ends up "in the shape of an ugliness, a drifting thing, a walking contradiction" (1919f, 26). He experiences a separation between himself and his physical form. This older version of the author thinks fondly of the original moment of inspiration, the "road to the splendid somewhere" that he had "conceived one day" and that is now lost (1919f, 27). He finally attempts to move again: "You know there is some greatness in me, you know that I always saw it, the beacon shining very far" (1919f, 28). Yet the narrator falls and breaks all his bones: the story ends with him lying on the ground, looking at the skyscrapers of New York in despair. The story deals with Carnevali's fear, at the beginning of his career, of ending up as a "warped effort" (1919f, 27) on his road to artistic fulfillment. References to "splendid somewheres" and "beacons" of light that he would never reach assume a much more concrete significance when placed at this moment in the *Autobiography*, which seems to realize the young Carnevali's worst fears.

Carnevali had already voiced his preoccupation with inhabiting a fine balance between aesthetic perfection and madness in his 1919 essay on the poetics of Rimbaud, where he first brought forth his idea of a language of "godhead." As noted by Congiu (2008, 122), that essay already hinted at the poet's transformation into a god. The correspondences are deep at a linguistic as well as a theoretical level. The Italian poet defends Rimbaud as a model poet-god, while he states that he can merely aspire to replicate Rimbaud's original: "I have gone on a great adventure, and I may sometime personify a god I have seen for a moment. I would, as much as I could, personify him" (E. Carnevali 1919c, 20). In light of Rimbaud's abandonment of poetry as he entered adulthood, it is possible to see the French poet's "utopian madness" as permanently "accompanied by a farewell," which "marks the failure to go beyond materialist science and the bourgeois culture" (Thiher 1999, 222). Rimbaud's parable of the poet-god contains his own annihilation. Carnevali played out the myth of Rimbaud: the god that he hoped he might come to "personify" one day would appear to him in a moment of crisis, followed by a descent into silence and oblivion. Writing the

Autobiography from his hospital bed, preoccupied with his fading and uncertain literary fame, Carnevali makes sense of the crisis through a supposedly failed transformation into a poet-god.[2]

The myth of Rimbaud also includes the possibility that youth might develop its own language, and that said language could reveal an otherwise unspoken truth. His poems contained the vision of Youth, the vision of the world as seen for the first time. In a word, Rimbaud had attained godhead:

> This is the consecration of the trinity, ethic-aesthetic-logic, which is godhead. To achieve liberty, to write perfect poetry, to sense perfectly, to love perfectly, to live—these are vague phrases, meaning to the great but one thing. And that thing, to me, to a man who has no sign from God otherwise than from books, is godhead itself. (E. Carnevali 1919c, 21)

This passage makes it clear that, to Carnevali, the word "godhead" initially had literary connotations—it was included in a vision of poetry as divine manifestation. He admits his dependence on tradition by depicting himself as "a man who has no sign from God otherwise than from books." These words assume a more literal meaning if placed next to the image of Carnevali in the midst of a psychotic crisis, looking for his "face" and finding refuge only in the "masks" of the nineteenth-century canon.

The "Rimbaud" essay demonstrates that Carnevali was thinking about poetic godhead before the onset of his illness and that he associated it with the language of youth. In Carnevali's own lexicon, built and expanded by reading and writing in his adoptive language, the word "godhead" assumed its own connotations, performing a definite function in both criticism and artistic work—or, more precisely, at their junction. He believed Rimbaud had revealed "axioms of Godhead" to the world in the form of simple statements (E. Carnevali 1919c, 23). The "Youths" are believed to be repositories of "godhead": "for this I believe in Arthur Rimbaud, and even in all the distorted and queer and desperate signs of godhead that Youths give the world as they pass" (E. Carnevali 1919c, 23). The universal truth that they communicate, on the other hand, expresses itself only in "distorted and queer and desperate signs." When Carnevali brings up the concept of "godhead" again in the *Autobiography*, it still has linguistic connotations. Instead of the perfect poetic understanding promised by Rimbaudian "godhead," he experienced the contrary: the real outcome of Carnevali's transformation into the "First God" is the impossibility of expression and creation.

Carnevali turned to Rimbaud for inspiration in the first phase of his career to develop a poetics of the outsider. In a moment of crisis, he depicts himself trying to enact his own transformation of reality. The episode becomes, in its literary rendition, a moment of apotheosis, in which he turns to nineteenth-century poetry for models of a poet-god and then attempts to become one. His attention in this regard turns to the language—the *Autobiography* is a tale of Carnevali's language as much as his life. Carnevali reports having, for a moment, a glimpse of the perfect language in which to write the perfect poem:

> YES-NO and YES and NO. This is the formula of acceptance and denial, at the same time and at different times, and if simultaneous acceptance and denial could be achieved, then godhead would be at your door. (E. Carnevali 1967, 178)

This formula seems to theorize linguistic divinity as the overcoming of difference. From a perspective above the concrete reality of language, opposite poles such as acceptance and denial may coincide. This could entail the creation of divine language, which does not realize only one side of the many dichotomies expressed in everyday language, but all of them at the same time. The formula goes beyond mere coexistence of opposites: it proposes the creation of a language beyond opposites. Its goal is the achievement of "simultaneous acceptance and denial." It takes two basic components of language, two of the simplest components into which the newcomer can break the language. It makes them coexist: "YES and NO." It reveals the degree of similarity, even identity that can be achieved between the two: "YES-NO . . . NO-YES." As Carnevali envisions himself as "the centre of the earth," with "the whole universe" revolving around him (E. Carnevali 1967, 179), he repeats the single simple phrase that could summarize the whole of existence: "Yes and no. Neither yes nor no. Yes or no." This proposition may contain the whole of creation, exhausting all linguistic and logical possibilities within itself. It seems to be a common temptation for translinguals in the modern era to "transcend language in general, to be pandictic, to utter everything": impatient with "the imperfections of finite verbal systems, they yearn to pass beyond words, to silence and truth" (Kellman 2000, 16). Carnevali's expression of such aspirations, his attempts to realize pandictism in practical human language, ultimately leads to annihilation. The supposed passing beyond the limits of human language leaves the poet with only two choices: silence, or the reiteration of the formula. Carnevali writes that he spent the night of his crisis repeating the formula aloud.

The time spent as a "God" separates the poet from common language: "a cyclone had struck me and whirled me from the earth of common-places" (1967, 181). The word "commonplace" is, as we explored in chapter 2, quite important in Carnevali's vocabulary. Mastering and overcoming the American commonplace was the goal of his first years as a poet, the very thing that would turn him from outsider to poet. The fact that the "formula of godhead" took him away from the realm of the commonplace may have meant a new phase in Carnevali's writing. Writing beyond the commonplace should have been the ultimate poetic achievement, moving from the poetic treatment of American speech to the ultimate poetic language, the language of god. Instead, Carnevali lost control of his literary and linguistic tools, drifting away from the American literary world and the niche he had carved for himself:

> Now the access to houses which remained open to anybody was denied to me. I was called "Carnevali" where before I had been simply Em. I had fallen, but I fell from high. This made it all the more painful, although more dignified too. (1967, 190)

Writing in the 1930s, Carnevali seems to regard this as the time in which he stopped living in the realm of infinite possibilities of youth. The procession of visitors to his first sanatorium in Chicago takes the form of a literary funeral, attended by McAlmon, Anderson, Sandburg, and Tennessee Williams. Thus started a period of his life mostly spent in hospitals: "hospitals are now the milestones which mark the different stages of my life" (Carnevali 1967, 183).

In retrospect, Carnevali characterized the immediate aftermath of the crisis as the beginning of death-in-life:

> Now I knew I was the master of death . . . I knew he was still far away, and I knew he would not hang around my bed for long, watching me lying there. But once, just once, I certainly did feel his hands go over my body and leave me

> coldly sweating, rigidity in my muscles, despair in my heart,
> fear in my mouth, and a new craze in my eyes. (1967, 182)

Death started to appear more and more in Carnevali's works: by the time he was writing the *Autobiography*, Death had become pervasive and omnipresent. It would sometimes be personified as a woman (in the Italian usage), and sometimes as a man (as in English). The poems written in the early 1920s express a certain closeness to death, in the form of "The curiosity of a word: / Forever" ("Invocation to Death" ll. 22–23), but also a challenge, as the poet "laughed at Death, as Death's brother, the devil, would" ("Lake" l. 19). An obsessive, almost personal relationship with death would become an integral part of Carnevali in his Bazzano years.

The aftermath of the crisis lasted, in fact, more than twenty years— during which time Carnevali attempted to keep his status as American writer, albeit one writing in Italy. His language was not the perfect language of godhead, capable of going beyond the commonplace by containing all the statements as well as their negations; rather, it was a language born out of his "Godhead" crisis. Because of the change of scenery and his faltering health, Carnevali's language in Italy became solipsistic, disconnected from both standard American English and Italian. The language of Bazzano bears the traces of Emanuel's many border crossings, rather than the language of "godhead," existing beyond constraints.

2. Return, Disappearance, and the Problem of the Audience

Bazzano is a small town on the hills near Bologna. Carnevali called it "one of the commonest little country towns of Italy" (1967, 202) and argued that it "deserves to be put on the map" for possessing all the features of a typical Italian village: a belfry and a castle, green fields surrounding it, and "even its own town idiot . . ." (1967, 206). It was the setting for much of his life as a returning migrant. On his return to Italy, he spent time in the Bazzano hospital before his editor Robert McAlmon paid for a sojourn (1924–26) for him in a private clinic near Bologna, the Villa Baruzziana. After the clinic, he went back to Bazzano, living in a rented room. Although he spent a short period of time in Rome in 1936–37 undergoing experimental treatments, he again returned to Bazzano, where he lived until his final stay at the Bologna hospital where he died in 1942.

Both the author and several witnesses mention the strength of the tremors that kept Carnevali away from his typewriter most of the time. In addition to its links to psychosis, patients afflicted with encephalitis lethargica suffered from high fever and headaches as well as lethargy and tremors; some even fell into a coma.[3] Kay Boyle recalls meeting Carnevali in his room, "shaking completely, all over, like a pinned butterfly" (Boyle 1967, 16). His life became an alternating routine of scopolamine-induced sleep and the "terrible shaking of every limb" that the drugs were supposed to alleviate (E. Carnevali 1967, 203).

Despite his illness, Carnevali was as active as he could be as a writer and translator, even though it took him

> a day to do a sentence, a week to do a paragraph, for while
> he shook with the terrible ague of his illness, he would have
> to hold his right hand in the grip of his left in order to be
> able to strike the keys. (Boyle 1967, 15)

A Hurried Man, a collection of his short stories, essays, and poems from the American period, came out in 1925 and included some material written in Italy. Around this time, he wrote autobiographical short stories, describing his illness, the clinic, and Bazzano: "Train of Characters through the Villa Rubazziana" (1927), with its "Continuation" (1929) and "A History" (1929), were published in This Quarter. Meanwhile, Poetry published some new poems between 1924 and 1931. In addition, he made some translations of Rimbaud and, most importantly, the first Italian translation of Pound's Cantos—of which only Canto VIII would be published in 1931. At this point he began writing his Autobiography, sending drafts to his friend Kay Boyle. In 1932, the first six chapters of the Autobiography appeared in the anthology Americans Abroad under the title "The First God." Boelhower has defined Carnevali's life after 1922 as a "posthumous, post-modern life" (1982, 138), hinting at his precarious health and his distance from the modernist groups he had participated in. Yet the analysis of his production while in Bazzano and Bologna highlights that Carnevali worked hard to make literature out of his suffering, while also proving him to be a keen observer of the Italian reality that surrounded him. At the same time, his language evolved in relation to the sociopolitical context and to his personal predicament, opening a new chapter in the story of Carnevali's developing relationship with the English language.

Translingual writing necessarily has dialectic aspects, as it:

> explicitly establish[es] a dialogic process between the culture of origin and the host culture by addressing various frames of reference (religion, food, landscape, traditions, etc) and by highlighting common and differing aspects in the two cultures. (Wilson 2012, 48)

The Bazzano works register a shift in this dialogic process. For Carnevali, the American culture stops being the "host" culture, becoming instead a distant target culture. These frames of reference are also addressed in different ways in an evolving language: an English with more relevant Italian interferences than in his American period. The notion of Carnevali as an author-in-between, suspended between cultures, takes on a very literal connotation as he stumbles in linguistic negotiation in an effort to give an American form to an Italian experience and to individuate an audience for it. What happens to all of his previous efforts to enter the American canon from the outside, now that Carnevali is also *physically* outside the United States? What is, conversely, his place in Italy?

The key text of his repatriation, the long poem "The Return" (1924), testifies to Carnevali's problem: who is the recipient of his poetry? The poem is a succession of brief descriptions of cities and landscapes in loose free verse, interspersed with the poet's contradictory feelings about returning to his home country. Carnevali recalls Gibraltar appearing on the horizon "after eight days of the monotony / of sea and sky" (1924, ll. 1–2); then Italy appears piecemeal—the Neapolitan coast, Genoa, Bologna, and, eventually, Bazzano. Distraught and disillusioned, Carnevali recalls America as "young" and "pitiless," while hoping that the eyes of Italian people will be "mellowed by the experience / of two thousand years" (1924, ll. 57–59). America and Italy often appear in contrast: a description of "Old Bologna, with her ancient red palaces / Defying the present" (1924, ll. 83–84) is interrupted by the poetic *I* exclaiming "Remember the lake of Chicago?" ("The Return" l. 86). The problem is perspective: "How everything has grown small since I went away / Since I am away!" (1924, ll. 88–89). The shift in outlook makes Italian cities look "small" to the returning migrant in comparison to New York and Chicago. That shift from "I went away" to "I am away" also seems to point out that in 1924, Carnevali still thought of himself as absent in some way. The last lines of the poem convey the returning emigrant's desperation:

I have come back with a great burden,
With the experience of America in my head—
My head which now no longer beats the stars.
O Italy, O great shoe, do not
Kick me away again!
(1924, ll. 114–18)

The poet's bitter comment transfers his own troubles onto the national context. Carnevali uses the very common metaphor describing Italy's shape as lo stivale ('the boot') translated into an English context. In his Bazzano years, Carnevali's personal plights are at the center of his writing, but there is also always the need to continue his conversation with the American public, as he found himself discussing and representing Italy for an English-speaking audience. Continuing the conversation with the American public was, after all, the poem's main goal, as he wrote to Monroe: "People still know that I have flown to Italy, but they soon shall forget it. It is good to remind them of this fact, namely, my return to the fatherland."[4]

At the same time, Carnevali was back in his fatherland, and while he was a recognizable presence in literary circles in New York and Chicago, he was virtually unknown in Italy. The only Italian intellectual who paid attention to Carnevali in the 1920s was Carlo Linati, an author and critic who "played an important part, in a particularly difficult period, in introducing foreign authors to Italy" via translation and criticism (Guzzetta 2004, 113). He introduced Anglophone modernists such as Joyce, Lawrence, and Hemingway to the Italian public, while his own work was translated for American magazines such as The Little Review. In 1925, when McAlmon put together Carnevali's writings and published A Hurried Man, Linati wrote an article about him in the major newspaper Il Corriere della Sera. The two established a correspondence in the following years.

Linati's "Un uomo che ha fretta"[5] presents Carnevali's "vita di ribelle,"[6] admiring his capacity to write in English "con una maestria e una freschezza davvero sorprendente"[7] (Linati 1925, 3). A translator himself, he admires Carnevali's translingualism. As we have already seen, he insisted also on the Italian roots of Carnevali's English ("lingua inglese irradiata da una vivacità tutta Latina") with nationalist overtones that would be reprised by all early commentators. Polezzi has noted the insistence on patriotic elements in early translations of Italian-American texts, particularly in relation to the 1941 Bompiani translation of Di Donato's *Christ in Concrete*. In that case, the editor's celebration of the book as "libro italiano" might have been motivated "by the fact that the translation of Di Donato's book had been subjected to the attention of Fascist censors" (Polezzi 2010, 141). Linati's 1925 article and translation was not necessarily consistent with Fascist norms—in the same year, Linati signed Croce's manifesto of anti-Fascist intellectuals. Yet the insistence on Carnevali's *italianità* might hint at a common reaction of the Italian cultural establishment to the first examples of Italian-American texts: in the need to place the migrant writer in a particular frame, there was a temptation to incorporate him or her into Italian culture at all costs and "claim" the writer by turning descriptions of emigrant suffering into celebrations of Italian strength, endurance, and adaptability.

"Un uomo che ha fretta" contains Linati's translation of some paragraphs from "Tale III" and a prose translation of "The Return." The translations of "The Return" (Linati would slightly rework the 1925 translation in 1934) eliminated Carnevali's puzzled depiction of Italian cities that he hardly recognized, skipping (especially in the 1925 version) directly from Carnevali's critique of America to the final appeal to the fatherland, leaving out pages of poetry in between and turning the poetry itself into prose:

> And hunger is the patrimony of the emigrant:
> Hunger, desolate and squalid—
> For the fatherland,
> For bread and for women, both dear.
> (E. Carnevali 1924, ll. 41–44)

> I have come back, and have found you
> All new and friendly, O Fatherland!
> I have come back with a great burden,
> With the experience of America in my head—
> My head which now no longer beats the stars.
> O Italy, O great shoe, do not
> Kick me away again!
> (E. Carnevali 1924, ll. 112–18)

E fame è il patrimonio dell'emigrante, desolata e squallida fame
di patria, di pane e di donne . . . Ma ecco sono ritornato, e ti
ho trovata tutta nuova ed amichevole, o Italia. Sono tornato
con un grave fardello in me: ho l'esperienza d'America dentro
al mio capo. O Italia, o grande Stivale, non darmi più calci,
non allontanarmi più da te. (Linati 1925, 3)

The translation leaves out the poet's displacement at finding Italy
so "small" on his return—probably to avoid casting doubt on Carnevali's
patriotism, stressing immigrant hardship and faith in the welcoming
fatherland instead. To use Lefevere's terminology, Linati's translation of
"The Return" "rewrites" Carnevali's trip, aiming to create a comprehen-
sible and acceptable "image" of a text for a public with no other access
to it (Lefevere 1992, 5). Although the translation skips the potentially
unsettling aspects of his trip (the double displacement of the returning
migrant), it nevertheless presents emigrant hardships to the Italian public.

Linati's *Corriere* article had little impact on the readership.[8] In 1934,
he wrote another essay on Carnevali, where he lamented:

Temo che di questo strano poeta non si sia mai fatto cenno in
Italia che in un'articolo [sic] ch'io scrissi anni fa nel Corriere
della Sera dove cercavo di definire la sua bizzarra personalità
di emigrato e di artista.[9] (1934, 59)

It is significant that Linati had in the meantime included the 1925 essay
in his 1932 collection *Scrittori Anglo-Americani d'oggi*,[10] granting Carnevali
a place in his canon of American authors while calling him "un artista
italiano" throughout the essay. This new essay includes translations of
excerpts from Carnevali's works, with some untranslated words testifying
to the Americanness of the text:

The homes are sitting together in the night, and their horrible
Congress is called City. (E. Carnevali 1920c, 54)

E tutti questi *homes* stanno insieme nella notte e il loro orribile
congresso si chiama città . . . (Linati 1934, 62)

The word "Wops" also appears untranslated, a choice that avoids discussing
controversial depictions of Italians abroad. Linati also reveals his doubts
about the most effective translation of Carnevali's poetic discourse—was

"Splendid Commonplace" to be translated as "Splendida Usualità" or "Splendore di Luoghi Comuni?" (Linati 1934, 63). Linati may have written of Carnevali as a reason for Italian pride, but his translations reveal Carnevali's foreignness.

There were very few other newspaper articles about Carnevali in this period, all of which refer to Linati, seek to establish Carnevali as an Italian author, and express puzzlement at his linguistic choices. The authors generally admit their ignorance about Carnevali ("avevamo a due passi, da oltre un decennio, un grande poeta . . . e nessuno l'aveva mai saputo"[11]) and praise his ability to learn and master a foreign language. This may reflect the norms of Fascist Italy, which often praised Italian intellect over that of foreign cultures. The journalists reprised Linati's hint of the "vivacità latina"[12] of Carnevali's English, exploiting the connection for nationalist praise. An article from *Il Messaggero* underlined how the young Florentine "seppe . . . conquistare il pubblico Americano con un soffio potente di latinità"[13] (Silvestri 1934, 5). A 1934 article from *Il Resto del Carlino* featured a brief account of Carnevali's "conquest" of America:

> Il Carnevali ha un suo fermo e appassionante sogno: essere scrittore. Studia l'inglese; in sei mesi egli è padrone della nuova lingua: grazie, segreti, incanti, armonie. . . . Assalto alle riviste; vittoria rapida e sicura. Arrivano i primi dollari, esplode, nella gioia, la prima sbornia. Curiosità e successo: gl'illustrissimi accolgono e salutano, con lieto stupore, il giovane poeta emigrato. Vibra nella letteratura americana una voce nuova, una voce nostra. (Palmieri 1934)[14]

Such articles narrate Carnevali's story as a triumphant Italian conquest of American culture, but also describe the poet's predicament in Bazzano, where he was sick and isolated. There are touching descriptions in Palmieri's article of the delight in Carnevali's eyes when the journalist quotes one of his poems and of a shaking Carnevali asking the journalist if he would help him light a cigarette or pour a glass of water.

The newspaper articles also address the matter of Carnevali's possible presence in Italian literature. Palmieri asked him if he could ever write in Italian now that he was back in his ancestral land. The poet's response was definitive: "In italiano non so scrivere. La lingua è una creatura, sangue, nervi, muscoli: bisogna conoscerla. Non conosco l'italiano."[15] This attitude toward Italian is rooted in Carnevali's entrance into literature:

he considered English as the language in which he had learned to write as a poet and the only one in which he could express himself literarily. He was not confident, on the other hand, that he would be able to build harmony ("una creatura") with the single elements of Italian ("sangue, nervi, muscoli"), which were familiar to him. The matter of the audience was obviously central as well: it is evident that he considered English speakers to be his natural audience. In a brief autobiographical note for the 1932 *Americans Abroad* anthology, Carnevali stated: "I do not brag of being a major poet, still I believe that I fill a certain space, unique, in American literature" (1932, 71). His continuous English production was intended to maintain that "space." Boyle wrote, in her preface to the *Autobiography*, that Carnevali's literary works were "the only speech left to him to exchange with the men of his time and kind" (1967, 18). The exchange would take place in English in the pages of reviews such as *Poetry* and *This Quarter*. The latter was a transnational, wandering magazine itself, established by Ernest Walsh and Ethel Moorhead. It was published at irregular cadence from Paris, Milan, and Monte Carlo for the cosmopolitan Anglophone youth inhabiting the south of Europe in the 1920s. Carnevali's Italian works exist in the cosmopolitan, traveling dimension of 1920s modernism, but his own predicament and background was quite different from the one where Hemingway, Pound, and Joyce created their European works. Nevertheless, he chose to keep writing in English and cling to cosmopolitan modernism as much as he could. He may have been living in Bazzano, but *A Hurried Man* appeared in Paris for Contact Press at a time when Contact was publishing Hemingway, Stein, H.D., and W. C. Williams.

Carnevali's diary-like short story "A History" (1929) has an entry where he discusses how his attitude toward language changed through the years:

> There was a time, when I did not know English, that English as I saw it written had a very strange effect on me; it appeared to be like freight trains clanging along; the W gave it a most mechanical air. It seems the most modern of languages, the machine language. (E. Carnevali 1929a, 131)

This passage points to the migrant's linguistic displacement in its basic, graphic, dimension. A young Carnevali associated the unfamiliar letter "W"—quite uncommon in Italian orthography—with his own alienating, "mechanic" experience of the modern metropolis. Then an increased familiarity with English made the language natural and organic to his eye: "now it has gained the look of an Italian dialect" (1929a, 131). Such acquired familiarity places English within the limits of his native tongue in the subordinate position of a "dialect." He concludes this brief excursus on the inner dialectics of language with this highly problematic comment: "but! notice that all languages have a similar look" (131). Carnevali's realization that the "mechanic language" had gradually turned into a familiar dialect implies that the translingual temptation to transcend languages may reside in an experience common to all bilinguals as they manage their linguistic resources. That is, the fact that our capacity to use language, our existence as language users, precedes the linguistic repertoires that we have access to in terms of importance. Carnevali's comments that all languages "have a similar look," rather than implying the existence of a further state of linguistic consciousness, may be closer to what linguists intend when they speak of (trans)languaging as the idea that our ability to use language is less important than the presence of individual, separate entities called languages (Jørgensen 2008, Garcia and Li Wei 2014, Li Wei 2018). A translingual like Carnevali not only acquires and masters different repertoires, but also becomes able to see them beyond their individual existence (English as a dialect of Italian) and must find a way to bend and combine all the different influences into a coherent text. This is all the more evident in the Bazzano texts, where the goal is no longer to tell, in English, the story of a clash with America, but the story of a linguistic return.

"A History" ends with the declaration, to his American audience, that he would make literature out of the village where he lived:

> Too much literature comes from the city and too little from the country. . . . Thoreau believed in the place where he was living and by his belief he made books where the essence of the place in which he lived shines and glitters. A great courage was his and with courage he won. I also believe in the place where I am living. I will have courage too. (E. Carnevali 1929a, 148)

Carnevali had rejected, upon emigration, the culture of small-town Italy. His rediscovered links with Italy passed through his ruinous experience of the American metropolis—and the Thoreau reference in this passage shows that the American tradition was still quite present in the author's mind. In Bazzano, Carnevali was a returning migrant, a condition that added further trauma to the shock of emigration. For him, this might have represented a return to the backward, narrow-minded "fatherland" that he had fled: he found himself in the Bologna area because his father still lived nearby. He was able, however, to use the town not only as the background for the story of his sickness (which remains the main preoccupation of those stories and poems), but also as a basis for discussing Italian culture with American readers.

3. Priests, Podestà, and Proverbs

The translingual, with all his or her vast repository of set phrases that mark the result of a polyglot experience, does not write in a vacuum: he or she takes part, more or less willingly, in a dialectic between cultures. He or she needs to communicate aspects of a culture to an audience that may not know much about it. Tymoczko employed the metaphor of translation to describe this challenge faced by postcolonial and minority authors writing in a dominant language. She argues that the presentation of different cultures is at the basis of both postcolonial writing and translation, and the difference between the two may be, in fact, only in terms of scope: unlike translators, literary authors are "transposing a culture" and not a text (Tymoczko 1999, 20). Translation and literary creation may become linked, in Tymoczko's argument, when representation of unfamiliar cultural elements is involved, and a strategy of cultural representation is needed on the author/translator's part. As an Italian writing in English, from Italy and about Italy, Carnevali needed a strategy of cultural representation for his Bazzano texts. These works conveyed an idea of Italy, and the matter of authorial perspective was crucial in this regard; a language came with it.

This type of text ultimately follows the author's perception of the represented culture, creating a unified image and discourse out of a multiplicity of inputs and voices. The final text represents the author's choice and approximations—his or her view of the home culture and what of that view is transposed in the text. A "minority-culture or postcolonial writer will have to pick aspects of the home culture to convey and to emphasize" (Tymoczko 1999, 23), and usually to keep the audience in mind. After picking which characters, rituals, and discourses might exemplify provincial Italy, Carnevali reframed them in English, explaining potentially obscure points with an anthropologist's zeal and a misfit's attitude of dissent. His views of Italian culture are necessarily partial and fragmentary, retaining the experience of an outsider. Yet there is, in the author's communication of this personal experience to the American public, a will to translate the Italian experience by translating its voices, rites, practices, and discourse.

Carnevali's operation of writing Bazzano and the Villa Baruzziana clinic into American literature implies a dialogic element that contrasts and compares cultures, even in texts that proclaim to have the author's inner world as their main preoccupation. For example, Carnevali starts a paragraph on a game of cards with the words "how noisy are Italians!" (1929a, 133). He then goes on to explain that "four Italians can beat a score of Americans in loud talking" and that a discussion on a card game could make them "more prepotent than Mussolini" and "louder than Niagara" (thus using both an Italian and an American image for his simile). The construction of a foreign audience allows Carnevali to cast himself as outsider and observer. He speaks of hidden sides of the quiet country town, describing alcoholics and extramarital affairs, town idiots, and loan sharks with vivid expressionistic tones. The style often betrays an outcast's pleasure in exposing this hidden side, as in the case of the anecdote on "young ladies" who "go for long walks with young men" in the countryside and "find after a time themselves possessors of a large belly . . . all because of some long walk in the country with some young man" (E. Carnevali 1929b, 123).

Carnevali's outsider's gaze is particularly evident and penetrating in his translational representation of Fascism and the Catholic Church: two institutions that he could only criticize as a total outsider, as he was not a participant in the social discourse of 1920s Italy. Catholic practices, rituals, and beliefs are an integral part of his representation of Bazzano. The 1925 poems collected in *A Hurried Man* cast Carnevali as a disturbing force in the placid certainties of Bazzano's Catholic society. One poem is significantly titled "The talkative Poet follows a Catholic Procession," and it counters the Latin words of "De Profundis" with Carnevali's English. The poet's images of individual desperation and isolation are a dissonant echo to the words of the prayer:

De Profundis clamavi ad Te Domine.
Out of an inscrutably deep grotto

Comes a white body.
He speaks: "I have lived under the sea,
The tremor of the surf reached my supine body."
("The Talkative Poet," ll. 1–15)

The juxtaposition turns into social critique: he follows the reference to law in "*et proper legem tua sustinui Te Domine*" with the image of "diplomats and lawyers" discussing "theft, raping, white slavery etc. etc." ("The Talkative Poet," ll. 25–27). In "Dolce Cuore," an old man is presented mechanically answering to the words of an ejaculation, repeating "Dolce cuore del mio Gesù, fa ch'io t'ami sempre più."[16] The poem presents rituals of popular Catholicism to an American readership while deconstructing them as superstitious. The old man is described in his religious zeal, trying to live as a saint but ultimately appearing "religious like a bug / that contemplates the ocean / and thinks of crossing it" ("Dolce Cuore," ll. 5–7); a life of pilgrimages made him "stink of sanctity" (l. 40). The expression plays on the Italian idiom *in odore di santità* (literally, "smelling like sanctity"), designating someone who might be proclaimed a saint by the church.

In "Catholic Sisters," the "barren" nuns are the unlikely interlocutors of Carnevali's philosophical disquisitions:

I told Sister Claire:

Why was Adam put into the world when God knew beforehand that he was going to sin. "*That is a matter of philosophy. Ask our priest!*" Thus Sister Claire.

("The Catholic Sisters," ll. 12–14)

Priests in particular are described with a number of anticlerical clichés. Carnevali writes of the priests' sexuality in a way that would certainly have been censored at the time had he written in Italian. A scandal concerning the chaplain of the Villa, who was accused of having an affair with a married woman, is taken as opportunity by the author to imply the chaplain's pedophilia. The chaplain, he writes, "is very fond of young boys . . . ; perhaps a bit too fond of young boys" (1929a, 127). Carnevali in Bazzano also chastises priests on the basis of their supposed homosexuality, which is an anticlerical commonplace: the chaplain, fleeing the scandal, "scutles by [sic] like any Miss" in his "long black skirt" (1929a, 127). Memories of youth find their way into the Bazzano stories to recall priests who were "notorious degenerates . . . expelled from the diocese for taking liberties with young people" (1967, 203). In the *Autobiography*, he wrote about a priest who was his teacher in "the third elementary grade" and who "would offer you wine and sweets, yet he was not a pederast" (1967, 156). In parenthesis, the author feels the need to add: "I say he was not a pederast because so many of the priests in my country are." Addressing an Anglophone readership is instrumental to framing his harsh accusations on Italian religious institutions: the English language is what enables Carnevali to make such disruptive statements.

The advantages of writing in English are even more evident in Carnevali's translations of the speech and everyday practice of Fascism. While Carnevali's writings do not extensively reflect on Fascism, the regime—whose pervasiveness in Italy was at its peak in the late 1920s—makes its inevitable appearance. Carnevali lived in a nation where any "oppositional discourse" to Mussolini risked being silenced, and artistic production implied "condescending attitudes, and the supposed neutrality of art" (Moroni and Somigli 2004, 24). Writing in English for a foreign audience allowed him to describe and expose Fascism as no other Italian writer still working in Italy could do. While he could not be described as a militant anti-Fascist, Carnevali never showed much enthusiasm for the regime. In a 1932 letter to Ezra Pound, he appeared puzzled at the latter's embracement of Fascism: "What was the interview where you declared that you were fascist: please tell me: I am in too big a bunch of murderers, here in Bazzano to have a heart for fascism."[17] In his literary works, Fascism appears rarely, and few political issues are addressed directly. Yet daily life under Fascism is a recognizable component of his Bazzano works. Carnevali exposes the discourse of Fascism by ridiculing its everyday, banal dimension. His critique of provincial life in the 1920s is also a critique of Italian complaisance toward the regime.

In the short stories he wrote about his stay in the Villa Baruzziana clinic (which he called "Rubazziana"), Carnevali befriends a young Fascist named Arches, wounded by a gunshot, who stands accused of murder. Arches appears as pleasant company and a womanizer, but Carnevali also notes that "His tragedy—hidden—was his insignificance" (E. Carnevali 1927, 145). A psychiatric patient of the Rubazziana, an aristocratic woman named Mrs. Thighs, is "continually writing to Mussolini" and urges Carnevali to write to the king of England to sponsor his career (E.

Carnevali 1929b, 110). By staging it in the life of psychiatric patients and renegades, Carnevali shows his American readership a less-than-grandiose side of Fascism.

The regime, in Carnevali's view, is a façade that does not change the timeless provincialism and misery of the typical Italian small town. The impression is stronger in the paragraph on the *podestà* of the town. *Podestà* was the title of the regime's nonelective mayors, taken from Renaissance history: as Carnevali informs the reader, "Mussolini has decided to make Italy look Roman or Medieval" (1929a, 132). The *podestà* of Bazzano is a "fat faced little gentleman" who is "the purest image of doing-nothingness" (E. Carnevali 1929a, 132). The passage comically underlines the contrast between the daily occupations of the *podestà* (which consist mainly of idling in the streets of the town) and his high-sounding title. The *podestà* holds his position because "Mussolini says so, and the Madonna is satisfied," symbolizing an Italy in which secular and religious power have always been intertwined, and Fascism only maintains this immutable order. Carnevali remarks that, "like all fascists" the *podestà* is a "man of strong opinions, borrowed of course from the men who stand higher up above him" (E. Carnevali 1929a, 132).

This seemingly mundane anecdote penetrates Fascist rhetoric on many levels, going beyond what Bhabha calls the "nationalist pedagogy" (1994, 145). This is a discourse that has the "people" of a nation as its primary object, giving the national discourse "an authority that is based on the pre-given or constituted historical origin *in the past*" (Bhabha 1994, 145, author's emphasis). Italy's past, renarrated in mythical form and reenacted in the everyday life of citizens, is the self-justifying tale of the regime. Carnevali underlines the fiction of the Fascist state's purported historical links, exposing the "borrowed" quality of the strong opinions taught under the national pedagogy—its aggressive reutilization of the past and the underlying system of power that is maintained (Mussolini and the Madonna acting in accordance). Carnevali ridicules the "nationalist pedagogy" aspects of Fascism, calling the podestà a "mask" in "Mussolini's great bal masqué" (1929a, 132), which begins with the Balilla ("kind of boy-scouts") and ends with the government itself. Carnevali's ironic remarks expose the process of how "scraps, patches and rags of daily life" are turned by an imposed Fascist discourse into "the signs of a coherent national culture" (Bhabha 1994, 145).

To communicate the fiction of Fascism to his American audience, Carnevali needs to convey its specific language; that is the opposite of what he did in America, where he had to learn how to master American speech, rather than reproduce Italian speech. A word like *podestà* needs to stay untranslated in the text to play its role of ancient word inserted in a modern discourse. Other words of Fascist language are translated. Arches was wounded, Carnevali tells us, in a "Fascist punitive expedition" (1927, 144). The phrase gains its full meaning as a direct translation of the Italian *spedizione punitiva fascista*: a practice with its own violent ritual, directed at political opponents in the years leading to Mussolini's rule. Italians of the time knew the expression all too well; translated so that it maintained the closest possible resemblance to the original, it carries an element of Fascist language into English, signifying a precise Italian referent. Sometimes the English language needs to be bent slightly to convey such elements, as in the case of the "boundary line" used as a threat by the podestà ("he can send you to the boundary line, oh boy!," 132). Carnevali here refers to the Italian *confino*. The word resembles the Italian for "boundary" (*confine*), yet it referred to the Fascist regime's practice of *confinare* ('segregating') dissidents in small villages, not necessarily at the national border. Out of similarities between Italian words, an English word is bent to signify another practice relevant to Fascist Italy.

Carnevali's American works had operated on the proximities of English and Italian, displaying his particular relations with words that had similarities with Italian words—yet such language tended mostly toward linguistic assimilation. Carnevali's Italian works, on the other hand, display strong Italian influences, pointing to their context and the personal history of Carnevali's language. Linguistic strategies, such as the one that Carnevali used to represent Fascist speech, imply that the languages involved in the formation of a translingual text may have different impacts in different contexts. The way in which a bilingual uses language generally depends on negotiations between the languages that he or she knows, what he or she expects the interlocutor to know, and what he or she assumes is appropriate to the context (Jørgensen 2008, 170). One may argue that while the streets of New York called Carnevali to respond to American slang and give his own version of the speech, Bazzano and the Baruzziana presented him with the problem of representing Italian speech in English. There is an eminently practical side to the question of Carnevali's medium, and it relates to a negotiation between the multiple influences of context and the audience. Bilinguals report being influenced by all of their languages when describing the world, with each language offering its speakers many different discourses and interpretive frames, that is assemblages of lexical items, metaphors, rhetorical practices and scripts that structure speakers' expectations, assign interpretations to social events, and serve as a kind of memory structure facilitating understanding, encoding, recognition, and recall. (Pavlenko 2014, 225)

Carnevali's peculiar situation, as well as his desire to make sense, through literature, of his predicament, brings life to a text in which "different discourses," "interpretive frames," and "lexical assemblages" compete, but—because he has decided that he is an American poet and will stay so until the end—everything needs to be brought into the boundaries of generally accepted English. At the same time, in Bazzano he reached a point where he could not and would not ignore the most evident Italian influences. Hence, as we have seen, he called English "an Italian dialect" and reflected that all languages have a "similar look" in his search for a synthesis. The practical result is a style where two languages (not "all") participate in the repertoire of an author and are made to have a similar look; the strain of doing so is more evident in the Bazzano texts than in the New York and Chicago texts.

Idioms that appear to be freshly translated from Italian occur quite often. The result of Carnevali's painstakingly literal translation of idioms is often odd: "the stick-to-lean-upon of his old age" translates *il bastone della sua vecchiaia*, an idiom indicating a person who supports someone in his or her old age (1929a, 140); "if they are roses they will bloom" derives from *se son rose fioriranno*, usually said to invite someone to patience (1927, 147). Translations of Italian phrases and idioms may be used to cast judgment on Italian society, as he mentions "women of the vulgus" (1929a, 139), using its Latin antecedent to bring into English the Italian word *volgo* ("common people"). He uses phrases such as "I detest him cordially" (1929a, 135), which translates the expression *detestare cordialmente*, used to indicate outward respect of someone who is actually despised; or "native town" (1929b, 107), instead of the more common "hometown," to translate the Italian expression *città natale*. At the same time, versions of American English's interpretive frames are evident in the use of certain expressions to interpret Italian reality. The "sweet sixteen" has no place as a concept in the Italian cultural landscape, yet Carnevali calls a character "as sweet as a sweet sixteen" (1929b, 118).

This operation of explaining Italy through concepts learned in America is sometimes made explicit:

> Once he tried to stop drinking and smoking, but two days after he had begun his abstinence (after he had gone on the water wagon, to put it more Americanly), he started to have fainting symptoms . . . (1929a, 145)

"Water wagon" is an expression that has no equivalent in Italian, while its more usual English form is "to go on the wagon." Carnevali's use of this expression is a sign of the persistent influence on him of the English language, even as his circumstances reduced his familiarity and confidence with American concepts.

At this point, it is worth noting that there is no apparent intention of writing *against* English here. Carnevali's Italian works precede the challenges of postcolonial writing by decades. Like a postcolonial text, Carnevali's Italian text "comes to encode messages which are not readily decoded by the monolingual reader" unfamiliar with "other referential worlds" (Mehrez 1992, 122). Yet, unlike the postcolonial language analyzed by Mehrez, his goal is not to "subvert hierarchies . . . by exploding and confounding different symbolic worlds and separate systems of signification" (Mehrez 1992, 122). The goal of Carnevali's language is to maintain his identity as a literary author—and preferably an American one. However, in doing so, he faces an increasing need to borrow from Italian, more so than when he was "simply" attempting to become an American author.

There are multiple phrases and structures in the text that appear to be caught in the passage between Italian and English, and this depends evidently on the task at hand. In one passage of "A History," the need to convey Italian cultural and social specificities gives rise to a unique wording, which requires notion of Italian lingua-cultural space to be understood: "He started to speak to me: 'I will tell thee a story.' 'How,' says his daughter, 'do you thou him?' 'Then,' said the old man, 'I shall tell us a story. I saw snow in Castelfranco'" (1929a, 135). The dialogue functions on an Italian opposition between the colloquial second-person pronoun *tu* and the formal way of addressing interlocutors in the third person (*lei*). Carnevali attempted to convey excessive familiarity to make readers know that it was a *tu* that the old man used by using the antique English equivalent of a singular *tu*. Such opposition does not have the same currency in English. This is directly related to the "interpretive frames" that according to Pavlenko compete in the bilingual mind, providing different linguistic interpretations of social contexts. In particular, the lack of such an opposition between formal and informal personal pronouns is often felt as a "conceptual loss" by translingual writers coming from languages in which this opposition is present: Besemeres observed it in Hispanic American authors who were bewildered as they went from "inescapable distinction between two forms of address in [their] native Spanish" to "the all-embracing English pronoun 'you'" (2002, 25).

Colloquial Italian is present in all its culturally specific framework in the simple exclamation of a hospital patient: "God is a hangman!" (1929b, 124). The expression renders into English the blasphemous expression *Dio boia*. Blasphemies have a certain pervasiveness in the colloquial speech of some Italian regions, and their "shock value" is difficult to render pragmatically in English (Bassnett 2002, 34). In this case, literal translation enables them to retain some of the shock value. The blasphemous expression is deprived of its Italian sociocultural subtext, but it works in the narration as a dying man's expression of revolt against his doom. Unsurprisingly, Italian characters, with their quirks and customs, are Carnevali's main source of expressions that exist in a space between English and Italian. His nurse and friend, Gilio, talks about the fields in winter as being "peeled" (1929a, 130). That translates a colloquial expression (*pelato/a*), which could refer to fruit as well as a bald man or to things stripped of growth/vegetation/fur in general. A man who walks into town poorly dressed and with a long beard is bound to be identified by Carnevali's neighbors as "the man of the caverns" (1929a, 146)—an expression that is rhythmically closer to the Italian *uomo delle caverne* than "caveman." Another man, an alcoholic, is described as "alcoolized" (1929b, 123) from the Italian *alcolizzato*. In another passage, Gilio swears:

> "That I may become blind and not see my own child anymore. That my child drop dead as I enter the house tonight and that I may bust this very instant, if it's true that Celia's baby is my own." (1929a, 130)

Carnevali uses English structures to mimic the Italian subjunctive mood (*congiuntivo*), which can be used for remote or hypothetical occurrences (or oaths, as in this case). The transference of everyday speech into English is not, of course, only a matter of morphology. Syntax is bent to this use; phrases and expression are translated; culture-specific situations are displayed and, to some extent, explained. These factors together make up the transcultural performance. The passage on Gilio's marital troubles also contains his wife's threat "to leave her home, to scream in the public square Gilio's infamy, to break up the family" (1929a, 130). The sentence includes a translation of the Italian idiom *nella pubblica piazza*, which does refer to the town square, but also carries the extended meaning of "openly, in public." In such a context, taking a fight into the "public square" means a blow to family respectability. In addition to translating Italian colloquial speech, the passage shows the American readership a sample of "*bella figura*, the code of proper presence of social behavior that governs an individual's public presence" (Gardaphé 1996, 20, author's emphasis).

The translation process does not deal only with the speech of the people of Bazzano and the Villa Baruzziana. Some cultural references may also depend on Carnevali's middle-class education before emigration. He uses, for example, the phrase "rustic chivalry" to describe the evenings in the streets of Bazzano (E. Carnevali 1967, 208). The phrase mimics the Italian *cavalleria rusticana*, popularized by an 1880 short story by Giovanni Verga, dealing with the culture of honor and duels in a small Sicilian village. Once featured in an 1890 opera by Pietro Mascagni, it entered the language as an idiom. Carnevali tries to make an English expression out of it. Popular operas from the time seem to be a source of idioms for him: he also translates some lines from Ruggero Leoncavallo's *I pagliacci* (1892), referring to the "Pagliacci psychology," while rendering the popular aria "Vesti la giubba" in English: "Laugh, O clown / of your broken love . . ."[18] (1929a, 139). These references exist on a different sociocultural level from the speech of Carnevali's Bazzano neighbors, but they are equally important in conveying the feeling of a space that is usually interpreted through Italian.

This assemblage of translated Italian phrases and idioms makes the need for the use of untranslated Italian somewhat less relevant in this phase of Carnevali's writing. Multilingual literature generally uses "non translation—that is, deliberately leaving a part of the text not translated in order to marginalize the monolingual readers" (Gentzler 2008, 143). The Bazzano texts did not seek to marginalize their American audience—Carnevali had that audience very much in mind. The linguistic oddities convey a sense of an Italian linguistic environment but keep the untranslated Italian to a minimum. One of the author's love interests, a

young girl from Cairo, rejects him by saying "*Basta!* I don't want . . ."
(1929b, 107, author's emphasis). Quite interestingly, the same character is given other multilingual cues in Italian, English, and French ("I
went to the door, *et voilà, vous étiez là!*" 107, author's emphasis). On a
different note, the Italian onomatopoeia "*kirikiki*" (1929b, 116) is used
instead of the English "cock-a-doodle-doo." Overt multilingualism seems
to be relegated to special cases (onomatopoeia, multilingual characters),
while a more subtle multilingual habitus lies beneath the surface in the
Bazzano texts. Even names, which would provide immediate signs of Italian in the text, are sometimes translated into English. Carnevali does not
translate names like Clelia and Cimbra (1929a, 130) and surnames such
as Rossi (131), Andreoli (143), and Degli Esposti (144), yet there are
almost as many cases of English nicknames that he gives to his Italian
characters. His version of the Baruzziana clinic is populated by people
with names like "Professor Komebacks," "Marquis Dumbs," "Fireplaces,"
"Coast," "Mrs Thighs," and "Nothrills." While "Professor Blacks" of Carnevali's Rubazziana (1927, 142) might be Professor Neri, who founded
the Baruzziana in 1911,[19] it is usually hard to ascertain which names are
nicknames and which are translated surnames. Carnevali's idiosyncratic
attitude toward names also includes "Signor Gallese" and "Signorina
Testadimoro" (1927, 147), the Italian names he comes up with for his
editors Ernest Walsh and Ethel Moorhead. They exist outside Italy,
and outside America as well—they are all part of Carnevali's Bazzano
language, one that he created for the purpose of the text and that was
bound to exist in the text alone.

    The idiosyncratic nature of this text is also apparent in its rela-
tionship with one of the most crucial facts of Italian linguistic reality,
in the 1920s as well as today: dialect. It is quite likely that dialect
(*Emiliano-romagnolo*) had a presence in Bazzano, competing with standard
Italian as in any other Italian town, giving the town a definite linguistic identity. Carnevali notes that Bazzano has its own speech and "its
own songs, songs heard nowhere except in Bazzano" (1967, 206). He
translates three of these songs into standard English, thus keeping the
foreign presence to a minimum ("Moretto, Moretto, he has in his hair /
The natural wave that comes from water . . ."). On the other hand, he
hardly includes dialect in his works. The passage that contains his "all
languages have a similar look" epiphany also discusses Italian dialect,
contextualized in English. The author writes that he "noticed that Italian
language is to the dialect what English written is to American spoken"

(1929a, 131). He explains this by comparing the relationship between the Italian *discorrere* ("talk, discuss") with the romagnolo dialect *dscarer*, which he deems the same as the relationship between the word *hot* and a pronunciation such as *haht*. The passage fails to make the crucial distinction between dialect and accent, while Carnevali hardly considers the emiliano-romagnolo words that he must have heard in Bazzano. Many Italian-American writers did not consider their native dialects at all when making the passage into literature; they mostly chose English as a way of interacting with the American public, but the "dismissal of dialect as a form of cultural expression" relates more generally to an idea of "cultural homogeneity" that was imposed throughout post-unification Italy and that Italian emigrants absorbed (Verdicchio 1997, 96). Carnevali was exposed through his education to the idea that Italian was the "proper" written language and must have taken it for granted, also relating it—as he often did—to his own experience of English. That prompted him to write that "it is the dialect that resembles the language and not the language that resembles the dialect" (E. Carnevali 1929a, 131). Any element of colloquial Italian in the text was influenced by the notion that the dialect was unimportant.

In general, the Bazzano texts are a document of a highly idiosyncratic language, fueled by the unique circumstances of Carnevali's return and sickness. In them, he does not completely change his language—which had been determined, also in New York and Chicago, by a very strong need to be understood as an Italian on his own terms. His grasp of linguistic boundaries, on the other hand, necessarily falters, influenced by the changing conditions. Still, his language does not dissolve into general confusion or become outright multilingualism (which would not have worked because he admittedly wrote for Americans, not for Italians); it evolves into a new strategy of translingual writing.

These texts show, to a greater degree but not in a different scope from the New York and Chicago texts, how the translingual writer is first and foremost a bilingual individual. Like any bilingual, he or she makes the best to communicate using all his or her linguistic resources and manipulating them to address an audience that presumably does not possess the same resources. If we look—as is increasingly the case among linguists—at language not in terms of discrete vernaculars, but in terms of our capacity to address and manage culturally determined repertoires, using translation to transfer resources between them, the Bazzano texts are a prime example of how this human capacity can be used to create literature. They are also an example of how translinguals who choose to stay well within the limits of their adopted language (as Carnevali did, with a few idiosyncratic features, in his first years as a writer) may still decide to employ their linguistic resources in a different manner.

The Bazzano texts arise from a highly unique situation: a returning migrant, sick and isolated, in a precarious position as a writer. Hardly any text could be more idiosyncratic than this, focused as it is on the inner workings of the author's mind in relation to very confined environments: a small town and a clinic. However, the crisis that took him away from America did not, as he briefly thought, take him to a language beyond other languages: the language of godhead; if anything, it made the contrasts between Italian and English more evident in his writing. The continuous workings of Italian and English in the Bazzano texts demonstrate that society and culture never stop influencing the translingual's dialogue between cultures, and that the host culture never stops being the direct recipient of the translingual's efforts, the one against which he measures his efforts—even after the return, as in this case.

Between the Atlantic and Oblivion

Carnevali in the 1930s

In the 1930s, Carnevali's career drifted toward oblivion as the world changed around him and encephalitis lethargica made his life increasingly intolerable. He did not, however, give in to the idea that he would simply disappear from the literary world. At Ezra Pound's request, Carnevali became the first Italian to attempt a translation of A *Draft of XXX Cantos*. Only his translation of Canto VIII was ever published, in 1931 in the magazine *L'Indice*, but several others survive in draft form and more may have been lost. During the same years, he also set out to write the story of his life. The project was left incomplete, but first Kay Boyle, and then Carnevali's stepsister, Maria Pia Carnevali (with help from David Stivender), used his drafts as a foundation for their versions: the English-language *Autobiography* (1967) and the Italian *Il Primo Dio* (1978), respectively.

These two projects, the Pound translations and the *Autobiography*, represent the culmination of Carnevali's career as a translator and migrant narrator, even as their outcomes were marked by the difficult circumstances of the author's final years. The first two sections of the chapter explore Carnevali's crucial relationship with Pound and with his work, respectively. Pound was a patron and an advisor of Carnevali's, one of the few American writers and intellectuals who stayed in touch with him and provided support during his illness. Pound also had a deep and complex relationship with Italian culture and society, which at one point led him to sponsor a translation of his own *Cantos* into Italian. The translingual Carnevali was a natural candidate: his translations reveal another layer of complexity in Carnevali's linguistic journey as he attempted to travel in the reverse direction, from English to Italian.

The final section analyzes the creation of the *Autobiography*, a task in which he brought his own idiosyncratic, transnational language. This work was written in English, translating into the uncertain English of the Bazzano years both the Italian of his childhood and the quasi-assimilated English of his American years. The resulting narrative, fragmented and incomplete, shows Carnevali interpreting his own life as literature in a final effort to ensure his place in American letters.

1. Carnevali, Pound, and the "eyetalian licherchoor"

The translation of *A Draft of XXX Cantos* was not a simple translation job: Pound appointed Carnevali as a member of a transnational network of collaborators, friends, and protégés. This project, as Pound explicitly wrote in an essay titled "Lettera al traduttore,"[1] aimed to renovate the (in his opinion) stagnant Italian culture with the help of the translated *Cantos*. With few exceptions, Italian intellectuals of the time were reluctant to consider Pound and his brand of modernism as a valuable cultural option despite Pound's presence in Italy since 1925. Even though he had been harshly critical of Pound in the early 1920s, Carnevali was part of the American modernist group, a somewhat experienced translator, and a man in need. Pound supported him financially and gave him the job of translating both the *Cantos* and an essay on the *Cantos* by Louis Zukofsky: the latter was explicitly aimed at defending Pound's idea of poetry.

It is not certain how many Cantos Carnevali translated: in addition to the published Canto VIII, six other Cantos (II–VII) survive in draft form. Translation of successive Cantos, up to XVII, are mentioned in correspondence but have not been found in the archives. As outlined in the previous chapter, Carnevali's language had evolved during his long period of sickness and isolation, and his grasp of English and Italian as two separate language systems was less and less firm. This also affected his work as translator: the *Cantos* translations, in their gaps and idiosyncratic language, show both the inherent difficulty of translating Pound and the effect of years of translingual writing on Carnevali's Italian. Just as Italian contextual influences appeared in his English writing, continual use of English had an impact on his return to written Italian. Carnevali's work on the *Cantos* puts to the test Kellman's claim that "translinguals are, by the very fact of not being limited to their native language, better equipped than most others to engage in translation" (2000, 33).

We still have a series of letters that Carnevali wrote to Pound from Bazzano. Pound's side of the correspondence was lost, reportedly destroyed by Carnevali's landlords after the poet's death during World War II. The side of the argument that is still available provides valuable insight into a particular relationship of dependence between author and translator: Carnevali lauds Pound as his benefactor and often mentions a monthly allowance of 200 lire that he received from him. In a 1930 letter, he calls Pound "the best human being in the wirld . . . AND this is no adulation at all, it is sheer grstitude."[2] Pound was also one of the few important literary contacts left to Carnevali. He helped Carnevali sustain his presence in the literary scene, for example, by including him in his 1932 Italian-published anthology *Profile*. When not writing to Pound for money (or books or clothes), Carnevali asks him for his opinion on poems and translations: "when you say that someting of mine is O.K., I feel happy" (1930).

Carnevali expressed his desire to continue translating, sending Pound some of his translations from Rimbaud. Mentioned in a 1930 letter to Pound, these were subsequently sent as a sample to Caresse Crosby of the Paris-based English language press The Black Sun. Pound had been Crosby's first choice for a Rimbaud translation, but he deemed it too difficult and suggested she turn to other associates of his (Ford 1975, 217). The Rimbaud translations ended up in Poetry after Crosby finally chose to focus on other editorial projects. Yet in the same year Pound assigned another translation job to Carnevali: Zukofsky's 1929 essay, mentioned above. It appeared in L'indice in 1931, months before "Canto Ottavo."[3] This magazine was published in Genoa, conveniently close to Pound's home in Rapallo. It was a favorite of Pound's and, together with its successor Il Mare, an important Italian outlet for his work. It was not particularly prominent in the Italian milieu, but Pound was then "content to remain an outsider, with little contact among prominent writers and critics, appearing only in local periodicals with small circulation" (Bacigalupo 1999, 46). Although it was carried out by a small circle, Pound intended this project as a response and critique of wider tendencies that he observed in Italian culture.

An admirer of the signori of the Italian Renaissance, Pound hoped to find sponsors who "exemplified what [he] appreciated about the great Renaissance patrons, their interest in bringing new art into being" (Dasenbrock 1991, 147). If he did not have the economic means or the decisive power to fund many of his projects by himself, nevertheless he was able to create links across a transnational community of authors. Pound's attitude toward the Italian translation of his Cantos reflected his status as modernist patron as well as his belief that "a great age of literature is perhaps always a great age of translations" (1968, 232). He was conscious that foreign influence on national canons worked through patterns of translation and criticism and could be directed by those with strong enough cultural authority.

Pound published his "Lettera al traduttore" in 1930 in the form of an open letter to an unnamed translator (this may be a reference to Carnevali, whose translation would be published in the same magazine the following year). Addressing the translator directly, Pound gives stylistic indications and makes a case for the brevity of the translation compared to the original in the name of a polished style and against the elaborate syntax of Italian: "Non fare complementi a cascate. Sono modi di condensazione tipici dell'italiano."[4]

Pound argues that clarity ("chiarezza"), rigorous thought ("il rigore del pensiero"), and a new and effective hardness ("durezza nuova ed efficace") should spring from the translation of his own poetry and change the very nature of early twentieth-century Italian. He often remarked that he found a certain weakness in the Italian language of his time (Zanotti 2009, 376), and some passages in "Lettera al Traduttore" reveal that he intended a translation of his work to have an impact in this sense: "Naturalmente un forestiero non può condurre tale rinvigorimento della lingua: bisogna qualche autoctono, che forgi la sua lingua natia."[5] These words spring from his firm conviction that Italian itself needed renovation and that such an overhaul could only happen through the influence of translated foreign work. In the essay, he acknowledges his status as a "forestiero" (foreigner) and puts emphasis on the "autoctono" (native). More than a mere mouthpiece, the native translator appears as someone who would eventually "forge" his native tongue into something different, using the Cantos as inspiration.

Pound addressed the plight of this ideal, unnamed young Italian writer: "Naturalmente lo scrittore italiano si sente rinchiuso, vedendo che si dorme, vedendo che le riviste italiane non vanno all'estero."[6] (Pound 1930, 1). In a 1935 letter to his Italian contact Carlo Izzo, Pound would make this point more strongly: he stated that "Eyetalian purrfessors" were acting as if they were "way back in 1860," while "eyetalian licherchoor" was "BACK in 1895" (Izzo 1956, 129). In 1934, in a letter to the New

England Weekly, he mentions "three Italys existing side by side": that is, he considered Mussolini's idea of Italy more advanced than the backward country of professors and literati (Jung Palandri 1972, 42). He evidently saw a translation of the *Cantos* as a means of advancement for Italian literature that the Italian literati should have welcomed. However, this was not always the case: at least until after World War II, there was no consensus among Italian intellectuals on any gaps in Italian culture that would be filled by a translation of Pound's.

Some Italian authors and intellectuals appreciated and supported Pound's efforts. They include his second Italian translator, Carlo Izzo, and Vanni Scheiwiller, who was a tenacious ally in his Italian editorial projects. Carlo Linati wrote an essay in praise of Pound in *Scrittori anglo-americani d'oggi* (1932)—a volume that also included the reprint of Linati's essay on Carnevali. Linati discussed Pound's early poetry, translating some lines and underlining the multiform character of his activity and the novelty of his style. Linati frequently remarks on Pound's admiration for Italian medieval poetry, contrasting it with the Italian audience's reluctance to appreciate Pound:

> Ma si sa come, per la generale, vanno queste cose in Italia. I valori spirituali stranieri entrano da noi per così dire alla spicciolata, a casaccio e quasi di straforo, spinti avanti o da una stamburata d'oltralpe o dalla réclame di qualche editore nostrano, per modo che i migliori ne restano sempre fuori.[7]
> (Linati 1932, 95–96)

Linati laments that the public did not welcome Pound despite what he deemed an explosive vitality fueled by Italian culture.

By contrast, the case of Mario Praz is a perfect example of how the Italian intelligentsia reacted to the *Cantos*. Praz, a professor at the Universities of Manchester and Rome in those years, wrote a review of Pound's latest edition of the Cavalcanti poems for the Turin newspaper *La Stampa* in 1932. He criticized not only the Cavalcanti book, but also the entirety of Pound's work together with his network of literary contacts. Praz was particularly disapproving of Pound's choices for the 1932 *Profile* anthology: among the "Americans" that he looked upon suspiciously, Praz listed Carnevali. Praz explicitly ridiculed the Italian intellectuals (e.g., Linati, Scheiwiller) who supported Pound. Of Pound's poetry, he claimed to appreciate some of his early work but commented harshly on the *Cantos*:

> Il resto dell'opera del Pound é abile mimesi di greci, di latini, di cinesi, di provenzali, di stilnovistici, di francesi moderni, arlecchinata universale, macedonia amenissima, aperitiva, stimolante, gustosa, vino mussante senza corpo. Dilettante é parola di suono ingrato, ma temo che definisca appropriata-mente la figura del Pound . . .[8] (Praz 1932, 3)

What Linati had praised, Praz did not regard as literature. He again criticized the *Cantos* in a June 5, 1933, article and reiterated his views in December 13, 1933, attacking Pound's "discepoli": Zukofsky, Hemingway, and Cummings (Praz 1933, 3).

Carnevali was aware, to a certain extent, of being caught up in a debate on the reception of Pound's modernism in Italy. He had no strength or authority to make his participation in this debate public, but he kept as informed as he could. He wrote to Pound in 1931:

> Youmust know that a losuy, clerical, (meaning catholic) newspaper of Bologna dared to tell its readers that Italian literati assume amost humble and servile attitude towards you: I have not read the note butI knowit is so: ther was also somefilthy allusion to your living luxuriously in the best country town of the Italian Riviera. These losuynewwpaper ours ought to be hung.

Carnevali went on to remark that the Italian intellectuals were really "honored to have [Pound] as a inhabitant of this soroowing country of ours."

"Lettera al traduttore" indicated that the man charged with the task of translating Pound was called to play a role in nothing less than the renovation of the Italian language. This ambitious enterprise was destined to be ignored or opposed by the majority of Italian letters, where the critical reevaluation of Pound would come later. Carnevali's faltering health, his peculiar background, and his outsider's attitude were to be tested by a very difficult translational task whose ultimate goal was intended to make a lasting impact in a reluctant target culture.

2. Carnevali and the *Cantos*

Before fulfilling its sociocultural implications, a translation is mainly a matter of "nouns and verbs and all kinds of lexical and grammatical patterns" with which the translator engages in "a detailed process of decoding" (Bassnett 1998, 60). Carnevali's letters to Pound testify to the difficulty of such a process when it comes to the *Cantos*:

> SoonI begin working at that tremoendous job; that of trans-
> lating your canti. I don't knowthat I shall ever be able to do
> that: some ofthe cantiareteribly difficult, like must havebeen
> to the assyrian sculptor to sculpt thosetremendous bulls. But
> this time they are difficult for apppoor translator (I mean poor
> comiseratingly not that I think of myself as a bad translator).
> (1930)

Carnevali perceived the difference between his own writing and the effort required to assemble a language appropriate for a work whose "province," latter critics noted, is "the entire human race speaking, and in time as well as in space" (Kenner 1975, 95).

In the letters, Carnevali seems to treat the translation as a challenge that he is almost sure to fail. In a 1930 letter, he complimented Pound on the "superb" *Cantos* before admitting: "but I must dole it out to myself: I cannot assimilate more than half a Canto a day." It is interesting that he used a word so similar to the Italian *assimilare*, which expresses the incorporation of the alien into the self or wrapping one's head around a concept. With their blanks, mistakes, and stylistic peculiarities, the typescript of his *Cantos* translation show Carnevali's extreme difficulties in assimilating the source text as well as his problems with reverting to his native language after years.

It is worth noting that the *Cantos* are indeed very difficult work to assimilate without a proper system of reference. Let us take these lines from Canto IV:

> Ityn!
> Et ter flebiliter, Ityn, Ityn!
> And she went toward the window and cast her down,
> "All the while, the while, swallows crying

Ityn!
"It is Cabestan's heart in the dish"
"It is Cabestan's heart in the dish?"
"No other taste shall change this."
(Canto IV, ll. 16–23)

With some research, a reader discovers that the Latin words are from
Horace, that Itys was the son of the king of Thrace who was killed and
cooked by his own mother, and that the Provencal troubadour Guillems
de Cabestanh was killed by a jealous lord, his heart served to his own
beloved (Terrell 1980, 11). The extremely wide scope of reference and
the composite nature of the work make volumes of glosses and indexes
necessary. This necessarily has an impact on the work of an isolated
translator like Carnevali, who was detached from the literary environment and lacked the necessary apparatus of glosses and commentaries.

Faced with this challenge, Carnevali generally provided a word-
for-word translation: words appear to be translated individually, often
without an apparent comprehension of syntactical structures. They
appear in precarious balance over the structure of the verse, which he
followed to the letter:

Itino
Et ter flebiliter, Itino, Itino
Ed Essa andò verso la finestra e si gettò giù.
Nel mentre, nel mentre, rondini cantanti:
"È il cuore di Cabestano nel piatto."
È il cuore di Cabestano nel piatto?
Alcun altro gusto cambierà questo.[9]

It almost seems a servile attitude toward the source text. Carnevali did
not allow himself any intervention in the translated text, following the
English as much as he could; he often seemed uncertain about which
Italian words to use. As Cronin emphasized, a translator is always in the
position of having to maintain links with his or her native language:
"translation only makes sense if Ithaca is in sight, if there is homecoming
in the target language" (2000, 99). As seen in chapter 4, Carnevali in
Bazzano had made a further step away from the monolingual certainties
that he had struggled to acquire in English without making decisive
steps toward Italian. Carnevali's linguistic uncertainties at the time
were responsible for a truly unique language, if sometimes unstable and

obscure, in his short stories and poems. Faced with a translator's job, whose intended target is usually a stable monolingual product, Carnevali's linguistic contradictions exploded. His illness also most likely had an impact on the amount of time and effort he could devote to the job because of his tremors as well as the tranquilizing effects of the scopolamine he took to alleviate them.

The translations' word-for-word style reflects Carnevali's familiarity with English as his language of writing, many features of which he assimilated into his own language. And yet, at the same time, he did not possess a total command of English: there are some passages in the drafts where it seems that the English proved too difficult. Carnevali sometimes left blanks in the typescripts, which Pound penciled in. Carnevali's Cantos drafts are a study in translingualism as a never-ending process, hovering between familiarity and strangeness in the management of a complex array of linguistic resources. The transition from one language to another can never be final or total, but it impacts all of the languages used, with unique effects on each of them.

Linguistic confusion characterizes the drafts as a document of linguistic in-betweenness. Carnevali's Italian in the translations is highly idiosyncratic at grammatical, syntactical and lexical levels. The typescripts are only a draft translation, yet some features of the texts seem to denote a deep-seated linguistic instability rather than a preliminary stage of work. Even small details such as the typescript's headings indicate an unstable language. Where he is simply supposed to write the title and the page number, Carnevali seems to be unable to decide whether to use Italian or English. In Canto II, the heading "pagina 2" is followed by "page three," and in Canto IV, "page three" follows "pagina two." He even comes up with a "Canto Settimo Page First."

Such peculiarities and oddities seem, in most cases, to follow a pattern. The language in continuous transformation assumes varied intermediate forms, but there seems to be some regularity in the way in which Carnevali bends Italian to fit the English original. He has a recurrent, Anglicized way of translating the same words, or constructs—a hint at the fact that those were not simply individual mistakes: he must have deemed those constructions acceptable, at least in the draft stage. Such departures from the standard forms of Italian bring the language closer to English syntax, sentence structures, and even vocabulary.

The phrase "swallows crying" in Canto IV is translated as "rondini cantanti"—a choice that, though not strictly incorrect, sounds unconventional to the Italian ear. Modern translators would have used "le rondini squittivano,"[10] using a finite form of the verb that is more common in Italian, though not syntactically equivalent to the concise English "crying." In English, it is normal to use an *-ing* form as an independent clause, but in Italian that clause is generally made explicit with a subject and a verb. Elsewhere, when Pound writes about "departed locusts / *speaking a shell of speech*" (VII, ll. 76–77), Carnevali translates it as "locuste partite / *parlando* un guscio di discrsi [sic]," seemingly ignoring not only that the *-ing* form is not translatable into one Italian word in that case, but also that *parlare*, unlike its English counterpart "to speak," may not always be used as a transitive verb.[11] This occurs even when the result borders on incorrectness in Italian. In an effort to translate "the fauns *chiding* Proteus" (II, l. 153), Carnevali comes up with "i fauni *ridentesi* di Proteo," trying to condense into one word a phrase that conventionally would have been *che se la ridono di*. In a 1919 letter to Papini, Carnevali showed a similar linguistic uncertainty when he was writing, in Italian, a sentence that in English would have required the gerund. Not knowing how to render it in Italian, he simply left it in English:

> Questa America leggera e poltrona. Co' suoi sforzi al modern-
> ismo e l'arte. Vecchia puritana che accorcia oggi la sottana
> *dust-stinking*, e s'imbelletta all'ombra dei bellissimi-bruttissimi
> *sky-scrapers*! (E. Carnevali 1981, 77)[12]

In his ideas about the renovation of Italian through translation, Pound may have expressed a desire for Italian to become a more concise language. Yet he thought mostly about Latin as an example, remarking that Caesar did not "need" things such as the determinative article when building an empire (Zanotti 2009, 378). In contrast, the concise-ness that Carnevali's Italian displays in the translated Cantos is not an erudite quest for the mythical origins of the language, but springs from prolonged familiarity with English.

Approaching the text as if he were afraid of going even a step too far from Pound's words, Carnevali elaborates new rhythms of discourse that are calques of English rhythms. There is no structure in Italian that would perfectly replicate a line like "flaming as if with lotus" (IV, l. 77), and that is why Carnevali's painstakingly faithful "fiammeggiante come se con loto" carries with it a sense of foreignness to Italian readers. The effect of disorientation is not necessarily negative, as it may have cre-ative implications. A structure like "male e più male . . . muove eppur si muove" is not quite common in Italian, but it well reproduces the sound of Pound's "evil and further evil . . . moves, yes she moves" (II, ll. 16–17). The most immediate Italian correspondent of "any" (*alcuno*) does not commonly perform the function of negation on its own: Carnevali uses *alcuno* like an English "any," as he translates "No other taste shall change this" (IV, l. 23) into "alcun gusto cambierà questo."

Syntactical uncertainty is not the only salient feature of Carnevali's drafts. Lexical idiosyncrasies also arise out of his long acquaintance with English. The first and most evident result is Carnevali's struggle with compound words. English seems to have a predilection for creating words from a union with other words, which Italian employs to a considerably lesser extent. In an Italian translation, this would usually be rendered with a single word (whose etymology may or may not be the same as the words that form the English compound) or with a phrase. Most of the time, Carnevali does not seem entirely in control of the translation of these compounds. A "fish-hawk" (II, l. 149) may be a *falco pescatore* in Italian, but for Carnevali it was a "falco da pesci." The "sea-crest" (V, l. 30), at the same time, can simply become *onde* ("waves"), or, in Carnevali's attempt to translate both of the words of the compound, it can become "la cresta del mare." The same happens to "churn-stick" (II, l. 131), for which *mestolo* is a precise translation; but Carnevali decided to render both words, resulting in an awkwardly literal "bastone agitatore."

English often turns nouns into verbs, a practice that native speakers tend to perform quite independently from the indications of dictionary and grammar. The same does not occur in Italian, in which speakers have limited possibilities for turning nouns into verbs without sounding odd. Carnevali follows the English habit in the *Cantos* translations, creating neologisms that existed for the brief space of the typescripts and fell into oblivion along with them. In the process of translating Pound's "moonlit velvet" (V, l. 122), he creates a "velluto lunato" out of the Italian for "moon," whereas translators usually resort to periphrasis ("velluto al chiaro di luna," Bacigalupo). In the same way, he invents the unlikely verb *petalare* when Pound uses "petals" as a verb (IV, l. 85), and *pilare* when Pound uses "piled up" (V, l. 63). Carnevali finds new use for Italian words by attempting to reproduce English sounds. The Italian *sorte* means "fortune," but Carnevali nevertheless translates "three sorts of blue" (V, l. 19) into "tre sorti di blu." In another instance, an Italian *duomo* is not a dome but a cathedral, but this does not prevent Carnevali from translating "domed head" (VII, l. 26) into "testa a duomo." In most cases, the word Carnevali uses belongs to the right semantic field, but the meaning appears somehow twisted. It is the case with Pound's "little slave money" (II, l. 51), which becomes "poche monete da schiavo": *monete* actually means "coins," and that is why Pound changed it to "profitto"—less similar in sound, but closer in meaning.

Toury has observed that translations may present "linguistic forms and structures . . . which are rarely, or perhaps even never encountered in utterances originally composed in the target language" (1995, 207–8). In Carnevali's case, the rarely occurring forms are peculiar to the point of sounding recognizably English. Toury attributed such phenomena "to the fact that the verbal formulation of a translation is partly governed by a felt need to retain aspects of the corresponding source text invariant" (1995, 208). Carnevali's Cantos translations are not, on the other hand, a simple case of "translationese": they reflect the surprising uneasiness that translinguals sometimes report feeling when using their native tongues. If Carnevali's second language had felt alien and artificial at the beginning, it nevertheless ends up opening expressive possibilities for the author, who considered it crucial to his intellectual life. In a time when he reportedly considered English as "an Italian dialect" (see chapter 4), Carnevali wrote English fiction in which the interference of Italian is palpable, while at the same time his Italian translations sound English at times. Together, the two bodies of work document the in-betweenness of Carnevali's language.

Carnevali's familiarity with English did not prevent him from being unable to understand it at times. The moments when English proves impenetrable to him are as relevant as the ones when he shows extensive familiarity with the language. It is significant that the words he could not translate are mostly in Canto II: focused on the Greek myths of the sea, Canto II is full of a specific vocabulary concerning ships, and ancient ships at that. Carnevali's English was the English of the metropolis. He probably had no idea how to translate words like "scupper-hole," "rowlocks," "oarshafts," or "fore-stays." Only in some cases does Pound help by writing down the right word (as in the case of "oarshafts," which he translates as "maniglia dei remi"). In other Cantos, uncommon and idiosyncratic language in the original results in blanks in Carnevali's translation: "slivver [sic]" (IV, l. 41), "but on the barb of time" (V, l. 20), "cygnet" (IV, l. 68), "song or land on the throw, and was dreitz hom" (V, l. 60). Carnevali was unable to decode some of Pound's modified spellings and bits of foreign languages. The lines of dots that in these cases he leaves on the typescripts symbolize, in visual form, the distance that most readers have to go before they can understand the *Cantos*.

There are also a few cases when the translation is simply and irrevocably wrong, mistaking one word for another. Carnevali writes "tartaruga" (tortoise) for "turquoise" in Canto III and "onda" (wave) for "waste" in the same Canto. Pound had to correct them, circling and crossing them out and writing "turchino" and "guasto" instead. These mistakes, unlike the aforementioned borrowings from English, obviously follow no pattern but are the product of occasional misreading. They are not a consequence of Carnevali's translingual upbringing, but probably reflect his difficulty in maintaining concentration for long periods. There are, in the letters, phrases that end abruptly; he adds excuses like "The last unfinished phrase indicates that I am now a prey to scopolamin. I not only think nonsese but speak an write ittoo" (1930 letter). Probably in a hurry to deliver the translations, working in the intervals between health crises, he translated almost on the spot. In at least one case (judging by the drafts that we have, which do not cover the whole work), he corrected himself right on the typescript; "fanning their hair in the dark" (IV, l. 46) is first translated as "funzionando il loro ventaglio nell'oscurità" and then as the much more viable "sventagliando i loro capelli nell'oscurità."

In such situations, Carnevali seems to rely on Pound to help him as a fellow translator. In a letter, he warns him that the manuscript would be "full of mistakes and badly typed and everything," concluding "you must work hard and correscy: you know Italian don't you?" (1930 letter). Pound had his say on the translations, as the signs of his pencil on the manuscripts show. It seems that, in any case, Pound did not give up hope for these translations, at least judging from Carnevali's responses to his letters. At times, he seems to be dealing with Pound's impatience about the work's progress, justifying delays with references to his health. This also enables us to know that there were other translations and other manuscripts that must have gone missing. In a 1930 letter, he apologizes for not having sent Canto XII, yet in 1932 he expresses his delight in knowing that Pound liked his translation of XI. As Carnevali's illness progressively worsened, his letters contain more and more excuses. The last mention of a completed translation is in a 1933 letter: "hav yu receibed my Canto diciassettesimo?"[13] Other sources let us know that Pound was quite reluctant to give up his hopes for Carnevali. In 1930, he wrote to Zukofksy about Carnevali's health. There was, he wrote, still "a personality intact in the middle of [his illness]," and he was still a "civilized male reading French, Italian and capable of discussion same" (1987, 57). He therefore asked Zukofsky to be patient with him: "He can't hold a pen. Typing full of errors."

Carnevali's translation of Zukofsky's essay on the *Cantos* appeared in *L'Indice* in 1930. Its goal was to defend the style and language of the *Cantos* from critics; as such, it also contained quotations from the *Cantos*, which Carnevali translated with the rest of the essay—the first small samples of his translation project to be published. They present many of the idiosyncrasies that were already in the drafts. At the same time, if we compare the lines from Cantos II–VII quoted in the essay with Carnevali's drafts, editorial intervention becomes evident. The editors of *L'Indice*, or Pound himself, corrected most of the drafts' linguistic uncertainties. A quote from Canto II, for example, displays some cosmetic changes in the published version with respect to the drafts ("Dio" instead of the more colloquial "Iddio" for "God"). Where the drafts present "spesse come un covone" for Pound's "thick like a wheat swath" (IV, l. 61), the edited version replaces "covone" ("sheaf") with the more precise "fascio di grano." When translating Pound's "slim white stone bar" (IV, l. 25) Carnevali had written "barra sottile e bianca" to keep the similarity in sound; the edited version, "colonnetta di pietra sottile e bianca," may be more precise, but it lacks that foreign quality that was present in the drafts. These brief quotations offer us a chance to confront the drafts analyzed above with what they might have become in print, as we do not have other finalized versions of the drafted Cantos II–VII translations, and we do not have the draft of the only one that was fully published. Although the drafts are now a valuable document of the influence of prolonged experience of the source language on translation, they were predictably edited before publication. Then most of the idiosyncratic elements were eliminated in favor of more common words. We do not have the drafts for "Canto Ottavo," but it is likely that the same process happened before its publication in November 1931.

The choice of starting publication with "Canto Ottavo" may not have been a casual one, as it is one of the most Italianate Cantos. The first of the so-called "Malatesta Cantos," it is dedicated to the *Signore* of fifteenth-century Rimini, Sigismondo (or Sigismundo) Malatesta, a warlord and patron of the arts. Based on his fascination with this historical figure, Pound evolves his technique of poetic impersonation, with which he had been experimenting from the early years of his poetry. Pound's way of conjuring and displaying the life of the Renaissance hero on the page has been defined as "Pound's most far-reaching experiment with the half-mask" (Albright 1999, 72). The story of Malatesta's exploits is not narrated, but shown through a collection of documents—letters, poems, and historiography. The poet appears only as editor and translator of Sigismundo's own words:

> And Malatesta
> Sigismund
> *Frater tamquam*
> Et compater carissime tergo
> . . . anni de
> . . . dicis
> . . . entia
> Equivalent to
> Giohanni of the Medici,
> Florence
> (VIII, ll. 4–13)

Historical and personal matters of Sigismundo's life are on display, but the poet gives the reader only scattered details (battlefields, numbers of horsemen and soldiers, and amounts of money) in the text. Pound's words "do not convey information" but "take certain facts and present them from different linguistic perspectives (formal, florid Italian; broken Italian words; English translation) as if to undercut their historicity" (Perloff 1981, 183). Carnevali, presented with the task of translating this collage for an Italian audience, did not have the original manuscripts available to him, and therefore no direct access to the "facts" that Pound presented in his text. In *L'Indice*, Carnevali's translation was followed by a short editorial note stating that the translator had not seen the original medieval document (1931, 5). Thus the editor, "per verificare la storicità del poema," presented the original document "verificato dal Pound."[14]

Carnevali was to produce, in fact, a translation of a translation, yet he could not take into account the first source text in a chain of originals and reproductions. If he had been able to access the first original, there would have been no need for an Italian translation to exist: it would have consisted of an arrangement of fragments written in Sigismundo's Medieval Italian. In later years, Pound's recommendation to translators was precisely that they use the original Malatesta letter—starting from his daughter Mary's 1961 translation (Bacigalupo 2012, 32). This of course presents issues, namely that of bypassing a great deal of Pound's work and his multilingual arrangement of words. The poet left bits of Italian on display for the reader, as if the English layer had not been applied uniformly over the Italian surface. The poem's intertextual aspects are exposed provocatively, turned against themselves, providing "a melange of conflicting, competing modes" instead of "affirming a single link with the homogeneous past," creating heterogeneity (Smith 1994, 65). The English repeats and complements the Italian, establishing its status as a translation and an inventive footnote:

> "With his horsemen and his footmen
> (gente di cavallo e da pie) etc"
> (VIII, ll. 75–76)

> "For two days' pleasure, mostly "*la pesca*," fishing."
> (VIII, l. 112)

Praz had ridiculed this technique in his articles, quoting the lines from the *Cantos* that Pound had inserted in the *Profile* anthology:

> Suppongo che il dodicesimo e ultimo frammento voglia dir poco da solo, ma siccome da solo il Pound l'ha dato, eccovelo nel testo originale: "And in August that year died Pope Alessandro Borgia, il papa morì." (Praz 1933, 3)[15]

To Praz, an Italian professor of English, the line seemed meaningless in its redundancy. He did not consider the English-speaking readership, who were exposed, through Pound's lines, to the linguistic sign of another historical moment, bearing the force of otherness and remoteness. Pound's English guided the reader toward the comprehension of the general meaning. This is a prime example of how modernist poetry existed in "more than one temporality: the historical temporality of its composition" and "the temporality of its sources and originals," so that translated lines, quotations, and allusions ultimately end up "complicating the relations between texts and time, temporality and form" (I. Patterson 2011, 176). In the case of Carnevali's "Canto Ottavo," they also hugely complicated the relationship between modernist poetry and its subsequent translation. As a conglomerate of times and languages, it takes the form of a speech act bringing together different spatial and temporal identities—but how can a translator negotiate a target text out of the fragments and complexities of the source text?

Carnevali was forced to downplay at least a part of the linguistic collage of the original, juxtaposing the Italian of his time with the Italian that Pound quoted or combining them in just one Italian sentence. Pound's "And it wd be merely work chucked away / (*buttato via*)" (VIII, ll. 32–33) becomes simply "e sarebbe solamente lavoro buttato via." The juxtaposition that was in the original disappears, also eliminating the sense of linguistic displacement. Even when the Italian insertions do not disappear, their role in the text becomes much less evident in the translation. In the original "with his horsemen and footmen / (*gente di cavallo e da pie*) etc" (VIII, ll. 75–76), the Italian insertion performed a function of underlining the strangeness of the source, the journey across time and space that those words had undergone. In the translation, they are puzzling to the reader only because of their redundancy: "con i suoi cavalieri ed appiedati / (gente di cavallo e da pie) etc."

A significant part of the Canto was a translation, in modern and colloquial English (provocatively using abbreviations like "shd" and "wd"), of a very ornate Renaissance Italian. As Carnevali did not have the Italian original, he had no choice but to translate Pound's modern English into modern Italian. Malatesta's original "Circha la pratica de la pace tra voi et el re de Ragona" becomes Pound's "As to arranging peace between you and the King of Ragona" (VIII, l. 18). At this point, no indication of the Renaissance Italian underneath was available. Carnevali translated the lines into modern Italian: "In quanto riguarda la pace fra di voi ed il re di Ragona." His work ends up giving centrality to Pound's translation over Malatesta's words, elevating it to the status of source text and, consequently, of an original work in its own right. Given that he instructed subsequent Italian translators to use Malatesta's letter in their translations, this is a centrality that Pound himself probably did not desire.

There is at least one attempt on Carnevali's part to play the card of the unexpected and return Pound's insertions of Italian into his English text by inserting some English. This is when "the respectable man Agnolo Della Stufa" (VIII, l. 65) becomes "l'uomo rispettabile Angel of the Stow." It is the only case in which there is an attempt in the translation to reproduce the sense of otherness and foreignness that the Anglophone reader experiences in reading the "Malatesta Cantos."

Without the philological reasons that made Pound juxtapose Italian with English, this insertion of foreignness into the *Cantos* loses its point. This may be the reason why Carnevali did not usually pursue this technique in the translation.

Carnevali kept working at the translations, but the problems were evident and his health was getting worse. Pound turned to other Italian contacts for help. Carlo Izzo's translations of some poems by Pound ("Ballad for Gloom," "Night Litany" and "The Return") appeared in 1935 in *Nuova Corrente*, together with some lines from Cantos II and III. From a 1937 letter (probably one of their last exchanges), it seems that there had been a misunderstanding between Pound and Carnevali,[16] yet even then the latter insisted: "amico finirei anche di tradurre i trenta canti."[17] It was work he would never finish. There is a difficulty inherent in translating such a complex work, especially at a time when its innovations had not yet been appreciated by the majority of critics and writers. Carnevali's attempt was the first, and his failure probably resulted in Pound's decision to give more advice to Izzo for the translation of the aforementioned poems (there are letters in which he gives advice on almost every word). The first complete Italian edition of the *XXX Cantos* would appear in 1961, translated by Pound's daughter Mary De Rachewiltz, who worked in close contact with her father (Bacigalupo 2015, 123).

The 1930s project involving Carnevali demonstrates that translation may be treated as a means of spreading ideas, expanding audiences, and conquering new markets only if we take into account the idea that translation is first and foremost the way in which we negotiate meaning from a foreign text. On the one side there was Pound, fighting against an intelligentsia that would not welcome his ideas. On the other was Carnevali, struggling against the text and his own health. The failure that resulted is all the more interesting for the multiple factors that determined it—ranging from power relations in the Italian press to Carnevali's faltering lucidity. More importantly for the purpose of this volume, the analysis of this translation project shows how the bond formed by the translingual writer with his or her adopted language can resurface in unexpected ways, sometimes placing him or her in a precarious position between languages. When Carnevali attempted to translate into Italian, he found out that English was an integral part of his speech. As he discovered, covering the distance back from English into Italian (particularly given the difficulties inherent in the *Cantos*) was far from easy.

3. From Italy to Italy: The Making of the *Autobiography*

Carnevali's last major effort, undertaken as his illness worsened, was writing the story of his life. The project conformed to a tendency for autobiographism that his work had always had. Throughout this volume, I have used the *Autobiography* as a major source of clues about the author's personal and linguistic development. It provided indications of how Carnevali construed his movements across language and culture. It is now time to consider how the *Autobiography* came into being and to place it in the proper stage of Carnevali's development as a writer—that is, at the very end of his career, as he cast the bitter look of a dying writer at his youth.

Carnevali mentioned the project to *Poetry* editor Harriet Monroe in 1930:

> It is hard, very hard for me to write, otherwise I should have long ago begun the story of my life, which should awake the echoes of all America.

> I think I shall do something pretty good with it. It is my last hope of earning something by myself for myself. I shall begin one for good, this coming week.[18]

He implied that it would be difficult to write, but he appeared sure that it would help him maintain his status as an American writer ("the echoes of all America"). Only a few chapters of the book saw the light of day during Carnevali's lifetime, and these were in relatively obscure publications. The first six chapters were published under the heading "The First God (A Novel), Part I" in the 1932 anthology *Americans Abroad*. Kay Boyle, a writer and friend of the poet, was appointed editor of the *Autobiography* in 1933, probably because of Carnevali's faltering health. The agreement between Carnevali and his publisher, Harcourt Brace & Co., listed as an "essential condition of this agreement that the work is to be under the editorial supervision of Kay Boyle who is to have full editorial liberty in regard to the manuscript."[19] A reference to Monroe's death ("Tireless little woman, you are now dead," 157) indicates that Carnevali was still writing after his former editor's death in September 1936. At least one other chapter appeared during Carnevali's lifetime as "Excerpt from Autobiography" (1939) in the British magazine *Kingdom*

Come.[20] However, Boyle lost touch with Carnevali in the early days of World War II (Boyle 1967, 18), and he died in 1942.

To understand the *Autobiography*, it is first necessary to understand how it came to exist in its later published forms: Boyle's 1967 volume and the 1978 Italian translation, *Il Primo Dio*. Boyle returned to the text in the 1960s, piecing together the published chapters and the autobiographical stories that Carnevali had collected in the 1925 book *A Hurried Man*; then she completed the book with the remaining "sections of the book he was trying to write in the public ward of the hospital in Bazzano" (Boyle 1967, 15).[21] She arranged the fragments to form a coherent story and inserted excerpts from texts published by Carnevali in the 1920s in the body of the 1930s narration.

Boyle showed her care for her dead friend by giving shape to the fragmented and multiform narrations of his life. In the same years, she was intent on revising another autobiography written by a friend of hers in the 1930s: Robert McAlmon's 1938 *Being Geniuses Together*. In McAlmon's autobiography, she not only rearranged the original narrative in chronological order, but also openly inserted chapters of her own, integrating a narration from her own point of view. Boyle saw her 1968 edition of "*Being Geniuses Together* as a dialogue with her dead friend" (Monk 2001, 492); Monk calls it an example of how "writing a community" constitutes "a gesture central to modernism itself" (2001, 495). Boyle's 1967 edition of *The Autobiography of Emanuel Carnevali* does not feature such an open dialogue between editor and author; it is more a collection and chronological rearrangement of texts. On the other hand, it does reopen a discussion in the modernist community, by publishing—and most likely saving from definitive oblivion—the last writings of a man who had worked hard to enter the modernist canon.

Boyle's rearrangement of the text is quite evident if we compare previously published versions of the same chapters. For example, the first chapter of the 1932 "First God" becomes the second chapter of the 1967 *Autobiography*, and bits of its text are moved around:

> I may have been from two to three years old. It was in the city of Florence which I had left when I was less than one year old, left for the country following a tremendous bronchitis and pneumonia that carried me near to the grave. (1932, 74)

It is in the city of Florence where a tremendous bronchitis
and pneumonia had carried me near to the grave. I may have
been from two to three years old . . . (1967, 26)

The 1967 version shortens the passage, rearranging it for editorial pur-
poses. Yet the words are preserved, and, more importantly, the peculiar
"Bazzano language" of Carnevali's last years is preserved in expressions
such as "carried me near to the grave."

If we go deeper into Boyle's typescript, we notice that some chapters
exist in more than one version. The editorial work is still in progress there,
albeit in its final stages, as Boyle attempts to give shape and direction to
the collection of fragments that Carnevali had sent her in the 1930s. The
book is there sometimes indicated as "Religious Stammering"[22]—one of
the titles that Carnevali reportedly had in mind (Boyle 1967, 15). The
chapter subdivision is probably entirely Boyle's: there are examples in
the typescript of material that was moved from one chapter to another.
For example, a chapter titled "First Loves"[23] in its earlier typescript version contains the chapter that would become "First Love" in the 1967
version, while some pages would be incorporated in a chapter titled
"The Third Boarding School" in 1967, which links the Venice period
of Carnevali's life with events that happened the following year. Boyle
put Carnevali's autobiographical fragments in order and probably wrote
the brief sentences that linked them with texts that had already been
published. For example, a chapter called "Beginning a Literary Career"
tells of Carnevali visiting the offices of various New York editors, sub-
mitting manuscripts and hoping for publication; the same chapter also
includes whole paragraphs from his 1920 review of Ezra Pound. The
editorial intervention frames it with a narrative device: "in this room
I discovered Ezra Pound. I read his *Pavannes and Divisions*, and I wrote
these words about him . . ." (E. Carnevali 1967, 118). It is more than
likely that Boyle's work was limited to this "compiling" (and linking) of
Carnevali's works, as indicated on the frontispiece of the 1967 edition.
Still, by giving shape and structure to Carnevali's words, recuperating
texts from the 1925 *A Hurried Man* (a book that was never widely dif-
fused) and from magazines, Boyle's work as editor was fundamental in
reinstating Carnevali in the literary canon.

Boyle's emotional investment in rescuing Carnevali from oblivion is
evident in her foreword, where she outlines a very personal relationship

between author and editor. She recalls hearing Carnevali's name when she was working for the literary magazine *Broom* in the 1920s and then starting a correspondence with him in 1923. Her account of their 1933 meeting in Bazzano shows the strong impression that the sick poet made on her: "the thing one feels when one walks into that cell and sees the figure on the bed can never be explained" (Boyle 1967, 16). Once they had met in person, she reports, the "compiling of his book" became "an obsession" (Boyle 1967, 18), which she would bring to fruition only three decades later.

In 1971, opera conductor David Stivender wrote to Boyle. He stated that since reading the *Autobiography*, he had become obsessed with Carnevali's story as well and started looking for writings by and about Carnevali at the New York Public Library.[24] In his quest to restore Carnevali's fame, Stivender came in contact with Maria Pia Carnevali. When the two set out to translate and edit Carnevali's book for the Italian market, they focused mainly on removing what evidently had been added in Boyle's text, comparing that work with *A Hurried Man* and Carnevali's published material from various magazines.[25]

The fragmentary and multiple nature of the book, in the forms that reached the public, is part of its essence. In English, it is known as *The Autobiography of Emanuel Carnevali*, the provisional title given to it in the 1933 contract with Harcourt, Brace & Co. The Italian edition, *Il Primo Dio*, uses Carnevali's 1932 title for the first chapters of the book, translated into Italian; this version removes all of the material from the 1967 edition that was not explicitly written for the autobiography. In any case, Carnevali's autobiographical fragments "always remain fragments, although all of them together would seem to form the most complete portrait," and both editions of the book can only be defined as "approximations" (Boelhower 1982, 140).

The lack of an authoritative text may reflect the content of the narration: the author's procession from silence to literary American English through the temptation of absolute language, and finally to linguistic confusion and silence once again. In the interplay between the sick author, the sick narrator, and the posthumous editor, the reality of Carnevali's life is transfigured one last time as a tentative legacy to the world of letters and a document of the author's language in its final stage. If translation and autobiography have in common the fact that they both supposedly point to an "original"—be it a "self" or a "source text"—which is assumed as "transcendental signified, the untranslatable 'presence' or the outside referent that arrests the process of supplementation" (Karpinski 2012, 9), then it seems even appropriate that a figure like Carnevali should have more than one "translation" of his life story. The analysis of his autobiography may only confirm Karpinski's observation that "translation can be replaced by retranslation just as life narratives are open to retellings and rewritings" (2012, 9). The text is one possible telling of his life, told from the perspective of a sick, dying, and isolated Carnevali. It was written in one of the languages of his life—or perhaps in his one true language, the one that he crafted in Bazzano out of multiple passages across linguistic boundaries. Out of such specific constraints, he created the fragments that were later collected by Boyle and Maria Pia Carnevali. The text gave Carnevali his last chance to exist as an author, to voice his feelings about his short and tormented life and to make literature out of it. To do so, it needed to be "translated," as Carnevali's autobiography could only exist in English. The translation into English of his life, his memories and frustrated aspirations, enabled the isolated author to communicate with his intended audience. Carnevali's last work seems to respond to Derrida's later intuitions on the need of an audience for an autobiographical text. The autobiography, usually identified closely with the self, fulfills its promise only by reaching an audience:

> The signature becomes effective—performed and performing—not at the moment it apparently takes place, but only later, when ears will have managed to receive the message. In some way the signature will take place on the addressee's side, that is, on the side of him or her whose ear will be keen enough to hear my name . . . (Derrida 1985, 50)

To take Derrida at his word, Carnevali's text owes its existence to the Other. This resonates with its unusual genesis, as it took three people (Boyle, Stivender, and Maria Pia Carnevali) who cared about his legacy to bring the text into existence for the English-speaking and Italian-speaking communities, respectively. But, most importantly, the "ear of the other" is present at the very heart of the process of writing in Carnevali's decision to write in English, address an English-speaking audience, and maintain his identity as an American author.

The most evident link between Carnevali in the 1930s and the *Autobiography* is the pervasiveness of the author's illness in the text. From the start of the 1932 installment of the text, Carnevali's tormented childhood and his mother's sickness are connected with his 1930s sickness. The narration starts with the author's birth in a Florentine hospital, framing his life in a full circle—from the Italian hospital of his birth to the Italian hospital of his impending death. He describes himself as a sickly and weak newborn, adding: "I think all the troubles I caused could have been evaded had I died, and a good riddance too" (E. Carnevali 1932, 74).

The chapter he dedicated to his mother is linked to his present condition: "What can I tell you of myself, mother, except that I have wasted in sickness a good half of my real life from fifteen up" (1932, 77). As discussed in chapter 1, in his autobiographical writing, Carnevali's mother represents an emotional kernel rather than an actual family figure. As he appeals in English to his Italian-speaking dead mother, this justification may serve more as consolation. The translation of his life into English offers him a chance to write his past and present torments and ultimately appeal to the literary audience in his chosen language. The importance of illness is all the more evident in the 1939 "Excerpt," written as his health worsened, beginning with Carnevali spreading "wide nets in the sea of [his] memory" and lamenting that "few fish are caught in them" (1939, 16). As memory starts to fail him, writing becomes a means to affirm his existence, which at this point had become both necessity and torture:

> Words, words, words . . . words which serve only to nail me to my cross, words which serve only to gag me, words which destroy one another and which leave me more lonely and wretched than I was before. (E. Carnevali 1939, 16)

Writing is the only activity left to him as he "courts" the "infamous figure of death," and "even she rejects me." In what was probably his last work published during his lifetime, Carnevali affirms both the necessity and the uselessness of writing.

The intimate aspects of the narrative are transformed and enriched, though, by the translational forces at work in the different stages of the autobiographical narration. The text has several intercultural, intertextual links offering multiple angles of analysis. The echoes of Papini in the *Autobiography*, noticed by Boelhower (1982, 145) and mentioned in chapter 3 of this volume, should be understood in the context of Carnevali's career to this point. The echoes of *Un Uomo Finito* were not inserted in the text by a young Carnevali, eager to imitate one of his favorite authors; they represent the last influence of an old model on an aging, dying Carnevali.

This intertextual relationship takes on an interesting role if we consider the ending of Papini's book in relation to the conditions in which Carnevali wrote the *Autobiography*. Papini writes about his youthful struggle for renovation in art and morals; he makes vague plans to emigrate to America but does not leave. He then experiences a crisis, finally returning to his birthplace in a Tuscan village. It is undeniable that, given the obvious differences in the outcomes of the two stories, the "theme is the same [as] the vision" as "Carnevali's persona goes to America to become Papini's first god, to conquer America and celebrate the modern man" (Boelhower 1982, 146). In the end, Papini's novel considers his failure to produce definite truths and become an artist-god ("Ma Dio non vuol parlare colla mia bocca,"[26] 238) by reflecting on his intertextual debt to the history of literature, lamenting his own influences on his quest for originality:

> Son tutto impregnato di teorie altrui, imbottito di libri, saturo di articoli, imbuzzato di parole e di immagini. Son figliolo della cultura e degli altri mentre vorrei essere genio e me stesso.[27] (Papini 1913, 239)

Carnevali's narration of the "First God" episode is also imbued with references to the literary canon, as discussed in chapter 4. Indeed, the whole *Autobiography* is an explanation of why he did not attain the powers of divine speech while defending his attempts, much like *Un Uomo Finito*. From his condition of post-authorship, aware of losing what little fame he had achieved, Carnevali also reflects on his place in literature, revealing a similar tension between literariness and the myth of originality:

> But above all I was, and I am, an envious man, madly jealous of all the writers who have got out more than one book. I was jealous (guess what I am jealous of!)—jealous even of Shakespeare. I was frantically in need of praise, crazy about my being considered a major poet. (1967, 93)

The difference lies in the context in which these final words are uttered—disillusion and resignation in Papini, bitterness and desire to cling to American literary fame in Carnevali. While *Un Uomo Finito* closed a phase in Papini's continuing career, Carnevali's *Autobiography* was his final effort before death, silence, and oblivion.

In his final effort, Carnevali collected the different ideas and words that he encountered into a series of fragments, which would later be compiled into more or less coherent book-like entities. The *Autobiography*'s fragmentary nature is made more complicated by the fact that Carnevali's book is an intercultural autobiography, a form of text establishing a peculiar relation between the individual and the canon(s):

> [It] is an amalgam of two cultures and sundry canons, but the only bridge spanning them is one individual, this singular self with uniquely intercultural perspectives and experience. (Hokenson 1995, 99)

On the other hand, the intercultural autobiography owes its existence to the "individual" as "bridge" connecting the multiple linguistic and cultural elements. The translational aspects of Carnevali's *Autobiography* set him apart from the Italian lyric autobiographers whom he had briefly translated (Papini, but also Slataper's *Il mio Carso* bears some indirect similarities) and turn the fragments into a sample of intercultural communication. The *Autobiography* does not simply communicate elements from one culture to another: it is written in English. Carnevali's fragments are positioned at the very end of his adventure through languages. They call into being the English-speaking Other that will in turn validate them: "the ear of the other says *me* to me" and "constitutes the *autos* of my autobiography" (Derrida 1985, 51, my emphasis). The existence of an English-language readership is the abstract pretext for writing, in correlation to the very concrete pretext of Boyle's editorial "ear." The choice of language could not be more central to Carnevali's memoir. Studies on autobiographical narrations by bilinguals have found evidence that bilinguals "produce different autobiographical narratives in their respective languages, and experience difficulties in translating the same memories and experiences into the other language" (Pavlenko 2014, 188). Of course, Carnevali never wrote an Italian version of his *Autobiography*, but in choosing to write in English, he had to overcome several linguistic constraints to tell a story that did not take place entirely in English. The language of the *Autobiography* exists in continuous negotiation between the subject matter (the Italian cultural setting, Carnevali's thoughts and impressions) and the target language of his choice.

The first installment of the *Autobiography* appeared in an anthology whose foreword declared that the artists in the collection may have chosen Europe for their residences, but "their service [was] dedicated to American art," and "the results of their arduous efforts" were "America's" (Neagoe 1932, xi). In Carnevali's case, this results in a dialogue with the American readership on Italian matters. For example, he follows an allusion to the fact that the author and a childhood friend "used to do dirty things together" with a comment that "this is a little thing I warn those American prudes who would make of it a big thing" (1932, 78). The comment acts as paradoxical link between an Italian subject matter and American audience, functioning much like the short stories of the late 1920s (the "Rubazziana" stories as well as "A History") to present Italian culture to America while reinforcing Carnevali's position as outsider in Italian society.

Carnevali's ongoing dialogue with the American audience in the "First God" takes the form of explanations about life in the small Italian towns of his childhood. After leaving Florence (of which, as we have seen, the author shows only a "white" hospital room), the narration then moves to less famous towns—Pistoia in Tuscany, and Biella and the village of Cossato in Piedmont. This personal geography is explained through similes and brief digressions addressing an English-speaking world. Pistoia is described as a "dead little town," while the industrial town of Biella is presented with a British analogy: "the Italian Manchester, tremendously industrious and variously industrial" (E. Carnevali 1932, 75). Nevertheless, this industrial town is divided into "Biella the High and Biella the Low" (1932, 79), referring to a common division of Italian towns between an upper fortified part and a lower modern part. Its geography is translated, and the town is given a street called Independence Street (1932, 79). Names like "Biella the High" and "Independence Street" do not exist in real-life Biella but are central to Carnevali's reframing of the place in an English linguistic environment.

This translated geography explores the same provincial Italy of Carnevali's Bazzano stories. Catholicism has a place in the narration, with its quasi-pagan rural aspects to be explained to Americans. One of the few images that Carnevali retains from the part of his childhood that he spent in Pistoia is the "congregation of the BROTHERS OF

MERCY" (E. Carnevali 1932, 78, author's emphasis). This religious group, which attends funerals in long robes and hoods, is likened by the author to "the great Spanish inquisitioners . . . in the olden days," using an image that might be more popular among the English-speaking public. Carnevali's relationship with religion is always uneasy, in his childhood as in his adult life: "these fools scared me stiff every time I saw them." As in the other Bazzano works, his treatment of Italian Catholicism is irreverent—the Oropa sanctuary near Biella is included as a place "where one may go and stay for fifteen days at a stretch without paying a cent for one's room" (1932, 79) as well as the main reason for building a rope railway that he fears would destroy the countryside (1932, 80). At the same time, elements from Italian Catholic speech are ingrained in the text, like the "eterno riposo" (*Lat.* "Requiem Æternam," usually translated in English-language Catholic liturgy as "eternal rest"), which appears in the story of Carnevali's aunt: "surely death had given her no repose" (1932, 81).

Places are also an important part of the construction of this language. Carnevali uses "villa" in the sense of "country house" and "pension" (80) to mimic the Italian *pensione*, a kind of boardinghouse. The sense of being in the presence of a bilingual struggling to balance different and contrasting linguistic repertoires is as strong as in the Bazzano works. The author's near-death experience shortly after his birth is described as an event that "carried [him] near to the grave" (1932, 75), an expression that literally translates the Italian *portare (quasi) alla tomba*. The author's cousins are described as "brigands" (1932, 81)—in Italian, the word *brigante* may mean "brigand" but also "scoundrel"—and the younger cousin is indicated as the "smaller cousin" (E. Carnevali 1932, 78), a translation of the Italian *il più piccolo* (*piccolo* meaning "young" or "small" depending on the context). This is the last stage of Carnevali's translingual journey. Carnevali finds himself within the constraints of a language that was at the same time the alien language (thanks to his increasingly loose ties to the English-speaking world) and completely his own: a language in which no one else was writing, forged through two passages across the Atlantic.

This type of language is also evident in the chapters of the *Autobiography* that he wrote after 1932, which the general public would be able to read only in 1967 after Boyle pieced it together and rearranged it. Even in such a composite work, however, the language of Carnevali's

Bazzano years finds its way to the surface of the text, showing continuity in terms of linguistic interference.

Many passages of the *Autobiography* are translations of various characters' Italian speech, reported in the text. Such is the case of a passenger on Carnevali's ship, who prays to the "Eternal Father" (1967, 69), a literal translation of the Italian *padreterno*, a common way to address God. Other cases of linguistic interference result in the quite literal translation of Italian idioms. He defines his younger self as "a little lion unchained" (1967, 44), with "unchained" translating the Italian *scatenato*, which has assumed the idiomatic meaning of "wild." His father's harsh comment on his decision to emigrate "filled the cup to the brim" (1967, 58), literally translating *la goccia che fa traboccare il vaso* (an idiom similar in meaning to the English "the last straw"). In another passage, the poet courts a young girl in New York, but she leaves him "alone with a fistful of flies" (1967, 97), which renders an Italian idiom (*con un pugno di mosche*) indicating the condition of being empty-handed. The text sometimes uses elements of Italian vocabulary, translated into English, for their metaphorical implications—dormant in Italian, where they have been part of the vocabulary for too long, but reactivated in translation. The procedure is sometimes foregrounded and introduced by the authorial voice: "The waves were what one calls in Italian 'Cavalloni,' equal to 'Great Horses,' so solid they were, large, majestic waves, grey-green" (1967, 69). Elsewhere their metaphorical meaning is implied as it would be if the text were written in Italian, as is the case when Carnevali recalls reading to William Carlos Williams his "latest parturition" (1967, 139)—meaning his latest poem, the latest parturition of his brain. In this case, the Anglophone reader is left to figure out the metaphorical implications of the word.

The text of the *Autobiography* in its earlier installments as well as in Kay Boyle's rearrangement of the whole work presents elements of tension between Italian and English. While the presence of Italianate phrases and expressions in the 1932 chapters—those extensively dealing with Italy—may have been dictated by the need to convey an idea of Italy to an intended American public, there are also several examples of Italian interference in the parts of the text that deal with America. In New York, Carnevali recalls receiving "a card from Europe advising [him] that [his] brother was in New York too" (1967, 85). The meaning of "advise" here is in fact closer to the Italian *avvisare*, "to notify." At the same time, he defines Harriet Monroe ironically as a "she-professor of English" (E. Carnevali 1967, 157), as if he needed to convey the difference between the masculine *professore* and the feminine *professoressa*, which could not be communicated with the English "professor."

Carnevali's language in the *Autobiography* is influenced by Italian when describing and reporting events that took place in Italy, yet the influence also permeates parts of the narration that take place in the United States. Carnevali had strong personal reasons for writing his memoir in English but was immersed in an Italian-speaking environment while writing. Judging from the thematic and stylistic links between his life-writing and testimonies of his life at the time of writing, this environment had an impact on the act of writing the autobiography. Some of the Italianate words in the narration ("Eternal Father" for *padreterno* or "pension" for *pensione*) actually relate to words heard in Italian at the time. Other Italianate expressions, such as idioms, reflect Carnevali's personal reflections on the episodes ("with a fistful of flies"). Their presence in the English text reflects a relationship with the English language that tended to stretch the limits of language to include linguistic elements from Italian, confirming the impression of a tormented relationship with language itself that is visible in other Bazzano works.

Carnevali's autobiographical fragments are contemporary with other "ethnic" autobiographies produced after the great wave of migration to America in the late nineteenth and early twentieth centuries—defined by Karpinski as "literacy narratives." Such autobiographies are linked to "the rhetoric of assimilation that dominated discussion about immigration early in the century" (Karpinski 2012, 42). These early stories of immigrant hardships and determination often have the author's successful integration (and acquisition of English) as their goal, representing "a Bildungsroman of acculturation" (Hron 2009, 18). By contrast, Carnevali's *Autobiography* contained the story of how a young man emigrated in search of fulfilment and became a published poet in New York and Chicago. As I demonstrated in chapter 2, Carnevali was preoccupied with his status as migrant, but undecided as to whether he could be placed on the same level with the other migrants he met. Most importantly, the book also contains the story of his crisis, failure, and subsequent return—as opposed to the stories of successful integration of other early immigrant autobiographers such as Mary Antin or Constantine Panunzio. The story is told in a language that reflects the author's changed attitude to language following his sickness and repatriation. The work, from his first 1932 installments, is preoccupied with Carnevali's fading status in the literary milieu as much as his status as migrant—and it may even contain a nod to the dormant, unrecognized canon of translingual authors of world literature. As he narrates his first trip across Italy in the "First God," he claims he saw the sea for the first time. The sick, aging writer Carnevali recognizes the sea of his childhood as already being "the sea of Ulysses and Herman Melville" (1932, 75). This attempt to write the sea into literature, and particularly into an account of his own entrance into literature, may also be connected to his identification of the sea with another translingual author. The sea is "the sea of that bourgeois, Conrad, and my own sea manufactured by my own imagination and by its presence" (E. Carnevali 1932, 75). Conrad, possibly the most famous translingual to write in English in Carnevali's time, is evoked as a rival. We may take this as a hint of a translingual dialectic, as translingual writers have sometimes been described as constituting a canon of their own in which they implicitly discuss their condition of "doppelgangers, veritable secret sharers of translingual virtuosity"[28] (Kellman 2000, 39). Carnevali's last works do not fail to signify his peculiar transcultural situation and the evolution of his translingualism, even if the author's preoccupation with his descent into sickness and oblivion is at their core.

Carnevali's life does not progress but comes full circle as the autobiographic fragments establish a link between the Italy he experienced as a troubled child and the Italy he narrated as a sick returning emigrant, with the American years in the middle. Such circularity is present in the way he frames his childhood, but it is made possible in book form by the effort of his editor—his original "ear" in Derrida's sense of the word. The commitment of a few dedicated people who had personal relationships with Carnevali—or who were fascinated by the bohemian, uprooted poet figure he represented—ensured his place in literary history. The work of Boyle, Stivender, and Maria Pia Carnevali made possible the inclusion of Carnevali in the tentative canon of Italian-American intellectuals, as well as sparked interest in Italy. Such recognition came because of Carnevali's unique life story and his claim to transnational dimensions at a time in which such links had yet to be recognized between the Italian community in America and the rest of the world. The *Autobiography*, in spite of its composite, fragmented nature, is what carved Carnevali's relatively small niche in twentieth-century literature. The book is made of auto-fiction, poetry, and criticism. It responds to the tropes of immigrant autobiography in the United States, while unsettling them from the point of view of the migrant's sickness, repatriation, and linguistic idiosyncrasies. It attempts to situate Carnevali in the modernist canon while debating the modernist experience. It provides closure with its last paragraph (in Boyle's version), in which Carnevali begs "Lady Death" to come closer, as he wants to "stammer a few words in [her] ear" (1967, 260). At the same time, the *Autobiography* continues an unfinished and provocative conversation between the canons (the Italian canon, the American canon, the Italian-American canon, the modernist canon, and the immigrant canon—if there is such a thing). The book *is*, in one word, Carnevali.

Conclusion

Emanuel Carnevali in the 21st Century

What does it mean to be writing about Emanuel Carnevali a little more than a century after he landed in New York? At the start of this volume I emphasized that it does not necessarily mean to rediscover him: scholars and intellectuals have been "rediscovering" him since the 1960s. At the present time, he is a niche figure in Italian and American cultures, but a recognized and appreciated one. In 2014, Columbia University organized a symposium in New York dedicated exclusively to Carnevali. In the same year, author and musician Emidio Clementi (who already dedicated a good part of his 2004 novel *L'ultimo dio* to his admiration for Carnevali) used texts by Carnevali for his show *Notturno Americano*, representing the Italian versions of *Il primo dio* in a work halfway between poetry reading and rock opera. The question now is not how to bring Carnevali to the public; rather, it is necessary to find the real significance of his brief and yet complex career and his place in the areas of interest of Italian studies, Italian-American literature, and modernist studies.

In the analysis of Carnevali's relationship with English and Italian, I have closely followed the evolution of a translingual author's language in relation to suprahuman entities and cultural constructs such as Italian and American cultures, literary tradition, or the modernist milieu. The focus has been on the creation of a language under conditions of cultural difference. In the last two decades, scholars have acknowledged how cultural difference opens the possibility for "new forms of meaning and strategies of communication," as it "interpellate[s] forms of identity which, because of their continual implication in different symbolic systems, are always 'incomplete' or open to cultural translation" (Bhabha

1994, 162–63). The problem with definitions of cultural translation such as Bhabha's is that, for their insistence on semiotic systems and cultures as texts, they fail to address "the passage from interlingual translation to cultural translation" (Wagner 2012, 64), although they still maintain that cultural translation has a performative quality.

The analysis of Carnevali's work has demonstrated that, for all the different strategies that a translingual author may assume, and for all the forms that translingual writing may take, the text comes into being through operations of positioning within (or against) more than one culture. These operations can be rooted in the author's background on a deeply personal level: Carnevali's relationship with his father was instrumental to his decision to write in English, although that also involved a view of Italian culture as backwards and conservative. Operations of positioning and repositioning include criticism as well as a discussion with the literary milieu through fiction and poetry, as seen in Carnevali's different treatments of the linguistic outsider in the various media.

Entering American literature as an outsider, Carnevali challenged the idea of cultural belonging on multiple levels. He made his cultural alterity a recognizable feature of his role in American modernism, while struggling with images of *italianità* that were projected onto him. Carnevali's work while in America poses his Italian identity as an open question, problematizing his relationship with the literary canon as well as the Italian migrant community.

The analysis has demonstrated that the operations of cultural repositioning, of adaptation to a new context, are interwoven with a number of linguistic and textual strategies, which were all at work at determinate points of Carnevali's career and evolved accordingly to his goal as well as the context. The main textual strategy allowing Carnevali to perform cultural translation was translingualism—which in itself includes several different, even conflicting strategies. At the end of her study on writers who went *Beyond the Mother Tongue*, Yildiz remarked on the lack of a singular "postmonolingual paradigm" and on the several ways to be a multilingual author (2012, 201). The analysis of Carnevali's works show that this variety can exist even in different texts by a single author. His American works signify an attempt at linguistic assimilation, but at the same time present stylistic elements that seem to point toward a common ground between Italian and English from which he crafted his American language. My treatment of translingualism has focused on the relationship between literary and cultural factors and the building of a literary language by navigating such factors. The analysis intended to counter totalizing ideas of linguistic assimilation or irredeemable difference by delving into the complex patterns of assimilation and resistance through which Carnevali entered American literature.

The evolution of the translingual language in a changing context is particularly evident and traumatic in Carnevali, determined as it was by sickness and repatriation, but, as we have seen, it generated texts that never lost touch with their literary and translational goals. The resulting language is evidently a product of the multiple cultural and linguistic border crossings that generated it; Carnevali may not have been in complete control of his linguistic media at the time (as the *Cantos* translations seem to attest), but the language he created was fertile and unique nonetheless. At the end of his life, he used this language to tell the story of how the language itself came into being, thus coming full circle.

My analysis of translingualism has focused almost exclusively on Carnevali, and it is important to stress the uncompromising individuality and specificity of the cultural and personal constraints that generated it. Carnevali's language may be best understood as a textual response to a particular cluster of constraints, which are evident in the text as Carnevali navigates the problem of being an Italian among the New York modernists, or a returning migrant author in Italy. If the text testifies mostly to the process that led Carnevali to write his own brand of English, it is also true that its analysis enlarges our understanding of a much wider range of critical issues, such as the development of Italian-American literature or ethnic presence in modernism.

Carnevali was involved with the beginning of Italian-American literature long before the question of its definition was posed. Carnevali did not engage with the collective dimension of the nascent Italian-American literature, as seen in his problematic treatment of the Italian-American community. Yet he mentioned and referred to the possibility of a culture that was both Italian and American even while declining to be its spokesperson. This ambivalent and problematic presence proved enough, over the decades, for Italian poets in America to place him at the beginning of their literary genealogies, as we have seen (Valesio 1993, 276; Fontanella 2003, 13). The fact that he could be inserted retrospectively into the canon of Italian-American literature means that, although most of his artistic efforts fell into oblivion at the time, their significance could be manifest once a general framework existed for where to place him.

Carnevali's progressive rediscovery goes hand in hand with the rediscovery of "African Americans, European immigrants, and members of other minority groups" who "participated in, and significantly advanced, the course of modernism in the United States" (Sollors 2008, 12), inserting him into a wider context of ethnic modernisms. As scholars increasingly find connections between canonical modernisms and their minority counterparts, Carnevali assumes significance: not just as the Italian whose work was acknowledged by modernists but as the figure who facilitates an understanding of American modernism from a migrant's and an Italian's point of view. The same applies to Carnevali's links with Italian modernism, an entity that only recently gained scholars' attention under this particular denomination, opening up comparisons of early twentieth-century Italian literature with contemporary global modernisms. Carnevali's work represents one of the very few points of contact between American and Italian modernisms as part of his unique point of view. Even though his work of translational connection did not have a large impact at the time, he can still be used to demonstrate similarities and differences between the Italian and Anglophone brands of modernism.

Carnevali's surviving body of work may be centered exclusively on the personal vicissitudes of the author, but its analysis makes it possible to reconsider several cultural entities as open containers in continuous definition as Carnevali asserts his individuality with respect to them. Writers who work outside national borders "cannot be bound by national borders, languages, and literary and critical traditions," but rather they "seek to name and configure cultural and literary production in their own terms and to enter novel forms of inter/transcultural dialogue" (Seyhan 2000, 4). The analysis of Carnevali's work brings such forms of dialogue to the forefront, enabling us to devise different forms of similarities and allegiances not only in synchronic, but also in diachronic fashion. In fact, part of present-day interest in Carnevali may be linked to the study of similarly bound-less, transnational writers across history.

Once the scholarly community has acknowledged that it is often "the permanent quantum duality of cultural experience that is the norm rather than homogenous national or imperial continuums occasionally disrupted by foreign adventures" (Cronin 2006, 26), it becomes possible to see Carnevali as one sample in a global flow that exists across time and space. A necessary premise for translingual studies is the acknowledgement that translingual authorship has in fact been the norm for millennia (Forster 1970, 1); the significance of translingualism in the present debate is on the other hand that of acknowledging the voices of those who live by crossing linguistic and political borders and find expression in a language that is not perceived as fully "their own."

Thus, Carnevali becomes not an exception, but a figure that demands its status in the global forum (together with the other migrants and translinguals) as well as a role in a transnational understanding of Italian culture. Carnevali stands out in the transnational discussion of Italian studies by virtue of his presence within modernism (as an outsider yet a recognizable presence) and his status within Italian America (a complex pattern of identification and rejection). The space "carved out within a broadened Italian canon for literary texts written by first, second, and subsequent generations of Italian migrants abroad" (Bond 2014, 419) is instrumental for a transnational definition of Italian culture with links to other seemingly unrelated aspects of the same field, such as contemporary migration into Italy and colonialism. This discussion aims to open up the Italian discourse to the discussion of difference, as well as disrupt through Italian the global hegemonic discourses of world literature (Polezzi 2008). It acknowledges Italy's links with the world, which are inherent to its nature as a nation of emigrants and immigrants, a Mediterranean crucible, and a nation perennially in the making. Carnevali was just an individual who struggled to find his own voice by renegotiating his Italian identity, but he can occupy a place within a migrating canon that opens up and does not eschew renegotiation (as canons usually do) but rather places renegotiations at its center.

Notes

Introduction

1. "Finally, the reason why Carnevali should be acknowledged as ancestor of Italian poets in the United States is that he lived and wrote in the interval or interstice between two different social milieus; that was neither Italian nor American or Italian-American, but truly (that is to say coherently, purely—even with the irresponsibility that often goes together with purity) a poet between two worlds." (All translations in endnotes to be considered mine unless otherwise stated.)

Chapter 1

1. Carnevali to Harriet Monroe, 1 September 1917, in *Poetry: A Magazine of Verse. Records* (Box 43, Folder 11), Special Collections Research Center, University of Chicago Library.

2. The editorial history of *The Autobiography of Emanuel Carnevali* is examined in more detail in chapter 5.

3. Carnevali to Harriet Monroe, September 1, 1917.

4. Carnevali to Monroe, September 1, 1917.

5. Carnevali translated parts of Slataper's book into English in 1919—see chapter 3.

6. "without any doubt more poetic than scientific."

7. For a more detailed analysis of Carnevali's "Tale I" in the context of colonialism and race relations in the United States, see Ciribuco, Andrea. 2019. "'White Queens' and 'Nubian Fiends': Early Italian American Fiction and the Problem of Colonialism." *borderlands e-journal* 18 (1) (forthcoming).

8. According to his biographer, Carnevali was expelled from the Collegio Marco Foscarini in Venice in 1913, possibly for his relationship with Giovanni (Cacho Millet 1994, xix). After that, he moved to Bologna, where he attended

another school. Only in 1914, after the new school principal called Tullio Carnevali to tell him that Emanuel was skipping school, father and son finally had an argument, and Emanuel decided to emigrate.

The causal link, in the *Autobiography*, between Carnevali's expulsion from the Collegio Marco Foscarini and his emigration is in large measure a result of the way in which Boyle has arranged Carnevali's autobiographical writings. In the "Kay Boyle papers, 1914–1987," Special Collections Research Center, Southern Illinois University, Carbondale, there is a version of the chapter ending with Carnevali breaking up with Giovanni (Series 9, Box 86, Folder 3); and another one (closer to the published version) in which the incident is followed by Carnevali falling out with his father and deciding to emigrate (Box 86, Folder 8). It is possible that Boyle rearranged Carnevali's chapters in a way that would highlight the link between Carnevali's rebellion and his decision to emigrate. In any case, contrasts between father and son were considered by the author as the main reason for emigration, as stated in the aforementioned 1917 letter to Harriet Monroe.

9. According to Cacho Millet, Augusto and Emanuel Carnevali actually emigrated together in 1914 (1994, xx). Yet in the narration of the *Autobiography*, Carnevali tells of how Augusto joined him after some time.

10. "The signifier's autonomy as a pole of attraction for the foreign poet."

Chapter 2

1. Associate editor Helen Hoyt wrote on the envelope, "Wonderful stuff but not to be put in Poetry or any magazine." In *Poetry: A Magazine of Verse. Records* (Box 32), Special Collections Research Center, University of Chicago Library.

2. Carnevali to Monroe, March 1919, in *Poetry: A Magazine of Verse. Records* (Box 32), Special Collections Research Center, University of Chicago Library.

3. In a passage, Williams mentions Carnevali going into "an acute mania" after receiving a rejection slip from *The Dial*, "attack[ing] insanely not the proprietor but an editor and say[ing] ALL the true things that should be said about an editor of such a magazine" (1919, 4).

4. Carnevali to Monroe, 1917 (month and day unknown), in *Poetry: A Magazine of Verse. Records* (Box 32, Folder 14), Special Collections Research Center, University of Chicago Library.

5. Carnevali to Monroe, answered February 1, 1918, *Poetry: A Magazine of Verse. Records* (Box 32, Folder 14), Special Collections Research Center, University of Chicago Library.

6. It is significant that the only apparently positive image of New York in his early poetry is in his 1919 "Variation" on Synge's *The Playboy of the Western World* (1907). The poem gives voice to an unnamed character, possibly the "Playboy" Christy Mahon, talking about his dream of moving to New York. Synge hints repeatedly that his character would flee Ireland eventually: in Carnevali's variation, he imagines a future in America: "It's New York I tell you . . ." (l. 1). Carnevali hints at an empowering transformation, in a "city that lives / with work / for men stronger than I / with duties / for a different conscience than mine" (ll. 12–17). The poem depicts a migrant's fantasy, not the migrant's reality: the New York home imagined by the character has "roses / from the roof down" (l. 5). A migrant with some years of experience in the city, Carnevali was aware of the reality of immigrant neighborhoods—as is evident from his description of tenement life in "The Day of Summer" or the "Tales of a Hurried Man."

7. Carnevali to Monroe, March 18, 1919, in *Poetry: A Magazine of Verse. Records* (Box 32), Special Collections Research Center, University of Chicago Library.

8. "Myth is still in action, or at least the psychological condition relating to myth is."

9. Carnevali to Monroe, April 17, 1918, in *Poetry: A Magazine of Verse. Records* (Box 32, Folder 14), Special Collections Research Center, University of Chicago Library. In 2006, Dennis Barone called his edition of Carnevali's poems and essays *Furnished Rooms*.

10. "Fascinated by the open writing of gigantic advertising banners, and shop signs."

11. Carnevali to Harriet Monroe, September 1, 1917, in *Poetry: A Magazine of Verse. Records* (Box 43, Folder 11), Special Collections Research Center, University of Chicago Library.

12. Carnevali, "Lean Woman" (unpublished, probably 1919), in Mitchell Dawson Papers (Box 21, Folder 699), The Newberry Library, Chicago.

13. Carnevali, "from The Day of Spring" (unpublished, probably 1919), in Mitchell Dawson Papers (Box 22, Folder 703), The Newberry Library, Chicago.

14. Boyle actually quotes it at this point of the *Autobiography*, creating a short-circuit between different stages of auto-narration.

15. Carnevali to Monroe, answered February 1, 1918, in *Poetry: A Magazine of Verse. Records* (Box 32, Folder 14), Special Collections Research Center, University of Chicago Library.

16. Carnevali to Monroe, March 1919, in *Poetry: A Magazine of Verse. Records* (Box 32), Special Collections Research Center, University of Chicago Library. Emphasis in the original.

17. Carnevali, "Lean Woman" (unpublished, probably 1919), in Mitchell Dawson Papers (Box 21, Folder 699), The Newberry Library, Chicago.

18. "English infused with a Latin vitality, almost Florentine I would say."

19. "Linguistic disguise."

20. "Behind the self-proclaimed American poet there always were Italian words and instinct."

21. "Radically alien phonemes."

22. Carnevali's notebooks of sketches and drafts include Italian phrases among other random jottings—and the fragment of a short poem in Italian, dedicated to a child in his neighborhood ("il bimbo Howard").

One piece of writing in the "Orders" notebook bears the crossed-out Italian title "Prolegomeni di un [sic] arte della ribellione" above its English title, "Poetic Pragmatism—Prolegomena of an Enacted Art of Rebellion." The poem is left unfinished after six lines, and its Italian title is an exception among Carnevali's drafts (Mitchell Dawson Papers [Box 22, Folder 703], The Newberry Library, Chicago).

23. Fowlie's 1966 translation of the whole stanza reads: "The young man, facing the ugliness of this world, / Shudders in his heart deeply irritated, / And, filled with the eternal inner wound, / Begins to desire his sister of charity."

24. The definition comes from "The Translator's Task" by Walter Benjamin, to whom Bhabha's reflection is directly linked.

Chapter 3

1. Parts of sections 3.1 and 3.2 appeared in their earlier forms as Ciribuco, Andrea. 2013. "Carnevali's Cultural Translation: Modernism, Dante and the Italian America." *Scritture Migranti* 7: 43–63.

2. Introducing himself to Monroe, Carnevali wrote that he "had studied in Turin, Venice and Bologna: technical schools (I do not know Latin and Greek)." (Carnevali to Monroe, September 1, 1917, *Poetry: A Magazine of Verse. Records* (Box 43, Folder 11), Special Collections Research Center, University of Chicago Library. He saw this fact as a shortcoming in comparison with the Italian intellectuals he had in mind, who generally studied Latin and Greek at a *liceo classico* (grammar school).

3. This Italian name is usually spelled "Oronzo." It is possible that this was a typo not recognized by Boyle.

4. Another anecdote possibly links Carnevali with Italian gangs in New York, although it is virtually impossible to prove. In her preface to *A Hurried Man*, Dudley speaks of the author's days of poverty, including a time when he went to "the lower end of town" and "found a small place for himself in a gang of crooks, who kept him going until again he had a waiter's job" (1925, 2). The episode is not found elsewhere, and it was possibly a rumor or an exaggeration on Carnevali's part. If it did happen, Carnevali excluded it from subsequent narrations of his life—and he was generally quite candid in retelling his thorny episodes.

5. D. Dudley, "Foreword to *Religious Stammering—An Autobiography*" (unpublished, presumably 1933). "Kay Boyle papers, 1914–1987" (Box 86, Folder 6), Special Collections Research Center, Southern Illinois University, Carbondale.

6. This and subsequent quotations are from "Fragments of a short story concerning Marcello at the Rale Club" in Mitchell Dawson Papers (Box 22), The Newberry Library, Chicago.

7. Italian curse: "By the Holy Mary."

8. Carnevali, "Lean Woman" (unpublished, probably 1919), in Mitchell Dawson Papers (Box 21, Folder 699), The Newberry Library, Chicago.

9. Carnevali, "My Home," (presumably) 1919, in Mitchell Dawson Papers (Box 21, Folder 696), The Newberry Library, Chicago.

10. "What is good in America" . . . "neither Giovannitti nor Ruotolo."

11. "I translated badly, for Mr. J. E. Spingarn, your *Breviary of Aesthetics*."

12. Dahlberg, Edward. "A memoir [of Emanuel Carnevali] Typescript (copy)," unsigned and undated. In New York Public Library, Henry W. and Albert A. Berg Collection of English and American Literature, Kay Boyle collection of papers, 1925–1988 (bulk 1952–1986).

13. ". . . in the Public Library I discovered all the issues of *La Voce*, and that left me very hungry for Italian stuff."

14. See Adamson 2004, 225–26.

15. "It is about giving back to Italy its contact with European culture, as well as the historical awareness of its own culture, which is after all such a great part of European culture. I shall be content with a few words: nationalists no, Italians yes!"

16. "This will be good publicity for you—and if someone will ever translate your books for an American publisher (perhaps I will have the time to do it myself) I will be honored to tell you that I, more or less, generated the interest among the American (il)literary audience."

17. "They need to know Palazzeschi, Govoni, Jahier, and Soffici. If I don't do that, nobody will."

18. "Fra poco sarò uno degli editori di un piccolo periodico 'Poetry'. . . . Lo voglio fare internazionale—Mi aiuti, vuole?" (1981, 68). ("Soon I shall be one of the editors of a little review 'Poetry'. . . . I want to make it international—could you help me?") Note that the translingual Carnevali used the words "piccolo periodico" as a literal translation of the English phrase "little review."

19. *La Vraie Italie* was a French-language journal of Italian culture and literature edited by Papini and Soffici in the years 1919–1920.

20. "A little Italianate professor."

21. "Small, chaotic and *wretched magazines* [in English in the source] are all ready and very happy to accept translations."

22. "We will have an exchange with those Italian and French journals that interest us."

23. *Poetry* had already dedicated a short article of praise to the Florentine review in 1917. Walter Pach had praised *La Voce*, declaring it the most promising place to look for heirs to Carducci, D'Annunzio, and Pascoli; and calling the magazine "distinctly modern in its whole viewpoint" while managing to "combat . . . , at least in many instances, the excesses of the futurists" (1917, 52).

24. Carnevali leaves this difficult-to-translate term in Italian. It is fundamental to the vocabulary of Futurism, indicating "those who love the past," often in a derogatory sense.

25. The translation ended up, among other drafts, in Mitchell Dawson Papers (Box 22, Folder 706), The Newberry Library, Chicago. The typescript appears ready for publication, also bearing Carnevali's New York address at the top of the page—which allows us to date the manuscript to early 1919, the time of the other translations.

26. "The soul of our flame."

27. Carnevali, "The Incendiary," translation of Palazzeschi's "L'incendiario." Unpublished typescript, probably 1919, Mitchell Dawson Papers (Box 22, Folder 706), The Newberry Library, Chicago.

28. Carnevali, "Half Hour," manuscript translation of Papini, "Mezz'ora," in Mitchell Dawson Papers (Box 22, Folder 703), The Newberry Library, Chicago.

29. Carnevali, "Half Hour," manuscript translation of Papini, "Mezz'ora," in Mitchell Dawson Papers (Box 22, Folder 703), The Newberry Library, Chicago.

30. Carnevali, "My Home," [presumably] 1919, in Mitchell Dawson Papers (Box 21, Folder 696), The Newberry Library, Chicago.

31. "Pretentious marionettes of my inner theatre."

32. "When we used to look at the city spreading out cowardly on the shores of the slow river and we used to say: you will be ours."

33. "But now I feel like starting a fire which may not be quenched and may set fire to the world."

34. "I dived headfirst into all the reading that my proliferating curiosities suggested me."

35. "So I, on a gray Winter's morning, married Fame."

36. "I cried over a simple and bare biography of Mazzini."

37. Fracassa (2005, 138) also recently advanced the hypothesis that Carnevali reprised famous lines from other Italian poets of his time, such as Sbarbaro and Corazzini.

38. "And maybe I won't translate *Un uomo finito*. Why do I always make promises?"

39. "Please don't be angry at me again. If I was insolent, I deeply regret it." Cacho Millet, in his edition of the letters, expresses his opinion that Papini was angry at Carnevali for having criticized some articles about America in *La Vraie Italie*.

40. "Unknown American brother of ours—of us from *La Voce*, I mean."

41. "[A look] more penetrating than that of so many professors, especially for a time in which the issue was discovering new values and not confirming or following them."

42. . . . "under many aspects could have 'talked with me.'"

Chapter 4

1. Carnevali to Dawson, August 30, 1920, in NLC Dawson, Box 4, Folder 273: "Syphilis, hell!—those profane doctors! I have had the most beautiful disease this side of heaven. Tell that to everybody you meet who knows me." Cacho Millet is of the opinion that Carnevali caught syphilis from a prostitute shortly after his breakup with Annie Glick (1994, xxvi).

2. Another possible reference, in terms of modernist *Bildungsroman*, comes from his Italian model Papini. *Un uomo finito* featured a chapter on "La conquista della divinità" (the conquest of Godhead). The episode is told in a more philosophical tone than Carnevali's: there is no psychotic crisis, no sleepless nights spent wandering in the streets of the city: instead, a period of reflection and readings convinces Papini that the power of human will could be enough to attain divine status. Papini claims that he thought, at one point in his project, that he believed in everyone's possibility to become a god (1913, 186). Papini's project included the creation of a religion of the "Uomo-Dio" ("Man-God"), and quite interestingly he wanted to found it "nella vasta America"("in vast America") (1913, 187). Before renouncing this idea, Papini went as far as recruiting companions, learning English, and raising funds for what he had imagined as an evangelical mission. Unlike Carnevali's episode, Papini's tale of apotheosis and self-abasement is a philosophical parable. Still, in those pages, Carnevali had read about the possibility that a poet might aspire to godhead—a notion that was also central to the work of his other models, such as Nietzsche.

3. See https://www.ninds.nih.gov/Disorders/All-Disorders/Encephalitis-Lethargica-Information-Page. The illness was recorded only once, during a global epidemic (1917–1928), and never again recurred. The peculiar nature of the disease, as well as the lack of clinical records, makes it difficult to ascertain whether Carnevali had suffered from it from during the 1920 crisis or developed it later on.

4. Carnevali to Monroe, [probably] 1923, in *Poetry: A Magazine of Verse. Records* (Box 32), Special Collections Research Center, University of Chicago Library.

5. The title of the article is itself a translation of *A Hurried Man*.

6. . . . "rebel's life."

7. . . . "with surprising mastery and freshness."

8. There is at least one account of the success of Linati's "Return" translations. The Milan magazine *L'Italia della Domenica* published the 1934 version, claiming that they had received several requests to print the poem after it was read on the radio ("Il Ritorno in Italia di un Emigrante"). It is interesting that an unnamed editor referred, in the introduction, to the "brividi di commozione" ("thrills of emotion") of readers who would find an echo in the poem of the "sofferenze che essi stessi hanno dovuto sopportare" ("sufferings they had to endure themselves"). Carnevali had a potential audience of returned migrants in Italy, but that population was infrequently addressed by mainstream culture.

9. "I am afraid that no mention of this strange poet was ever made in Italy apart from an article which I wrote years ago for *Corriere della Sera* in which I tried to define his bizarre personality as a migrant and an artist."

10. "English and American Writers of Today."

11. "We have had, for more than a decade now, a great poet living around the corner from us, and nobody ever knew it."

12. "Latin liveliness."

13. ". . . was able to win the admiration of the American audience with a powerful breath of Latin soul."

14. "There, Carnevali has a firm, passionate dream: to become a writer. He studies English; within six months he is fluent in the new language: knows its grace, its secrets, its charms, its harmonies. . . . He launches an assault on magazines; his victory is fast and sure. The first dollars come, and drunkenness and joy with them. Curiosity and success; the most illustrious writers welcome and salute, gladly astonished, the young migrant poet. A new voice resonates in American literature, a voice that belongs to us."

15. "I can't write in Italian. A language is a living creature, of blood, sinews, and muscles. One needs to know it. I don't know the Italian language."

16. "Sweet heart of my Jesus, make me love you ever more!" (Carnevali's translation provided in the poem.)

17. Carnevali to Pound, [presumably] 1932, Ezra Pound Papers, Yale Collection of American Literature, Beinecke Rare Book and Manuscript Library (hereafter Yale Beinecke), Series I, Box 8, Folder 344.

18. In the original: "Ridi, pagliaccio / sul tuo amore infranto . . ."

19. See https://www.villabaruzziana.it/.

Chapter 5

1. "A letter to my translator," published in the magazine *L'indice*: *Quindicinale di Lettere, Arti e Scienze*, I, 12, October 1930.

2. Carnevali to Pound, (probably) 1930, Yale Beinecke, Series I, Box 8, Folder 344. All of Carnevali's letters to Pound are from this folder. The letters are all typewritten; they were not dated, and only some show the year when they were probably sent, written in pencil (in this case I give a parenthetical reference of the year). Throughout this chapter I faithfully reproduce the spelling and word spacing used in the letters, which probably reflect Carnevali's tremors due to encephalitis lethargica.

3. I refer to Carnevali's translation of Canto VIII as "Canto Ottavo," while using the academic convention of Pound studies for the original *Cantos*.

4. "Do not generate cascades of complements. Those methods of condensation pertain to Italian."

5. "Naturally, a foreigner cannot direct such a renovation of the language: one needs a native who will forge his own native language."

6. "Naturally, the Italian writer feels trapped, seeing that everyone is asleep, seeing that Italian reviews do not go abroad."

7. "It is well known how things generally go in Italy. Spiritual values from abroad enter, so to speak, in dribs and drabs, in random and almost clandestine fashion; kept up by the beat of the French drum, or by advertisement from some Italian publisher. Eventually, the best ones are always left out."

8. "The rest of Pound's work is a skillful imitation of the Greek, the Latin, the Chinese, the Provençal, the *Dolce Stil Novo*, the modern French, a universal masquerade, a delightful fruit-salad, an aperitif—stimulating, tasteful, wine without strength. 'Amateur' is a harsh word, but I am afraid it aptly describes Pound . . ."

9. Carnevali, "Canto IV" (unpublished, date unknown), Yale Beinecke, Series IV, Box 143, Folder 6280. All quotations from Carnevali's translations of Cantos II–VII are from this folder.

10. For the sake of comparison, Massimo Bacigalupo's 2012 translation is used here as example of modern Italian translation of the XXX Cantos.

11. *Parlare* is usually transitive only when the object is a language: "parlare italiano," "parlare francese," and so on. In fact, Bacigalupo, in his translation, preferred to change the verb into *pronunciare* (utter): "locuste dipartite / *che pronunciavano* gusci di discorsi."

12. "This light-headed, lazy America. With all her efforts toward modernism and art. An old Puritan lady, cutting her *dust-stinking* gown shorter and putting on make-up in the shade of her wonderful-horrible *skyscrapers!*"

13. "Canto XVII."

14. . . . "to prove the historicity of the poem . . . verified by Pound."

15. "I suppose that the twelfth and last fragment does not mean much on its own, but since Pound printed it exactly on its own, here it is in the original version: 'And in August that year died Pope Alessandro Borgia, *il papa morì.*'"

16. It is not possible to ascertain what the misunderstanding really was. The letter starts with Carnevali writing, "Andiamo vecchio mio facciamo la pace" (Come on old friend, let's make up") and refers to an event in which Carnevali admits having been "sanguinosamente offensivo" ("bloodily offensive").

17. "My friend, I would also like to finish the translation of the thirty cantos."

18. Carnevali to Monroe, (probably) January 1930, in *Poetry: A Magazine of Verse. Records* (Box 32), Special Collections Research Center, University of Chicago Library.

19. Series V, Box 144, "Emanuel Carnevali" Watkins Loomis Records, Rare Book & Manuscript Library, Columbia University in the City of New York.

20. In the 1967 *Autobiography*, the chapter would appear as "Annie Glick."

21. Boyle indicates in the preface that, at the time of putting the book together for the 1967 edition, Carnevali's original manuscript was lost (1967, 15). The book's acknowledgements include "a debt of gratitude" to scholar Norman Holmes Pearson "for supplying the typescript of the book, which the editor had made a gift of to him in 1964" (Boyle 1967, 8). It is likely that the original manuscript was lost after Boyle lost touch with Carnevali and that her work on the book in the years 1964–1967 was based on the typescript she had made of the manuscript in the 1930s.

22. "Kay Boyle papers, 1914–1987" (Box 86, Folder 4), Special Collections Research Center, Southern Illinois University, Carbondale.

23. "Kay Boyle papers, 1914–1987" (Box 86, Folder 3), Special Collections Research Center, Southern Illinois University, Carbondale.

24. David Stivender to Kay Boyle, July 29, 1971, New York Public Library, Henry W. and Albert A. Berg Collection of English and American Literature, Kay Boyle collection of papers, 1925–1988 (bulk 1952–1986).

25. In an October 31, 1972, letter to Boyle, Stivender claimed that the method he adopted in rearranging the *Autobiography* was that of removing all parts of the text that had been published in magazines during Carnevali's lifetime. New York Public Library, Henry W. and Albert A. Berg Collection of English and American Literature, Kay Boyle collection of papers, 1925–1988 (bulk 1952–1986).

26. "But God won't speak through my mouth."

27. "I am all soaked with other men's theories, filled to the brim with articles, force-fed with words and images. I am the son of culture, of others, while I would only be a genius, and be myself."

28. Kellman's passage relates to another attack on Conrad on the part of another translingual: Igbo-to-English author Chinua Achebe, who gave his "An Image of Africa: Racism in Conrad's *Heart of Darkness*" lecture in 1975. Achebe's attack on Conrad, writes Kellman, is "all the more severe for the fact

that he and the novella's Polish-English author, Conrad," are both translinguals (2000, 39). The nature of the debate seems to imply that there are many ways and many points of view from which to interpret translingualism and that they often clash because of the individuals' respective strategies and cultural agendas.

Bibliography

Adamson, Walter L. 2004. "Modernism in Florence: The Politics of Avant-Garde Culture in the Early Twentieth Century." In *Italian Modernism*, edited by Mario Moroni and Luca Somigli, 221–42. Toronto: University of Toronto Press.

Ahearn, Barry, ed. 1987. *Pound/Zukofsky. Selected Letters of Ezra Pound and Louis Zukofsky*. New York: James Laughlin.

Albright, Daniel. 1999. "Early Cantos I-XLI." In *The Cambridge Companion to Ezra Pound*, edited by Ira B. Nadel, 59–91. New York: Cambridge University Press.

Amati Mehler, Jacqueline, Simona Argentieri, and Jorge Canestri. 1994. *La Babel de L'inconscient. Langue Maternelle, Langues Étrangères et Psychanalise*. Translated by Maya Garboua. Paris: Presses Universitaires de France.

Anderson, Benedict. 2006. *Imagined Communities. New York*. 2nd ed. London: Verso.

Bacigalupo, Massimo. 1999. "Pound and Montale—Nature, History, Myth." *Journal of Modern Literature* XXIII (1): 45–58.

———. 2012. "Nota Testuale." In *XXX Cantos di Ezra Pound. A cura di Massimo Bacigalupo. Testo originale a fronte*, edited by Massimo Bacigalupo, 31–32. Parma: Guanda.

Ballerini, Luigi. 1978. "Emanuel Carnevali tra autoesibizione e orfismo." In *Il Primo Dio*, edited by Maria Pia Carnevali, 413–33. Milano: Adelphi.

Bassnett, Susan. 1998. "Transplanting the Seed: Poetry and Translation." In *Constructing Cultures: Essays on Literary Translation*, edited by Susan Bassnett and André Lefevere, 57–75. Clevedon: Multilingual Matters.

———. 2002. *Translation Studies*. Edited by Mona Baker. 3rd ed. London: Routledge.

Benjamin, Walter. 1996. "On Language as Such and on the Language of Man." In *Selected Writings*, edited by Marcus Bullock and Michael Jennings, 62–75. Cambridge, MA: Harvard University Press.

Besemeres, Mary. 2002. *Translating One's Self*. Oxford: Peter Lang.

Beyers, Chris. 2001. *A History of Free Verse*. Fayetteville: University of Arkansas Press.

Bhabha, Homi K. 1994. *The Location of Culture*. London: Routledge.

Bloom, Harold. 1997. *The Anxiety of Influence*. 2nd ed. New York: Oxford University Press.

Boelhower, William. 1982. *Immigrant Autobiography in the United States*. Verona: Essedue.

Bond, Emma. 2014. "Towards a Trans-National Turn in Italian Studies?" *Italian Studies* 69 (3): 415–24.

Boyle, Kay. 1967. "Preface." In *The Autobiography of Emanuel Carnevali*, 9–19. New York: Horizon.

Buonomo, Leonardo. 2003. *From Pioneer to Nomad: Essays on Italian North American Writing*. Toronto: Guernica.

Buonomo, Leonardo, and John Paul Russo. 2011. "Forum: The Emerging Canon of Italian-American Literature." *RSA Journal* 21–22: 77–83.

Cacho Millet, Gabriel. 1981. "Emanuel Carnevali: Un discepolo de *La Voce* in esilio." In *Voglio disturbare l'America: Lettere a Benedetto Croce e Giovanni Papini ed altro*, 9–56. Firenze: La Casa Usher.

———. 1994. "Cronologia della vita e dell'opera di Emanuel Carnevali." In *Emanuel Carnevali—Diario bazzanese*, edited by Gabriel Cacho Millet, XVIII–XXXIX. Bazzano (BO): Quaderni della Rocca.

Campbell, Stuart. 1998. *Translation into the Second Language*. London: Longman.

Caparoso Konzett, Delia. 2002. *Ethnic Modernisms*. New York: Palgrave Macmillan.

Carnevali, Emanuel. 1918a. "Colored Lies." *The Forum* (January): 83–84.

———. 1918b. "The Splendid Commonplace." *Poetry, A Magazine of Verse* 11 (6): 298–304.

———. 1918c. "As He Sees It." *Poetry, A Magazine of Verse* 12 (2): 113–15.

———. 1919a. "Five Years of Italian Poetry (1910–1915)." *Poetry, A Magazine of Verse* 13 (4): 209–18.

———. 1919b. "Procession of Beggars." *The Lyric*, February.

———. 1919c. "Arthur Rimbaud." *Others* 5 (4): 20–24.

———. 1919d. "Synge's Playboy of the Western World. Variation." *The Dial* 66 (787): 340.

———. 1919e. "Walt Whitman." *Poetry, A Magazine of Verse* 14 (2): 60.

———. 1919f. "Dancing as an Art." *The Little Review* 6 (2): 26–28.

———. 1919g. "Bogey Man." *Others* 5 (6): 22–23.

———. 1919h. "The Day of Summer." *Poetry, A Magazine of Verse* 14 (6): 314–28.

———. 1919i. "Tales of a Hurried Man, I." *The Little Review* 6 (6): 16–23.

———. 1920a. "Irritation." *Poetry, A Magazine of Verse* 15 (4): 211–21.

———. 1920b. "Tales of a Hurried Man, III." *The Little Review* 6 (10): 28–37.

———. 1920c. "Tales of a Hurried Man, III (Continued)." *The Little Review* 6 (11): 51–58.

————. 1920d. "Immigration and Importation." *Poetry, A Magazine of Verse* 16 (5): 278–79.

————. 1921a. "Our Great Carl Sandburg." *Poetry, A Magazine of Verse* 17 (5): 266–72.

————. 1921b. "Dante—And Today." *Poetry, A Magazine of Verse* 18 (6): 323–27.

————. 1921c. "Neuriade." *Poetry, A Magazine of Verse* 19 (3): 139–45.

————. 1922a. "Giovanni Papini." *The Modern Review*, no. 1, 11.

————. 1922b. "Review: Asia." *Poetry* 20 (6): 346–48.

————. 1924. "The Return." *Poetry, A Magazine of Verse* 24 (2): 85–89.

————. 1925. *A Hurried Man*. Paris: Contact.

————. 1927. "Train of Characters through the Villa Rubazziana." *This Quarter* 1 (4): 141–51.

————. 1928. "Furnished Room Rhapsody." *Poetry, A Magazine of Verse* 32 (4): 180–82.

————. 1929a. "A History." *This Quarter* 1 (4): 127–48.

————. 1929b. "Train of Characters Through the Villa Rubazziana (Continued)." *This Quarter* 1: 107–26.

————. 1932. "The First God. Part I." In *Americans Abroad*, edited by Peter Neagoe, 71–82. The Hague: Servire.

————. 1939. "Excerpt from Autobiography." *Kingdom Come: A Magazine of War-Time Oxford* 1 (1): 16–17.

————. 1967. *Autobiography*. Edited by Kay Boyle. New York: Horizon.

————. 1981. *Voglio disturbare l'America: Lettere a Benedetto Croce e Giovanni Papini ed altro*. Edited by Gabriel Cacho Millet. Firenze: La Casa Usher.

————. 1994. *Saggi e recensioni*. Edited and translated by Gabriel Cacho Millet. Bazzano (BO): Quaderni della Rocca.

————. 2006. *Furnished Rooms*. Edited by Dennis Barone. New York: Bordighera.

Casanova, Pascale. 2004. *The World Republic of Letters*. Translated by M. B. DeBevoise. Cambridge, MA: Harvard University Press.

Casillo, Robert, and John Paul Russo. 2011. "Preface." In *The Italian in Modernity*, edited by Robert Casillo and John Paul Russo, vii–xxx. Toronto: University of Toronto Press.

Churchill, Suzanne W. 2006. *The Little Magazine "Others" and the Renovation of Modern American Poetry*. Aldershot: Ashgate.

Ciribuco, Andrea. 2013. "Carnevali's Cultural Translation: Modernism, Dante and the Italian America." *Scritture Migranti* 7: 43–63

Congiu, Francesca. 2008. "Una parabola letteraria: Il caso di Emanuel Carnevali." PhD diss., Università degli Studi di Cagliari.

Connell, William J. 2010. "Darker Aspects of Italian American Prehistory." In *Anti-Italianism: Essays on a Prejudice*, edited by William J. Connell and Fred L. Gardaphé, 11–22. New York: Palgrave Macmillan.

Corngold, Stanley. 2004. "Kafka and the Dialect of Minor Literature." In *Debating World Literature*, edited by Christopher Prendergast, 272–90. London: Verso.

Courtivron, Isabelle De. 2003. "Introduction." In *Lives in Translation. Bilingual Writers on Identity and Creativity*, edited by Isabelle De Courtivron, 1–10. New York: Palgrave Macmillan.

Cronin, Michael. 2000. *Across the Lines: Travel, Language and Translation*. Cork: Cork University Press.

———. 2006. *Translation and Identity*. London: Routledge.

Dasenbrock, Reed Way. 1991. *Imitating the Italians*. Baltimore: The John Hopkins University Press.

Deleuze, Gilles, and Félix Guattari. 1986. *Kafka: Towards a Minor Literature*. Translated by Dana Polan. Minneapolis: University of Minnesota Press.

Derrida, Jacques. 1985. *The Ear of the Other*. Edited by Christie V McDonald. Translated by Peggy Kamuf. New York: Schocken.

Dewaele, Jean Marc. 2008. "The Emotional Weight of *I Love You* in Multilinguals' Languages." *Journal of Pragmatics* 40 (10): 1753–80.

Di Pietro, Robert J. 1977. "Language, Culture and the Specialist in Ethnic Literature." *MELUS: Multi-Ethnic Literature of the U.S.* 4 (1): 2–7.

Domenichelli, Mario. 1998. "Emanuel Carnevali's 'Great Good Bye.'" In *Beyond the Margin: Readings in Italian Americana*, edited by Paolo A. Giordano, 83–94. Cranbury, NJ: Dickinson.

Dudley, Dorothy. 1925. "Foreword." In *A Hurried Man: Emanuel Carnevali*, edited by Robert McAlmon, 1–10. Paris: Contact.

Eliot, Thomas Stearns. 1964. "Tradition and the Individual Talent." In *Selected Essays*, 2nd ed., 3–11. New York: Harcourt, Brace and World.

Ferraro, Thomas J. 1990. "Avant-Garde Ethnics." In *The Future of American Modernism: Ethnic Writing between the Wars*, edited by William Boelhower, 1–32. Amsterdam: VU University Press.

Finch, Annie. 2000. *The Ghost of Meter: Culture and Prosody in American Free Verse*. 2nd ed. Ann Arbor: University of Michigan Press.

Fink, Guido. 1973. "Le bugie colorate di Emanuel Carnevali." *Paragone* 280: 85–88.

Fontanella, Luigi. 2003. *La parola transfuga: Scrittori italiani in America*. Fiesole: Cadmo.

Ford, Hugh. 1975. *Published in Paris: A Literary Chronicle of Paris in the 1920s and 1930s*. New York: Collier.

Forster, Leonard. 1970. *The Poet's Tongues: Multilinguism in Literature*. Cambridge: Cambridge University Press.

Fracassa, Ugo. 2005. "Carnevali e Hajdari. Paradossi di estraneità." In *Presenze in terra straniera*, edited by Graziella Pagliano, 133–54. Napoli: Liguori.

Garcia, Ofelia, and Li Wei. 2014. *Translanguaging. Language, Bilingualism and Education*. Basingstoke: Palgrave Macmillan.

Gardaphé, Fred L. 1996. *Italian Signs, American Streets*. Durham, NC: Duke University Press.

———. 2004. *Leaving Little Italy: Essaying Italian American Culture.* Albany, NY: State University of New York Press.

———. 2010. "Invisible People. Shadows and Light in Italian American Culture." In *Anti-Italianism: Essays on a Prejudice*, edited by William J. Connell and Fred L. Gardaphé, 1–11. Basingstoke: Palgrave Macmillan.

Gardner-Chloros, Penelope. 2013. "On the Impact of Sociolinguistic Change in Literature: The Last Trilingual Writers in Alsace." *The Modern Language Review* 108 (4): 1086–102.

Gentzler, Edwin. 2008. *Translation and Identity in the Americas.* New York: Routledge.

Gramling, David. 2016. *The Invention of Monolingualism.* London: Bloomsbury.

Grinberg, Leon, and Rebeca Grinberg. 1989. *Psychoanalytic Perspectives on Migration and Exile.* New Haven: Yale University Press.

Grosjean, François. 2008. *Studying Bilinguals.* Oxford: Oxford University Press.

Guglielmo, Jennifer. 2003. "Introduction: White Lies, Dark Truths." In *Are Italians White?*, edited by Jennifer Guglielmo and Salvatore Salerno, 1–16. New York: Routledge.

Guzzetta, Giorgio. 2004. *Nation and Narration. British Modernism in Italy in the First Half of the 20th Century.* Ravenna: Longo.

Harissi, Maria, Emi Otsuji, and Alastair Pennycook. 2012. "The Performative Fixing and Unfixing of Subjectivities." *Applied Linguistics* 33 (5): 524–43.

Hokenson, Jan Walsh. 1995. "Intercultural Autobiography." *Auto/Biography Studies* 10 (1): 92–113.

Hokenson, Jan Walsh, and Marcella Munson. 2007. *The Bilingual Text.* Manchester: St. Jerome.

Hron, Madelaine. 2009. *Translating Pain.* Toronto: University of Toronto Press.

Inghilleri, Moira. 2017. *Translation and Migration.* New York: Routledge.

Izzo, Carlo. 1956. "23 Lettere e 9 cartoline inedite di Ezra Pound." *Nuova Corrente*, 5–6: 123–54.

Jørgensen, J. Normann. 2008. "Introduction: Polylingual Languaging Around and Among Children and Adolescents." *International Journal of Multilingualism* 5 (3): 161–77.

Jung Palandri, Angela. 1972. "Ezra Pound and His Italian Critics." *Tamkang Review* III (2): 41–56.

Karpinski, Eva C. 2012. *Borrowed Tongues: Life Writing, Migration and Translation.* Waterloo, Ontario: Wilfrid Laurier University Press.

Kellman, Steven G. 2000. *The Translingual Imagination.* Lincoln: University of Nebraska Press.

Kenner, Hugh. 1975. *The Pound Era.* London: Faber.

Kessner, Thomas. 1977. *The Golden Door: Italian and Jewish Immigrant Mobility in New York City 1880–1915.* New York: Oxford University Press.

Kövecses, Zoltán. 2002. *Metaphor.* Oxford: Oxford University Press.

Lefevere, André. 1992. *Translation, Rewriting, and the Manipulation of Literary Fame*. London: Routledge.

Levenson, Michael. 2011. *Modernism*. New Haven: Yale University Press.

Li Wei. 2018. "Translanguaging as a Practical Theory of Language." *Applied Linguistics* 39 (1): 9–30.

Linati, Carlo. 1925. "Un uomo che ha fretta." *Corriere della Sera*, September 25.

———. 1932. *Scrittori anglo-americani d'oggi*. Milano: Corticelli.

———. 1934. "Un poeta italiano emigrato." *Nuova Antologia*, no. 375: 59–68.

Luperini, Romano. 2012. "Il modernismo italiano esiste." In *Sul modernismo italiano*, edited by Romano Luperini and Massimiliano Tortora. Napoli: Liguori.

Malena, Anne. 2003. "Presentation." *TTR: Traduction, Terminologie, Rédaction* 16 (2): 9–13.

Mao, Douglas, and Rebecca Walkowitz. 2008. "The New Modernist Studies." *PMLA* 123 (3): 737–48.

Marazzi, Martino. 2011. "What Fodder for the Canon?" *RSA Journal* 21–22: 95–98.

———. 2012. *Voices of Italian America*. Translated by Ann Goldstein. New York: Fordham University Press.

McAlmon, Robert. 1931. "Fortuno Carraccioli." *Poetry, A Magazine of Verse* 37 (5): 247–51.

———. 1938. *Being Geniuses Together*. London: Secker & Warburg.

McDougal, Stuart Y., ed. 1985. *Dante Among the Moderns*. Chapel Hill: University of North Carolina Press.

Mehrez, Samia. 1992. "Translation and the Postcolonial Experience." In *Rethinking Translation*, edited by Lawrence Venuti. London: Routledge.

Micale, Mark S. 2003. "The Modernist Mind: A Map." In *The Mind of Modernism. Medicine, Psychology, and the Cultural Arts in Europe and America, 1880–1940*, edited by Mark S. Micale, 1–19. Stanford, CA: Stanford University Press.

Miller, Cristanne. 2007. "Tongues 'Loosened in the Melting Pot': The Poets of Others and the Lower East Side." *Modernism/Modernity* 14 (3): 455–76.

Monk, Craig. 2001. "Textual Authority and Modern American Autobiography: Robert McAlmon, Kay Boyle, and the Writing of a Lost Generation." *Journal of American Studies* 35 (3): 485–97.

Monroe, Harriet. 1918. "Notes." *Poetry, A Magazine of Verse* 11 (6): 343–44.

Moroni, Mario, and Luca Somigli, eds. 2004. *Italian Modernism*. Toronto: University of Toronto Press.

Neagoe, Peter. 1932. "Foreword." In *Americans Abroad*, edited by Peter Neagoe, VII–XI. The Hague: Servire.

Nicholls, Peter. 1995. *Modernisms*. Basingstoke: Macmillan.

North, Michael. 1994. *The Dialect of Modernism*. New York: Oxford University Press.

Otsuji, Emi, and Alastair Pennycook. 2010. "Metrolingualism: Fixity, Fluidity and Language in Flux." *International Journal of Multilingualism* 7 (3): 240–54.

Pach, Walter. 1917. "*La Voce* and Its Poets." *Poetry, A Magazine of Verse* 10 (1): 50–52.

Palazzeschi, Aldo. 1910. *L'incendiario: col rapporto sulla vittoria futurista di Trieste.* Milano: Edizioni Futuriste di Poesia.

———. 1914. "L'indifferente." *La Voce*, December 15.

Palmieri, E. Ferdinando. 1934. "Destino d'un poeta." *Il Resto del Carlino*, November 25.

Papini, Giovanni. 1908. "L'Italia risponde." *La Voce*, December 20.

———. 1913. *Un uomo finito.* Firenze: Quaderni della Voce.

———. 1919. "Leavetaking." Translated by Emanuel Carnevali. *Others*, July.

———. 1920. *Cento pagine di poesia.* 3rd ed. Firenze: Vallecchi.

Patterson, Anita. 2008. *Race, American Literature and Transnational Modernisms.* Cambridge: Cambridge University Press.

Patterson, Ian. 2011. "Time, Free Verse and the Gods of Modernism." In *Tradition, Translation, Trauma*, edited by Jan Parker and Timothy Mathews, 175–90. New York: Oxford University Press.

Pavlenko, Aneta. 2006. "Bilingual Selves." In *Bilingual Minds. Emotional Experience, Expression and Representation*, edited by Aneta Pavlenko, 1–33. Clevedon: Multilingual Matters.

———. 2012. "Affective Processing in Bilingual Speakers: Disembodied Cognition." *International Journal of Psychology: Journal International de Psychologie* 47 (6): 405–28.

———. 2014. *The Bilingual Mind.* Cambridge: Cambridge University Press.

Perloff, Marjorie. 1981. *The Poetics of Indeterminacy: Rimbaud to Cage.* Evanston, IL: Northwestern University Press.

Pickering, Michael. 2001. *Stereotyping: The Politics of Representation.* Basingstoke: Palgrave Macmillan.

Polezzi, Loredana. 2008. "La mobilità come modello." *Studi europei e mediterranei, studi (e testi) italiani* 22: 115–28.

———. 2010. "Polylingualism and Self-Translation in Pietro Di Donato's *Christ in Concrete* and Giose Rimanelli's *Familia.*" In *Into and Out of Italy: Lingua e cultura della migrazione italiana*, edited by A. Ledgeway and A. L. Lepschy, 137–46. Perugia: Guerra.

Pound, Ezra. 1913. "Contemporania." *Poetry, A Magazine of Verse*, April.

———. 1930. "Lettera al traduttore." *L'indice. Quindicinale di lettere arti e scienze* 1 (12): 1.

———. 1931. "Canto Ottavo." Translated by Emanuel Carnevali. *L'indice. Quindicinale di lettere arti e scienze*, November 10.

———. 1968. "Notes on Elizabethan Classicists." In *Literary Essays of Ezra Pound*, edited by Thomas Stearns Eliot, 2nd ed., 227–48. New York: New Directions.

———. 1975. *The Cantos*. London: Faber & Faber.

———. 2005. *Early Writings*. Edited by Ira B. Nadel. London: Penguin.

———. 2012. *XXX Cantos. A cura di Massimo Bacigalupo. Testo originale a fronte.* Translated by Massimo Bacigalupo. Parma: Guanda.

Praz, Mario. 1932. "Ezra Pound." *La Stampa*, August 13.

———. 1933. "Arte d'oggi." *La Stampa*, December 13.

Prendergast, Christopher. 2004. "The World Republic of Letters." In *Debating World Literature*, edited by Christopher Prendergast, 1–25. London: Verso.

Prezzolini, Giuseppe. 1963. *I trapiantati*. Milano: Longanesi.

Putnam, Samuel. 1922. "The Mad Wop." *The Milwaukee Arts Monthly*, October.

Ramazani, Jahan. 2009. *A Transnational Poetics*. Chicago: University of Chicago Press.

Redding, Patrick. 2010. "Whitman Unbound: Democracy and Poetic Form, 1912 to 1931." *New Literary History* 41 (3): 669–90.

Ricciardi, Caterina. 1986. "Le tentazioni di Calibano: Emanuel Carnevali e il rinascimento poetico americano." In *L'America degli italiani*, edited by Vanni Blengini, 172–215. Roma: Bulzoni.

Rimbaud, Arthur. 1966. *Complete Works*. Edited and translated by Wallace Fowlie. Chicago: University of Chicago Press.

Saba, Umberto. 1994. *Tutte le poesie*. Edited by Arrigo Stara. 4th ed. Milan: Mondadori.

Sandburg, Carl. 1970. *The Complete Poems*. New York: Harcourt Brace Jovanovich.

Scholes, Robert, and Clifford Wulfman. 2010. *Modernism in the Magazines: An Introduction*. New Haven: Yale University Press.

Seyhan, Azade. 2000. *Writing Outside the Nation*. Princeton, NJ: Princeton University Press.

Shklovsky, Viktor Borisovich. 1998. *Theory of Prose*. Translated by Benjamin Sher. 2nd ed. Elmwood Park, IL: Dalkey.

Silvestri, Ubaldo. 1934. "Il poeta 'incatenato' Emanuele Carnevali." *Il Messaggero*, November 27.

Simon, Sherry. 2012. *Cities in Translation. Intersections of Language and Memory*. New York: Routledge.

Slataper, Scipio. 1920. *Il mio Carso*. 4th ed. Roma: La Voce.

Smith, Stan. 1994. *The Origins of Modernism*. New York: Harvester Wheatsheaf.

Sollors, Werner. 1986. *Beyond Ethnicity: Consent and Descent in American Culture*. New York: Oxford University Press.

———. 2008. *Ethnic Modernism*. Cambridge, MA: Harvard University Press.

Somigli, Luca, and Mario Moroni. 2004. "Modernism in Italy: An Introduction." In *Italian Modernism*, edited by Luca Somigli and Mario Moroni, 3–31. Toronto: University of Toronto Press.

Tamburri, Anthony Julian. 1991. *To Hyphenate or Not to Hyphenate*. Montreal: Guernica.

———. 2003. "Beyond 'Pizza' and 'Nonna'! Or, What's Bad about Italian/American Criticism?: Further Directions for Italian/American Cultural Studies." *MELUS* 28 (3): 149–74.

Taylor-Batty, Juliette. 2013. *Multilingualism in Modernist Fiction*. Basingstoke: Palgrave Macmillan.

Templeton, Erin E. 2013. "'For Having Slept Much the Dead Have Grown Strong': Emanuel Carnevali and William Carlos Williams." *William Carlos Williams Review* 30 (1–2): 137–57.

Terrell, Carroll F. 1980. *A Companion to the Cantos of Ezra Pound*. Berkeley: University of California Press.

Thiher, Allen. 1999. *Revels in Madness. Insanity in Medicine and Literature*. Ann Arbor: University of Michigan Press.

Toury, Gideon. 1995. *Descriptive Translation Studies and Beyond*. Amsterdam: John Benjamins.

Tymoczko, Maria. 1999. "Post-Colonial Writing and Literary Translation." In *Post-Colonial Translation*, edited by Susan Bassnett and Harish Trivedi, 2nd ed., 19–40. London: Routledge.

Valentine, Kylie. 2003. *Psychoanalysis, Psychiatry and Modernist Literature*. Basingstoke: Palgrave Macmillan.

Valesio, Paolo. 1993. "I fuochi della tribù." In *Poesaggio*, edited by Paolo Valesio and Peter Carravetta, 255–90. Treviso: Pagus.

Varzi, Achille. 2017. "'All the Shadows/Whisper of the Sun': Carnevali's Whitmanesque Simplicity." *Philosophy and Literature* 41 (2): 359–74.

Vellon, Peter G. 2014. *A Great Conspiracy against Our Race: Italian Immigrant Newspapers and the Construction of Whiteness in the Early 20th Century*. New York: New York University Press.

Venuti, Lawrence. 2008. *The Translator's Invisibility*. 2nd ed. London: Routledge.

Verdicchio, Pasquale. 1997. *Bound by Distance: Rethinking Nationalism Through the Italian Diaspora*. London: Associated University Press.

Viscusi, Robert. 2003. "Son of Italy: Immigrant Ambitions and American Literature." *MELUS* 28 (3): 41–54.

———. 2006. *Buried Caesars and Other Secrets of Italian American Writing*. Albany, NY: State University of New York Press.

Wagner, Birgit. 2012. "Cultural Translation: A Value or a Tool?" In *Translatio/n. Narration, Media and the Staging of Differences*, edited by Federico Italiano and Michael Rössner, 51–68. Bielefeld: transcript Verlag.

Walsh, Ernest. 1925. "A Young Living Genius." *This Quarter* 1 (2): 322–39.

Weston, Daniel, and Penelope Gardner-Chloros. 2015. "Mind the Gap: What Code-Switching in Literature Can Teach Us about Code-Switching." *Language and Literature* 24 (3): 194–212.

Whitman, Walt. 1998. *Leaves of Grass*. Edited by Jerome Loving. Oxford: Oxford University Press.

Williams, Raymond. 1989. *The Politics of Modernism*. 2nd ed. London: Verso.

Williams, William Carlos. 1919. "Gloria!" *Others*, July 30 (1): 60–61.

Wilson, Rita. 2012. "Parallel Creations. Between Self-Translation and the Translation of the Self." In *Creative Constraints: Translation and Authorship*, edited by Rita Wilson and Leah Gerber, 47–66. Clayton, Victoria: Monash University Press.

Wolf, Michaela. 2012. "Cultural Translation as a Model of Migration?" In *Translatio/n. Narration, Media and the Staging of Differences*, edited by Federico Italiano and Michael Rössner, 69–88. Bielefeld: transcript Verlag.

Yao, Steven G. 2002. *Translation and the Languages of Modernism. Gender, Politics, Language*. Basingstoke: Palgrave Macmillan.

Yildiz, Yasemin. 2012. *Beyond the Mother Tongue. The Postmonolingual Condition*. New York: Fordham University Press.

Zabus, Chantal. 1991. *The African Palimpsest: Indigenization of Language in the West African Europhone Novel*. Amsterdam: Rodopi.

Zanotti, Serenella. 2009. "Da Dante a Mussolini: Appunti sull'italiano di Pound." In *Scrittori stranieri in lingua italiana, dal Rinascimento a oggi*, edited by Fabio Brugnolo, 375–94. Padua: Unipress.

Index

Made in the USA
Columbia, SC
15 September 2020